SACRED
Parenting

Books by Gary Thomas

Authentic Faith
Devotions for a Sacred Marriage
Devotions for Sacred Parenting
The Glorious Pursuit
Not the End but the Road
Sacred Marriage
Sacred Parenting
Sacred Pathways
Seeking the Face of God

GARY L. THOMAS

SACRED
Parenting

HOW RAISING CHILDREN
SHAPES OUR SOULS

GRAND RAPIDS, MICHIGAN 49530 USA

ZONDERVAN™

Sacred Parenting
Copyright © 2004 by Gary L. Thomas

Requests for information should be addressed to:
Zondervan, *Grand Rapids, Michigan 49530*

Library of Congress Cataloging-in-Publication Data

Thomas, Gary (Gary Lee)
    Sacred parenting : how raising children shapes our souls / Gary L. Thomas—
1st ed.
       p. cm.
    Includes bibliographical references.
    ISBN: 0-310-24734-9 (hardcover)
    1. Parenting—Religious aspects—Christianity   2. Parents—Religious life.
I. Title.
BV4526.3.T46 2004
248.8'45—dc22

    2003020213

Softcover ISBN-10: 0-310-26451-0
ISBN-13: 978-0-310-26451-4

All Scripture quotations, unless otherwise indicated, are taken from the *Holy Bible: New International Version*®. NIV®. Copyright © 1973, 1978, 1984 by International Bible Society. Used by permission of Zondervan. All rights reserved.

Interior design by Michelle Espinoza

Printed in the United States of America

---

05 06 07 08 09 10 /❖ DCI/ 10 9 8 7 6 5 4 3 2 1

To Brady and Shirley Bobbink,
whose example and teaching have left
a spiritual inheritance of the highest order

Acknowledgments

I'd like to thank my children, Allison, Graham, and Kelsey, who graciously allowed their lives to be captured on paper. They have read all the stories and have given their consent to anything that appears in this book that is related to them.

I want to thank my own parents, E.J. and Geneva Thomas, who have faithfully fulfilled the role of being sacred parents and modeled for me what it is all about.

There were a number of readers who provided helpful comments on an earlier draft. The volume you hold in your hands is much different because of their insightful comments and suggestions. They are: Jim and Connie Schmotzer, Jill Takemura, Shirley Bobbink, Nicole Whitacre, Annie Carlson, Larry Gadbaugh, Jerry Thomas, Mary Kay Smith, and Dr. Melody Rhode.

I'd like to offer special thanks to Drs. Steve and Rebecca Wilke. Their support and encouragement, and their insight on the content of this book, cannot be overstated. Lisa and I are in awe of the people God has blessed us with as friends and coworkers in his kingdom.

Dr. Cathy Carpenter and her husband, Gordon, also reviewed this book. I'm particularly indebted to Cathy for permission to quote from her unpublished manuscript on raising difficult children. It's my hope that a publisher will recognize the value of her contributions and evaluate her manuscript for publication.

I also want to thank Dr. Kevin Leman, whose friendship, support, and informal mentorship in the writing and speaking ministry has been invaluable, and Chip MacGregor, my agent, just for being there. Thanks are also due my assistant, Laura Thompson, whose manifold gifts allow me to pursue my own, and her husband, Steve, for his great advice, friendship, and support.

Because I wanted to include a mother's perspective, I was dependent on insightful and often witty writers whose reflections added a touch I as a man couldn't achieve. I especially want to acknowledge Rachel Cusk, Iris Krasnow, and Rabbi Nancy Fuchs-Kreimer.

The Zondervan team did their usual superlative job: John Sloan and Dirk Buursma provided their customary top-of-the-line service in taking a coarse manuscript and making it much better. John Topliff and Greg Stielstra — thank you for enduring the emails and for making sure people find out about this book! A special thank-you to Scott Bolinder for your personal encouragement.

Finally, and foremost, I'd like to thank my wife, Lisa, whose patience borders on saintliness. She gently responded when I'd interrupt her homeschooling to see if a paragraph worked or a story fit. Lisa has greatly influenced this book. I can't imagine having written it without her being within earshot of my office.

Contents

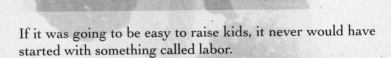

If it was going to be easy to raise kids, it never would have started with something called labor.

Anonymous

It is in families we are broken and it is in families that we are healed.

Carl Whittaker

Dear friends, let us purify ourselves from everything that contaminates body and spirit, perfecting holiness out of reverence for God.

2 Corinthians 7:1

Chapter 1

Papa God

One day, when our daughter Kelsey was two years old, she started pointing at every family member's chair around the table. I was gone at the time. "Mommy," she began, "Allison, Graham, Kelsey . . ." She then pointed to my empty seat and said, "God."

"That's not God, Kelsey," Lisa, my wife, said. "That's Papa."

"Jesus," Kelsey replied with a smile.

Three days later, all of us were together in a hotel room when Kelsey did it again. She started pointing to everybody and announcing his or her name. When she got to me, she said, "Jesus."

"I'm not Jesus, Kelsey," I said. "I'm Papa."

"You're Papa God," Kelsey replied.

I was flabbergasted and earnestly tried to talk it out with her, but you parents know what a two-year-old is like. By the time I had made my point, Kelsey had found something vastly more interesting than theology — her little toe, and how it could be made to wiggle in all directions.

To me, this is one of the greatest ironies of parenting. I think about how big I seemed to my kids when I was just in my twenties, and how little I knew. Now, a bit more experienced in my forties, it's almost laughable how much smaller I seem to my children! Graham knows he could take me in a math test (though as I write this, thankfully, he still hasn't beaten me in a round of golf), and there's no chance either one of my daughters would mistake me for deity.

But these early episodes of mistaken identity truly opened my eyes as a young parent. The more time I spent with my kids as they became toddlers, and then preteens, and then teens, the more open they seemed to God's presence in their lives. The less time I spent with them, the less they seemed to pray. The observation both sobered and humbled me; somehow, in their minds, I helped shape their passion and hunger for God.

I soon discovered that my own passion and hunger for God seemed just as directly related to my duties as a parent. I've been at this business of parenting for less than two decades, but I think it's fair to say I have been stretched more in these past sixteen years — spiritually, emotionally, and relationally — than perhaps in all the previous years combined.

Why does parenting offer such a potent pathway to personal growth and reflection? The process of raising children requires skills that God alone possesses, and we are decidedly *not* God. As much as our kids may even call us "Papa God," parenting regularly reminds us of our absolute humanity. We do not love perfectly, as God loves. Our ability to relate, to understand, and to build intimacy comes up short in a way that God's does not.

While I count raising children as one of the most profoundly meaningful and rewarding things I've ever done, it also has humbled me, frustrated me, and at times completely confounded me. I could never write a book about how to raise a toddler or a teen, because in many ways I still don't have a clue! If you thought this book would give you five steps to help your daughter succeed in school or ten steps to prepare your son for adolescence, you're in for a big disappointment. Instead, it approaches a much different territory — how God uses these children to shape *us*, spiritually speaking.

I knew the rules had changed just a few weeks after the birth of our oldest daughter. We were driving south to Oregon when we stopped at a restaurant to get a bite to eat. At one time in my life, my favorite food on earth was a Dairy Queen Blizzard. I just knew that the creator of this fine confection had to be a Christian, because I thought it would take nothing less than the Holy Spirit's inspiration to come up with anything that tasted as good as an M & M Blizzard.

We ordered our burgers and fries, and I had my Blizzard. We took it outside on a sunny day, and at exactly that moment our daughter had her once-every-three-day diaper blowout. Our first-born, as a baby, liked to "save it up." She preferred to wait until we were on our way to church, had just sat down for dinner, had just given her a bath, or some other convenient moment before she expunged the previous seventy-two hours' worth of digestive effort.

I remember the helpless feeling. Cold fries don't taste very good, and melted Blizzards lose a lot — yet I knew I had a good ten to fifteen minutes' worth of work ahead of me. Because this baby did it all at once, changing her meant not just a new diaper but a veritable bath and a full change of clothing. And we were on the road.

"Don't just stand there," Lisa said. "*Help* me!"

"But — " I looked at my fries, already wilting with a shelf life of about ten minutes. I stared forlornly at my Blizzard, teasing my tongue with its promise, yet already looking as though it were about to start boiling in the hot sun. I put the food bag on top of the car and went to work.

Life had changed, indeed. It may sound like a small sacrifice to you — and even now, as I look back a decade and a half later, it seems insubstantial — but it marked a major turning point for this then-twenty-five-year-old. I was learning to put someone else's needs ahead of my own. Little did I know that I had just begun the spiritually transformative journey called parenting.

My wife and I have benefited greatly from books and seminars that teach us how to shape our children, but along the way we've realized that our children also have molded us. Parenting is a two-way street! Our kids have taught us how to sacrifice (chapter 12) and how to handle guilt (chapter 3); they've schooled us in the art of listening and forced us to our knees in prayer (chapter 4); they've shown us how to laugh (chapter 5), how to grieve (chapter 9), and how to live courageously (chapter 6); they've helped us face our inadequacy, need, and reliance on One who is greater than we are (chapter 13). The experience of parenting comprises one of the most influential aspects of spiritual formation I've ever known.

Tiny Teachers

This idea that God can use children to teach *us*, that we have an opportunity to gain spiritual insight from those we are called to raise and teach, comes from our Lord himself, who in this regard was something of a revolutionary.

In the first century, children enjoyed little esteem and virtually no respect. While families appreciated their own children, society merely tolerated them. The very language of the day reveals this first-century prejudice. One Greek word for child *(pais* or *paidion)* also can mean "servant" or "slave." Yet another *(nepios)* carries connotations of inexperience, foolishness, and helplessness. Greek philosophers regularly chided a stupid or foolish man by calling him *"nepios."* Indeed, even biblical writers admonished Christians to "stop thinking like children *[paidia]*" (1 Corinthians 14:20).[1]

Imagine, then, the people's astonishment when Jesus brings a troublesome, noisy child and places him in front of the crowd (Matthew 18:1–9). With his hand on the lad's shoulder, Jesus has the audacity to suggest that this small tyke provides an example to be followed.

Even the boy himself had to feel great surprise! Young children couldn't *wait* to reach adulthood. They eagerly looked forward to shedding their lowly station. But Jesus said, "No, you're missing it entirely. Unless you humble yourself like one of these, you'll never enter the kingdom of God." He means, "Look at them *now*, learn from them *now*, and aspire to become like them."

Then Jesus does it yet again, just after he clears the temple of the money changers (see Matthew 21:12–16). Jesus not only chases off the thieves, but he heals the blind and the lame as well. The kids start shouting, "Hosanna to the Son of David."

The chief priests and teachers of the law were furious and demanded of him, "Do you hear what these children are saying?"

"Yes," replied Jesus, "have you never read, 'From the lips of children and infants you have ordained praise'?"

What went on here? The religious leaders scoffed at Jesus: "Rein in these ignorant, foolish, and lowly children who treat you like the Messiah. You might be able to fool *them*, but we see right through you!" Jesus shrewdly turned the tables, in essence saying, "*You* were fooled, but not the 'ignorant' children!"

Jesus seemed to delight in the fact that "inexperienced, simple" children had an understanding superior to the trained adults. Speaking to the crowds in Galilee, Jesus declared, "I praise you, Father,

Lord of heaven and earth, because you have hidden these things from the wise and learned, and revealed them to little children. Yes, Father, for this was your good pleasure" (Matthew 11:25–26).

We find the genius of children, spiritually speaking, in their help-less state. The Bible, as well as Christian spirituality, has consistently held pride as the greatest spiritual failing known to humankind. The message of the gospel scandalizes the proud: it insists that we admit we are fallen, helpless, and in need of someone to pay the price on our behalf and then to imbue us with a foreign power so that we can live life the way it was meant to be lived. An infant incarnates this truth perfectly.

The message of this book, however, goes beyond the idea that we can learn something by watching children. It insists that *the process of parenting* is one of the most spiritually formative journeys a man and a woman can ever undertake. Unless we are stone-cold spiritually — virtually spiritual corpses — the journey of caring for, raising, train-ing, and loving children will mark us indelibly and powerfully. We cannot be the same people we once were; we will be forever changed, eternally altered. Spiritually speaking, we need to raise children every bit as much as they need us to raise them.

Why Have Children?

If I want to get heads wagging during my "Sacred Marriage" semi-nars, all I have to do is to ask people why they got married. Many of us entered matrimony at a pretty young age, and a lot of us got mar-ried for rather superficial and selfish reasons. Few of us understood the deep commitment and call to service that biblical marriage asks of us.

Sadly, most of us end up having kids for equally superficial rea-sons. Some single young women tell crisis pregnancy center coun-selors that they wanted to get pregnant to create someone who would love them. Some men think it's important to "carry on the family name." Other couples have children because little babies "seem so cute." Still others get lost on a narcissist's binge to create another human being who looks just like the two of them combined. A few may even think having a baby will save a lonely marriage.

I have to confess that I felt eager to have kids, in part because I longed to experience a close father-son relationship as well as an intimate father-daughter relationship. I wanted to be a hero to my kids, as my dad was a hero to me. I had a sense that these children would validate me as a man. Yet these motivations, as noble as they may sound, are still narcissistic at root, based on an idealized notion of children and a romanticized view of what family life is really like.

Before long I discovered what every parent has discovered: babies come to us as sinners in need of God's grace and as dependent human beings demanding around-the-clock care. This reality will melt sentimentality and our romanticized notions of family life before we reach the end of the very first jumbo pack of Pampers!

We need something more concrete, something more eternal, to see us through the challenges of parenting. The best reason to have kids — the one reason that will last beyond mere sentiment — is so simple that it may not seem very profound: God commands us to have children (Genesis 1:28). It's his desire that we "be fruitful and increase in number," and this fruitfulness includes raising spiritually sensitive children who will serve God and work for the glory of his kingdom on earth. Deuteronomy 6 and Psalm 78 expand on the Genesis instruction by telling us that not only are we to love the Lord, but we are to raise children who will love God and obey his commandments.

In other words, having kids isn't about *us* — it's about *him*. We are called to bear and raise children for the glory of God.

Most of us are inherently selfish when it comes to raising children. We're hoping for some benefit to come our way, and when we wake up to the truth that children can be embarrassing as well as exemplary, we become resentful and bitter, and a foul spiritual climate can soon take over the home. When we don't understand the purpose of parenting, the process becomes tedious.

When we realize that having children isn't about us but is rather about God, then the trials and sacrifices of parenting are more easily borne. We see the purpose behind the difficulty, and we remind ourselves, "This isn't about me; it's about him." The ultimate issue is no longer how proud my children make me, but how faithful I've been to discharge the duties God has given me. To pin our hope and joy on the response of any given sinner is a precarious move at best. To pin this same hope and joy on the response of a sinner in his or her toddler years or teen years is to beg for disillusionment and to risk waking up in despair.

Parenting (and marriage) will disappoint us, wound us, and frustrate us. Yes, there will be moments of sheer joy and almost transcendent wonder. But make no mistake — family life can cut us open. If we have only a selfish motivation, we will run from parenting's greatest challenges. Once disappointment seeps in, we'll pull back into the same shells we inhabited as children and run from the pain, not by retreating to our bedrooms or backyards (which we did as children), but to our offices, boardrooms, workout clubs, Starbucks, or even churches.

Here's a thought: Let's accept that both marriage and parenting provide many good moments while also challenging us to the very root of our being. Let's admit that family life tries us as perhaps nothing else does; but let's also accept that, for most of us, this is God's call and part of his plan to perfect us. Once we realize that we are sinners, that the children God has given us are sinners, and that together, as a family, we are to grow toward God, then family life takes on an entirely new purpose and context. It becomes a sacred enterprise when we finally understand that God can baptize dirty diapers, toddlers' tantrums, and teenagers' silence in order to transform us into people who more closely resemble Jesus Christ.

What I've just said, most of us already know in our hearts; we simply haven't put words to it. A pastor-friend of mine asked me what I was writing about, and when I described this book, he related some of the problems he and his wife faced while raising their son. "My wife and I," he confessed, "would certainly consider our experiences with Jeff to be one of the most influential things in our lives, spiritually speaking."

Prize-winning novelist Rachel Cusk admits, "As a mother you learn what it is to be both martyr and devil. In motherhood I have experienced myself as both more virtuous and more terrible, and more implicated too in the world's virtue and terror, than I would from the anonymity of childlessness have thought possible."[2]

A mother who gave birth to a child with a developmental disability said, "I wouldn't change anything. I'm glad I had him, because I wouldn't be the same person. I would have desired for him to be normal, but I'm not sorry I learned what I've learned."

I'm not sorry I learned what I've learned.

In many ways, that's the message of this book. The goal is to get you to the place in this journey of sacred parenting where you can say the same thing: "It may have been difficult at times, but I'm not sorry I learned what I've learned."

My wife and I have three children. As I write this, Allison is sixteen years old; Graham is thirteen, and Kelsey is eleven. We're still in the thick of this process, which is why I shy away from trying to write a how-to book. This is more of a "why" book and a "what happened" book.

Along the way, we've discovered that difficult children and gifted children, children who make us cry and children who make us laugh, children who send us to our knees in gratitude and children who send us to our knees in fearful prayer, children who excel and children who fail — all of them have something to teach us. It's all part of God's master plan for parenting.

Why Parent?

Once you have children, what motivation drives your parenting?

Some parents bring a child into the word but refuse to make the sacrifices necessary to *truly* parent that child. One well-known real estate mogul recently told a reporter, "If I can see my daughter for dinner once every two months, I'm happy. I don't have to be around all the time to be a good father."[3] Deciding to conceive children is one thing; daily parenting them requires an entirely different set of decisions. What moves you to get up early in the morning to help your child with his homework, or to stay up late at night talking to your daughter about her day? Why do you go without certain things so that your children can have other things? Why do you give up doing some of the things you like to do so that you can stay at home with your kids?

If you're a single mom, why do you keep doing it all, even when exhaustion makes you feel as though you're wearing a fifty-pound coat? If you're a stepparent, why do you bother with all the hassles, negotiate the volatile relationships, and try to do what some have said is virtually impossible — successfully blend two different and often wounded families? If you're an adoptive parent, what makes you willing to take on such an unbelievably high commitment for some-one who used to be someone else's child?

We spend so much time talking about the "how-to" of parenting that we neglect the equally important "why" of parenting. This is unfortunate, because the "why" eventually drives and even shapes the "how-to." With the wrong "why," our motivations will get skewed, and while the "how-to" may be effective, it'll be effectively wrong!

Paul gives us a very clear "why" in 2 Corinthians 7:1. At first, this verse may not sound like a parenting verse (and in context it's not), but it may be the most helpful verse on parenting in the entire New Testament:

> Dear friends, let us purify ourselves from everything that contaminates body and spirit, perfecting holiness out of rev-erence for God.

Paul first tells us to focus on purifying *ourselves*, not our children. Many of us are so tempted to focus on purifying *our children* that we neglect our own spiritual growth. As Dr. Kevin Leman once told me, parenting is like an airline emergency. Before takeoff, every plane passenger is instructed that if the oxygen masks come down, parents should put on their own masks first before attending to their kids. Why? Because in an emergency, kids need their parents to be able to think clearly and act effectively. If we don't take in oxygen, our think-ing will grow fuzzy, and then our kids — dependent on us to get it right — will ultimately suffer.

What's true in the air physically is equally true on the ground spiritually. If we neglect our own "spiritual oxygen" — our walk with God — our motivations will become polluted. Our ability to discern, empathize, encourage, and confront will waste away. We must see parenting as a process through which God purifies *us* — the parents — even as he shapes our children.

This extensive purifying involves "everything that contaminates body and spirit." This takes us far beyond the obvious "physical" sins of substance abuse, physical abuse, sexual immorality, coarse lan-guage, and so on, and into the more hidden contaminations of jeal-ousy, fear, bitterness, resentment, control, and possessiveness. Paul warns us that this purification process is both deep and thorough —

a spiritual root canal. Parenting will lead us to confront spiritual sins that we never even knew existed. It will point out inner weaknesses that we saw as strengths. It will reveal holes big enough to drive our minivans and SUVs through.

Paul defines this process as "perfecting holiness." This may be my favorite phrase of Paul in the entire New Testament — I just love it! As fallen sinners, we won't fully mirror the image of Christ until that day in which he appears. In the meantime, we are to rub off the smudges, perhaps sand out some of the cuts and abrasive edges, letting Christ's spirit shine through as much as possible. This process of spiritual growth isn't just pervasive ("from everything that contaminates"), it's also ongoing ("perfecting," present tense).

And *why* do we put in such strenuous effort? What motivates us to approach parenting this way? Paul couldn't be clearer: we do it "out of reverence for God." When we are motivated out of reverence for God, we lose 99.9 percent of the excuses that we make in family life. God remains forever worthy of reverence, so we never get excused from acting in a way that moves us along toward holiness.

Consider an example from my own life. I returned from a weekend speaking trip late on a Sunday evening. Because I hadn't seen my daughter for a couple of days, I got up after less than five hours of sleep to drive her to school. She could have caught a bus, but if I drove her to school, she could sleep in a little later and we could talk on the way.

Or so I thought.

It was a Monday, and my daughter was in a Monday sort of mood. I couldn't pry a sentence out of her any more than I could lift Mount Everest. She got out of our silent car without so much as a "thank you." Normally, Allison is quick to express her thanks — but this was just one of those mid-adolescent days.

If I were a child-centered father, I'd feel resentful and immediately start stewing: *I get up after just a few hours of sleep, and this is how she treats me? Well, she won't get that chance again! Next week, I'm sleeping in and playing golf!* Child-centered parents act nicely toward their children only when their children act nicely toward them. A child-centered parent goes out of her way as long as her children appreciate her sacrifice. A child-centered parent bases his or her actions on the kids' response.

A God-centered parent, on the other hand, acts out of reverence for God. Regardless of how my children treat me, I know that God wills that I move toward my children, to get engaged in their lives, to offer biblical correction and loving support. It doesn't matter how they respond to me as much as it matters what God has called me to do. Though I adore my daughter, I don't get out of bed on just a few hours of sleep solely out of love for her, but out of reverence for God.

Do you see the difference? I hope you also see the importance. When God does not supply our motivation, we tend to major in the minors and minor in the majors. We may raise a more courteous and obedient child, but we won't pass on what is of ultimate importance. If parenting were only about behavior modification, Jesus would have praised the Pharisees and kicked dirt on the adulterous woman.

In other words, I'm saying that *our own spiritual quest must drive our parenting.* Unfinished or neglected spiritual business inevitably works its way out through our relationships in a negative fashion: we become more demanding, more controlling, more intolerant, more resentful. Our spouses and our children cannot quench the God-given spiritual hunger in our souls. When we neglect God, we ask our marriage and our parenting to become stand-ins for God — something they were never designed to do.

In this book, I hope to seize this spiritual quest and sanctify it for the good of our families and God's kingdom. Christian parenting is truly a *sacred* journey. It invites us parents to purify ourselves, to use the process of raising kids to perfect holiness, and to do this consistently, every day, out of reverence for God. If we enter it armed with this understanding, each segment will gain new meaning and purpose — even the difficult ones.

We live in the midst of holy teachers. Sometimes they spit up on themselves or on us. Sometimes they throw tantrums. Sometimes they cuddle us and kiss us and love us. In the good and the bad they mold our hearts, shape our souls, and invite us to experience God in newer and deeper ways. Although we may shed many tears along this sacred journey of parenting, numerous blessings await us around every bend in the road.

Sunshine without rain is the recipe for a desert.

Arab Proverb

I consider that our present sufferings are not worth comparing with the glory that will be revealed in us.

Romans 8:18

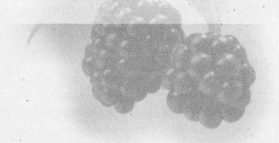

Chapter 2

The Hardest Hurt of All

How Raising Children Teaches Us to Value Character and Service over Comfort

Abigail Adams lived during a time when allowing your children to travel overseas to accompany their father on an important diplomatic mission meant that *years*, not weeks, would pass before you saw them again. Before one such trip, nine-year-old John Quincy had second thoughts; he wasn't sure he wanted to leave his mother for that long.

In a heartrending farewell letter to her son, Abigail showed what she valued most. Instead of pulling John Quincy back into her skirt, Abigail worked to strengthen her son's resolve. She admitted that, yes, the separation would be hard and that, yes, real dangers lay ahead (sea travel in the eighteenth century could be an iffy affair). But she also reminded her oldest son of his duty to take full advantage of the benefits he enjoyed as the son of an influential man. Some of those benefits entailed corresponding sacrifices and risks; but in the end, embracing those benefits with their risks would create a full life.

Abigail wrote this profound comment to her son:

It is not in the still calm of life ... that great characters are formed. The habits of a vigorous mind are formed in contending with difficulties. Great necessities call out great virtues. When a mind is raised, and animated by scenes that engage the heart, then those qualities which would otherwise lay dormant, wake into life and form the character of the hero and the statesman.[1]

A spiritually weak parent would have a grueling time writing such a letter, because no hurt can compare to watching your kids hurt. Abigail once said of her husband, "When he is wounded, I bleed." Most parents could say the same about their children. What mother or father hasn't pleaded with God at some point, "Lord, let *me* feel that pain, if it will spare my daughter or son"? But Abigail had a bigger view in mind: without "great necessities," her son would never know "great virtues." She realized that a life full of challenges is a soul-forming life, and since she wanted a mature son, she told him to look his trial in the face and say, "Give me your best — and I'll give you mine." Otherwise, those latent characteristics of greatness in her son might lay dormant and never come to the surface.

Abigail's approach worked. John Quincy grew up to be a very successful man, perhaps one of the most creative, competent, and effective secretaries of state our nation has ever had — from which he ascended to our nation's highest office, president of the United States. Following that, he served as a congressman, working diligently to bring an end to slavery. What mother wouldn't feel proud to raise a man with such influence and impact on our nation?

To what do you most aspire for your children — comfort or character? On almost a daily basis, we have to choose between the two, as they inevitably come into conflict. Sacred parenting matures the parent by inviting us to choose service and character for our children over pain-free living.

You're Special

Contrast Abigail's attitude with today's all too common alternative: frantically working to spare our children from any stress or pain. In this cowardly new world, competition is verboten.

Sports Illustrated's Rick Reilly wrote a column about how some school districts in New York, Texas, Utah, and Virginia have outlawed the game of dodgeball, with many additional school districts considering the same course of action. Dodgeball has clear winners and losers. If you get hit, you're out. Some believe this could damage a kid's self-esteem. Some experts also fear that the game gives a certain vent to aggression; after all, you're throwing a ball directly at another kid.

But without risks, can there be true, substantive rewards? I remember few things as satisfying as sneaking up on some testosterone freak of nature who shaved in the third grade and watching the shock on his face as my punky little throw caught him unaware — or the even bigger thrill of taking the strongest guy's best throw and catching it. Today's kids may never experience this, thanks to some of our nation's leading educational minds. Dodgeball appears headed to the same place as drive-in movie theaters and 8-track tapes. Sportswriter Rick Reilly expresses this lament:

> I know what all these NPR-listening, Starbucks-guzzling parents want. They want their Ambers and their Alexanders to grow up in a cozy womb of noncompetition, where everybody shares tofu and Little Red Riding Hood and the big, bad wolf set up a commune. Then their kids will stumble out into the bright light of the real world and find out that, yes, there's weak and there's strong and teams and sides and winning and losing. You'll recognize those kids. They'll be the ones filling up chalupas. Very noncompetitive.[2]

Apparently, some of these educators aren't content with stopping dodgeball; they also have a problem with musical chairs. *Seriously.* After all, every round of musical chairs potentially destroys the self-esteem of the child who gets pushed out.

Few games are safe from these guardians of the correct. Franklin Elementary School in Santa Monica, California, has now banned "unsupervised" tag. Reilly suggests how the game might be saved. Maybe, he says, we should change the rules so that instead of the child hollering, "You're it," she should say, "You're special!"

The sad truth is, these games don't hurt our kids nearly as much as they hurt *us*, the parents. We're sparing ourselves, not our kids, when we go to such ridiculous extremes. It takes twice as much courage to watch your son or daughter suffer as it does to take a hit yourself — and through a nifty little denial device we parents try to project that pain back onto our children.

The point here is not just competition. Dr. Melody Rhode, a marriage and family therapist friend of mine, has found from her experience that children raised under a coddled philosophy that avoids adversity and pain at all costs are likely to be addicted, obese, dependent, suicidal, incapable, and frequently overwhelmed by life. She points out that the phrase "growing pains" goes beyond aching knees to describe aching hearts and disappointed souls — essential experiences on the path toward maturity. If we protect our children from all risk, challenge, and possible rejection, they likely will become developmentally stunted and will therefore remain immature.

Out of love for our children, we must become strong enough spiritually to watch them hurt, to see them become disappointed, to hear their cries. Otherwise, we risk raising safe and compliant kids with an empty core. In this area our own immaturity and spiritual weakness can handicap our children.

Safe, Compliant Kids — with an Empty Core

Marilee Jones is dean of admissions at the Massachusetts Institute of Technology (MIT), one of the most prestigious schools in the nation. In April 2002, she received a letter from the father of a son who didn't make the cut: *You rejected my son. He's devastated. See you in court.*

This is far more than an isolated incident. Ms. Jones warns that "more and more, today's parents are getting too involved in their child's college admissions process, and in many cases, their actions and attitudes are getting out of hand."[3]

A friend of mine, Jim Schmotzer, would agree. Like Marilee Jones, Jim makes his living working with kids. A former schoolteacher, he now heads up a large college ministry in the Pacific Northwest. As such, Jim has had a front-row seat observing the fruit of modern parenting styles. In Jim's words, "This is the first generation of kids where their parents were hypervigilant advocates at every point: If the kids got bad grades, it was the teacher's fault. If they didn't get enough playing time, the coach heard about it. Everybody assumes that their kid is special, at least above average, even though it seems to me that *most* kids *must* be about average." Jim doesn't exclude himself from these comments, by the way. He freely confesses that he has struggled with this and even, on occasion, has fallen into the same mistakes he sees other parents making.

Jim continued, "In this generation, we parents have gone out of our way to protect our children from pain and to see that they succeed. The problem with this approach is that the kids don't learn wisdom, and they don't learn decision-making skills. I believe we learn more from failure than success, but when parents keep kids from failure, our children inevitably end up lacking wisdom."

Jim added, "Today's kids have a high standard of living, eat in good restaurants, wear nice clothes, and drive nice cars — whether they work or not. The kids start thinking this style of living is the norm, and they don't realize they will have to work for it. In this sense, they live in a fantasy world because they never have to deal with life's realities. Though they are highly trained intellectually, many lack the practical skills to know what to do with that training."[4]

In an article written for the April 2001 issue of *Atlantic Monthly*, David Brooks calls those born between 1979 and 1982 "the most honed and supervised generation in human history."[5] Brooks points out how seriously parents pursue the grand quest of giving their child every advantage. Evidence of this comes in the *WombSong Serenades*, a musical collection specifically designed to stimulate babies' fetal brain activity — while they remain in their mothers' wombs. If you somehow fell asleep and neglected to give your developing child this early advantage, you can try to catch up with *Mozart for Babies' Minds* (which features the Violin Concerto no. 3).

In such a society, our kids don't need character — they just need the right drugs! In fact, the United States produces and uses about 90 percent of the world's Ritalin and its generic equivalents.[6] As two researchers note, if Dennis the Menace was born today, he'd immediately be placed on Ritalin, and Charlie Brown would be a prime candidate for Prozac. (There are, of course, children who genuinely need the help that some of these drugs provide, but just about any educator will tell you that drugs are all too often the *first* resort for unruly children.) Kids are overprotected, too frequently drugged, and unnecessarily coddled.

This has produced, in some sectors, remarkably compliant kids with an empty core. In Brooks' estimation, "They are responsible. They are generous. They are bright. They are good-natured. But they live in a country that has lost, in its frenetic seeking after happiness and success, the language of sin and character-building through combat with sin. Evil is seen as something that can be cured with better education, or therapy, or Prozac. Instead of virtue we talk about accomplishment."[7]

All this results, I believe, from seeking happiness over holiness. Not that happiness and holiness are mutually exclusive (in fact, they often go hand in hand), but we face an ever-present temptation to choose stress-free living for our kids over character-building experiences. I by no means put myself above this. Recently, my youngest daughter, Kelsey, and her best friend, Laura, accompanied me on a trip to Orlando, Florida. We arrived early and stayed late, so that around my day-and-a-half speaking schedule, we found time to visit the Magic Kingdom, Sea World, and Disney-MGM studios. Even on the day I had to speak, Kelsey and Laura spent about three hours in a resort pool and got to watch two videos in our luxury room. We ate room-service meals and had twice-a-day cleaning service with a maid who always left extra mints for the girls.

But the plane trip from Seattle to Orlando is a long one, so Lisa and I, as well as Laura's mom, purchased some presents for the trip, which Kelsey dutifully proclaimed as her "survival" kit. When she called it that, I laughed in spite of myself. Only in America could parents think a kid on her way to a resort and four days of theme-park attendance needed a survival kit to make it there. Though I teach in my seminars about the importance of embracing boredom if we ever want to learn how to pray, here I was as a father trying to make sure my little girl kept busy at all times.

The same week I took Kelsey to Orlando, my son, Graham, went to summer camp. Lisa told me that parents could send care packages for their children, so I dropped forty bucks buying some snacks, a cartoon book, some water pistols, gum, a disposable camera, mints, and so on. After I delivered the goods, I laughed at myself once again. You go to camp *to have fun*. Why did I feel obligated to give Graham a care package for a place where he was playing eighteen hours a day?

Though I believe kids could stand a little boredom and a few difficulties, I still hate to see my own kids suffer. It pains me more than I can believe when they face difficulties. And I grieve over their failures perhaps more than they grieve over their own. Compared to Abigail Adams, I'm still a very weak parent. But I'm trying. I'm *trying* to help my kids see that this world is a tough place and that they have to become even tougher to make it. I want them to see the value in taking a risk, in overcoming challenges that at first seemed too big to manage, in learning how to rebound from failure without giving up.

Why? Because in learning this, they will understand the need to put first things first.

First Things First

Our natural (but not necessarily holy) inclination to make life as easy as possible for our children, coupled with our focus on what we really want them to achieve, ultimately tells us parents what we value most about life. In what we stress with our children, we reveal the true passion of our own hearts.

In a remarkable message titled "Gospel-Centered Parenting,"[8] pastor C.J. Mahaney of Gaithersburg, Maryland, warns that when we spend most of our parenting energy on producing "successful," intelligent, well-behaved children, our good intentions can suffocate even better aims. What is *the* most important thing for our children? Mahaney asks. Is it to make it into Harvard or Yale law school? Is it to make it to age twenty-one without suffering a single scar or a single broken heart? Is it to raise a child who says, "Yes, sir," and "No, ma'am," and who becomes financially independent? Though these are worthy goals, ask yourself a question. Is a child who has never been in the hospital, who is comfortable and familiar with the protocol of eating at a fancy restaurant, and who is a managing partner at a major law firm — but whose soul is in eternal peril — really the kind of son or daughter you want to produce?

The Bible gives us a strong warning in 1 Samuel. High Priest Eli had two sons who slept with women workers and who gorged themselves on God's offerings. Their father's position allowed them to live in relative luxury, and though Eli despised what they did, he didn't stop them. You might say he chose his sons' happiness over their holiness and, in doing so, elicited God's wrath. "Why do you honor your sons more than me?" God scolded Eli (1 Samuel 2:29). Eli's sons became God's enemies, to the point that the Bible tells us, "It was the LORD's will to put them to death" (1 Samuel 2:25).

How terrifying to think that my kids could feel happy on the way to receiving the full brunt of God's wrath! Which is why C.J. Mahaney reminds us that the "main thing" of parenting is praying, working, and striving for our children's salvation — and not just their salvation, but that they, too, will become servants of the gospel of Jesus Christ. I want my children to echo Paul, who called himself "a servant of Christ Jesus, . . . set apart for the gospel of God" (Romans 1:1). Rather than seeking mere behavior modification, sacred parenting points our children to their need for a relationship with God and his wonderful answer to this need. If they never experience this emptiness, they will never appreciate God's remedy.

If behavior is about achieving the right chemical balance more than looking honestly into our own sinful hearts, then the gospel message of forgiveness, repentance, and the empowering presence of the Holy Spirit becomes irrelevant. Mahaney tells his son after a bout of discipline, "You see now why both you and Daddy need a Savior?" This is sacred parenting — it looks at the heart, it admits real failing, and it recognizes the real solution: salvation.

If our kids never hurt; if they never sin but are only "sick"; if they never "fail" but just get "cheated" by an unfair coach, teacher, principal, and so on — they will never sense their need for a Savior. They will always take Adam's lame approach, blaming someone else for their own spiritual failing. And ultimately they may face God's wrath because of it.

Yes, it hurts us when our kids hurt, but it devastates our kids' eternal perspective far more when we hide their need for a Savior. *Our* hardest hurt may actually be their *most important* hurt. What a tragic loss if the hurt we spare ourselves is bought at the price of our children's salvation.

C.J. Mahaney's teaching reminds this dad to keep first things first — beginning with the gospel. This means accepting a very difficult but very important truth: Ultimately God's kingdom far outweighs in significance the personal comfort of my children. As much as I adore my children, as crazy as I feel about them, I betray them if I put their happiness and comfort over God's overall purpose in their lives and in our world.

I confess that it hurts even to type those words! Of course, I want my kids to be safe and well fed, and to achieve their full potential, educationally and otherwise. But even more important to me is that they become recipients of God's salvation and servants of their Savior. If they reject this gospel, they will be justly condemned. Even more difficult, *I will have to agree with that condemnation* — which means that if I try to craft a world without pain and consequences, I blind them to the reality that there will be *eternal* consequences, involving *great* pain, if they persist in rebellion against their Creator.

One time, one of our children got upset with us following a bout of discipline occasioned by an improper attitude toward us. I told her, "Look, this isn't just about the attitude you have toward your mother or me; it's about the health of your soul as you accept the authority God has placed over you. If I simply turn a blind eye to your attitude, I risk putting your eternal soul in peril, and I love you too much to do that."

How do I know if I'm keeping first things first? C.J. Mahaney encourages every parent to ask their children a very insightful question: "What do you think your daddy and mommy feel most passionate about?" If the gospel doesn't come to mind, they may have picked up that we *really* care about avoiding embarrassment over their behavior, having a clean house, getting them into the best schools, or having a straight-A report card to boast about in the Christmas letter.

In *Sacred Marriage* I call my wife my "God-mirror."[9] In a similar way, I think children are our heart's mirror. How we interact with them truly does reveal what we value most about life. Paul was "not ashamed of the gospel" but rather "eager to preach the gospel" (Romans 1:15–16). Our kids probably best reveal whether or not our hearts are mirroring what God desires us to be.

The Forgotten Father of Calvary

Sacred parenting leads us into a very severe truth. Consider what our heavenly Father allowed *his* Son to go through on the cross. Every Good Friday, we celebrate Jesus' heroic sacrifice — and well we should. But what about the "Forgotten Father" of Calvary? Imagine watching *your* son being humiliated before your eyes, stripped and pierced and beaten and ridiculed and then crucified. Now imagine your son looking into your eyes as he suffers, then uttering the agonized words, "My father, my dear father, why have you forsaken me?"[10]

Is it heretical for me to suggest that those words uttered by Jesus hurt our heavenly Father even more than the nails hurt Jesus? I don't think so. And I don't think any parent would disagree with me.

No father has loved his son as our heavenly Father loved Jesus, yet his love made room for his Son's suffering. In a way that is hard for us to understand, Jesus the Son, the perfect God-man, needed to suffer for his own sake, and for our sake. The writer of Hebrews explains that Jesus "learned obedience from what he suffered and, once made perfect, he became the source of eternal salvation for all who obey him" (Hebrews 5:8–9). If the Father had not allowed the Son to suffer, Jesus would still bear glory as the deity he is, but he would not wear the glorious victory that he won on the cross. You can't talk about Jesus having less glory without getting heretical, but certainly, without the cross, he wouldn't be the Jesus we know him to be.

Here's the sobering truth: If God allowed his own Son to suffer — and he is our model as a parent — we can expect times when we will have to watch our children suffer for a greater good. When this happens, we will know how Mary felt when Simeon warned her that "a sword will pierce your own soul too" (Luke 2:35).

But please remember, *suffering isn't the end of the story!* Luke takes great pains to express the united purpose of Father and Son after the terrible judgment of sin had been paid. The same Son who said, "My God, my God, why have you forsaken me?" left this world with the words, "Father, into your hands I commit my spirit" (Luke 23:46) — a ringing statement of absolute trust, relinquishment, and love. What a tender comment for any son to say to his father!

So, parents, take courage. Occasional frustration and even rage last only for a moment; they pass away. Do not forsake eternal truths for temporal gain. Mimic your heavenly Father, who courageously allowed his Son to suffer, knowing their relationship would survive.

This is truly the hardest hurt of all. If parenting weren't a sacred journey, we could avoid this truth. We could spend all our time trying to shield our children and ourselves from pain. But because parenting is a sacred task, God calls us to submit to a transcendent will far beyond our own — the Creator's plan for us and for his world, a plan that occasionally will take us through suffering and pain.

In God's worldview, some values rise higher than comfort and happiness. It's spiritual cowardice to shield our children from difficulty and suffering, the very things that temper us. Consider the most concise verse in the Bible on spiritual formation: "We also rejoice in

our sufferings, because we know that suffering produces perseverance; perseverance, character; and character, hope" (Romans 5:3).
In Paul's mind, character gets built by learning to persevere through
difficult times. If we never let our kids face difficult times, they'll
never become strong enough to make a difference in a very cruel
world — as Jesus made a difference on behalf of all of us.

This understanding may cause some of us to reconsider what we
regret most about our children's current situation. One mother,
bedridden by a lifelong hip problem, had to watch while her children
did many chores. Her kids couldn't take part in as many activities as
other kids because they had a mom to look after, and she couldn't get
around easily enough to take them two or three places every afternoon and evening. Further adding to their difficulty, the mom had to
lean on her boys as she walked with a cane. For self-conscious adolescents, having such a parent can feel rather embarrassing.

Yet, as the mom recounts it, instead of making her children bitter, their experience of life with a near invalid turned her boys into
"nurturing, caring people." Because they had so many chores to do,
they had to learn how to work together. The result? Each considers
the other his best friend (how many brothers today can say that?).
The mom's conclusion: "I do not believe that pain is good. But when
I look at my children, I think that my life has been good, and I would
not wish away the parts that have been hard."[11]

I would not wish away the parts that have been hard. This woman has
an Abigail Adams' heart; she is a woman strong enough to bear the
hurt her children will feel in the short term for the sake of the
rewards that hurt will produce in the long term.

We cannot feel unmoved watching our children suffer, yet living
in a fallen world ensures that they will. So what's the alternative? We
parents can be so conscientious, so concerned, and so seemingly caring that we inadvertently raise overly soft boys and spoiled girls.
Spared from any real pain, kept hidden from any real sacrifice,
removed from any real sense of loss, they grow up without any sense
of the agony experienced by Jesus on the cross. And if you remove
the cross from Christianity, all that remains is some wise moral teaching not terribly different from any other religion.

In the name of sparing our children these difficulties, in reality
we are trying to spare ourselves the hurt of seeing them hurt. This

cowardice must not stand. Coddled kids rarely have the mettle to succeed. When critics tear them apart, instead of setting their faces like flint, these pampered puppies will scamper off to the nearest corner, whimpering in self-pity.

Have we lost Abigail's understanding of the pain that purifies?

Two of our closest friends, Boone and Annie Carlson, noticed a major shift in their children's attitudes when they moved from the country to the suburbs. In the country, chores made up a regular part of their kids' lives, but when they moved to a city "with a postage-stamp yard," they started spending most afternoons and evenings taxiing their children to various sporting events. Living on a much smaller parcel of land, they had far fewer chores to do. Over a period of months, Annie noticed that this lifestyle seemed to be creating lazy, self-centered, and demanding kids — so she and Boone sat down and worked hard at creating a chores list, nobly trying to defeat the quiet seduction of the suburbs that was giving their children an unrealistic view of life.

Sadly, many parents travel the opposite direction. They say, "My kids have it so much better than I did" — but to them I want to ask, "Is better *better?*" If by "better" they mean their own rooms, affluent lifestyles, busy schedules (creating "more opportunities"), state-of-the-art sports equipment, sports camps, and so on, then we should stop and ask ourselves if all of that *really* is a superior environment for raising children. My father grew up sharing a bed with two siblings; he worked for his own clothes from the time he was twelve years old. Even a young child's loss of a job seriously affected the family — so much so that when his older sister got too sick to wash dishes at a restaurant, my dad walked in, on his own accord, to replace her. The restaurant owner laughed when he saw the little boy who had come to work. "You can't even reach the sink!" he said, whereupon my dad pulled up a bucket, went to work, and gave the money he earned to his sister.

Today it would be illegal for him to do any such thing. Child labor laws would forbid a young boy from filling in for his older sister. From this perspective, my dad certainly didn't have it better. He had none of the advantages enjoyed by most kids today (my own included). But oh, for another thousand men of his character! The question I ask when raising my own son is this: Is my dad's character an accident, or did he learn some valuable lessons from what he suffered?

This doesn't mean we should intentionally deprive our kids so they can become strong; this world will provide enough suffering without us artificially manufacturing it. There is a way to create a healthy family without undue coddling, but this isn't the book that discusses that. This is a book from the parents' angle, which for me means that I need to develop the courage to allow my children to face some difficulties and even suffering. This truly is "sacred parenting."

It comes down to this: Am I raising kids who believe that some things, namely, the kingdom of God and family life, are worth sacrificing for? Do our kids see me and my wife spending our time and effort focusing on something bigger than ourselves, bigger even than our family? Would I allow my son to put himself in harm's way for a cause more important than us?

Sacred parenting calls me to accept the hardest hurt of all — for the sake of God's kingdom and for the sake of our children's own development. I need to allow my kids to face challenges, failure, rejection, and pain, and then teach them to use these seemingly negative events to fuel their sense of mission and to foster their dependence on God.

Repentance, contrary to popular misconception, is not a heroic first step I make toward Christ, nor is it a feeling-sorry-for my sins. It is the divine gift of being turned toward truth.

William Willimon

There is in repentance this great mystery — that we may fly fastest home on broken wing.

William Sullivan

My guilt has overwhelmed me
    like a burden too heavy to bear.

Psalm 38:4

Chapter 3

The Gold behind
the Guilt

How Raising Children Teaches Us
to Deal with Guilt

I don't know that I've ever witnessed a more bizarre scene. Lisa and I were out on a walk when we saw a little boy, about sixteen months old, running in the middle of the street. We live on the end of a cul-de-sac so we don't get a lot of traffic, but still we could hardly believe we saw no parent anywhere.

The temperature had barely crept into the mid-forties, yet the young lad wore no shoes or coat. In forty-five minutes, it would be dark. I stepped out into the street and said, "Where are you going there, buddy?" He ran straight into my arms, smiled, and barked, "Hi!"

"Where's your mom?" I asked.

"Mom!" he said.

We soon realized we wouldn't get anything more than one-word sentences out of him.

We didn't recognize him, so we took him to a house where we knew small children lived, hoping they would recognize him. The young mom had never seen him before, but she lent us a blanket to keep his bare feet warm while Lisa and I walked around the neighborhood trying to find this boy's home.

Another neighbor called the police to let them know a little boy had been found. Lisa and I figured there had to be a frantic parent somewhere, so we walked up and down the sidewalks, asking at houses where we knew the occupants.

About fifteen minutes later, we saw a car coming down the road. A young mother saw us through her windshield, covered her mouth, parked the car, and ran toward us.

She was crying. She hugged Lisa and me and then said, "I can't believe I lost him. Stupid me! How could I lose my baby?"

An older brother and sister stood behind their mom, both of them fighting back tears of relief. Grandma came running up the sidewalk, probably setting a record for the uphill fifty-yard dash in the senior women's age division.

Then the mom recognized me — I had preached at her church. "And now you probably think I'm totally ditsy that I could lose my child!" she said.

In fact, we thought nothing of the sort. We found out from her (and from a close friend's daughter who baby-sits the boy) that little Dawson is a renowned escape artist. This mom had no fewer than three locks on her front door to keep him inside, but Dad had rushed out to the grocery store and had secured just two of the locks. While Mom talked with Grandma in the living room, little Dawson saw his opportunity for a joyride. He had run a good three blocks from home by the time we'd discovered him.

What parent would think that this mom was irresponsible? Things like this just happen. What struck me, though, was what followed her immediate reaction of relief and joy: extreme guilt.

When one of my friends found out I had begun writing this book, he immediately said to me, "Gary, please don't make me feel guilty about my parenting. I feel guilty enough already."

If this were a how-to book, I could pour the guilt on pretty thick. It's not hard to make any parent feel guilty, because we know we can always do more than we do. We can spend more time with the kids, provide a better house or living environment, listen to them more, pray for them more, respond in a more patient manner. The list of things we could do better never ends.

But we're fallible human beings. We get tired and grouchy. We don't always think before we act. We're far from perfect. And parenting puts the spotlight on our imperfections like nothing else.

I have faced tremendous guilt over my own parenting. As a father and husband, I am close to worthless after 9:00 p.m. I'm a morning person, I love to get up early, and I work hard throughout the day, but this means that by a relatively early hour I'm dead to the world. I hear about fathers and mothers who have long, soulful discussions late into the night with their children, and I feel ashamed at how frequently I hibernate in front of the television. On a vacation with my brother, I remember watching as Jerry talked his boys through their day, offering lessons and meaningful prayers. I guiltily compared that to my "Love you, bud. God bless you. Good night."

The thing is, I *want* my kids to think of me as the best father in the world. From a selfish perspective, that's been my goal for many years. But as they get older and as they see other dads, they're going to realize that in some areas — *many* areas — their dad falls short.

Thus I lived for many years fearing my children's inevitable date with disillusionment. Sure, in their youngest years they regularly called me "the very best daddy in the whole wide world," but I knew I lived on borrowed time.

Getting It Right

Parenting is a complex process. As mothers and fathers, we are simultaneously in charge of a child's emotional, physical, intellectual, social, and spiritual well-being. This gives us a million things to worry about every day.

When Allison was quite young, I told her to pick up her toys. She did it perfectly, without complaining and without being told twice. I wanted to thank her and reward her, so I reached for the cupboard to get out some chocolate chips, when a little voice in the back of my mind warned, "Didn't you read a book or article that said you shouldn't use food as a reward, or else risk giving your daughter an eating disorder?"

Immediately I took off on a furious mental deliberation. I wanted to reward my daughter, but I didn't want to plant the seeds of a future eating disorder. Should I just ignore the fact that she did something I wanted to reinforce, and hope that the lack of a negative response would keep her acting this way in the future? Or should I reward her, which some experts say can produce all kinds of negative effects? But maybe I could reward her with something besides food; maybe I could take her out for a walk, or we could go to Baskin-Robbins — but no, that would be food, too.

My wacky internal debate finally ended when a little three-year-old looked up at me and asked, "Daddy, are you gonna share your chocolate chips or are you just gonna stand there and eat 'em all by yourself?"

Great, I thought, *now Allison's probably going to grow up with feelings of insecurity since her dad is so mentally unstable that he can't decide whether he should just give her some stupid chocolate chips for picking up her toys!*

Since parents so often get the rap for everything bad their kids do, regardless of their parenting style, some character flaws in our children inevitably get traced back to us. Maybe we were too strict. Maybe we were too permissive. Some experts say reward; others say reward is a form of punishment. They all have Ph.D.s; we have only a pile of dirty diapers. We want to do the right thing — but what *is* the right thing?

End result?

Guilt, guilt, guilt, guilt, guilt.

One mother I know felt terrible that she missed early warning signals of a mental illness in her oldest child, in large part because the second child was a virtual tornado. She spent so much time and energy trying to keep this boy from burning down the house or jumping off a cliff that she missed some small, subtle signals that something very serious was afflicting her overly compliant and quiet daughter.

Anybody with such a child can understand how something like this can happen. Extremely difficult kids resemble a raging forest fire — when you try to douse the most dangerous flames, the more subtle fires get ignored. Parenting is a complex game, infinitely more difficult than chess, yet we often have to play it when we don't feel that we're at our best.

This reality, like a sliver of light that appears just above the horizon during a sunrise, provided the first glimpse of a new understanding as I sought to face my own parental guilt. I had to accept the fact that parenting demands skills of me that I don't possess. It requires an understanding and wisdom that I lack. It also puts me on the spot, in charge, twenty-four hours a day, seven days a week, 365 days a year — and even 366 days in a leap year!

A High-Speed Game

Rabbi Nancy Fuchs-Kreimer speaks for many parents when she says that she doesn't find it all that difficult (once the angry moment has passed) to forgive her children. What she finds far more difficult is learning how to forgive *herself*.[1]

I think it helps to realize how taxing any job is that requires giving care twenty-four hours a day. I made one group laugh by claiming that I'm a tremendous father when I feel rested and not stressed-out; I'm a wonderful husband when I don't feel exhausted and have no pressing deadlines. But Christmas comes only once a year, and I'm supposed to be a good husband and father for 365 days a year — that means 364 days when my scores go way down.

But if I think *I* deal with guilt, I have to admit that I don't come close to the world of guilt inhabited by working moms. If you want to see a guilt-ridden group, just talk to some of *them*. Some mothers work out of choice. Others work out of economic necessity. But almost all of them confess to regular pangs of guilt when work and child raising collide. Why? Journalist Lisa Belkin put it succinctly: "Being a working parent means having at least one moment of the day when you push your children away."[2]

You just can't do that without paying an emotional price. That's part of the reason Lisa Belkin decided to start working at home — but even that move didn't erase the guilt feelings. Her son's elation at having his mom home soon collapsed into consternation once she closed the door. "He stood and cried on his side of the office door. I stood and cried on mine."[3]

But even stay-at-home moms without careers become familiar with guilt. Just because you're home doesn't mean you're always at your best! My wife heard someone in a woman's group only half jokingly state that she wished there were a book titled *Parenting with PMS*. How do you nurture a bunch of toddlers — or even handle two teenagers — when you feel as though you're about to explode emotionally?

That's one problem with so many how-to parenting books. They assume, first, that you're calm and, second, that you have the time and energy to write out reward charts, draw up discipline contracts, and still have the peace of mind to administer them calmly and peacefully. On top of this, they assume that you and your spouse are on the same page, that you don't feel buried under financial pressure, and that you don't have a headache, cramps, or a pressing deadline at work.

In reality, parenting can resemble a blur. So many athletes who make it into the National Football League say the first thing they notice is the speed of the game. Everything happens *so fast*. The quarterback has just a few seconds to release the ball; the linebacker has half a second to slip a block or he becomes irrelevant on the play. If a player could just slow the pace down, he could make all-star plays — but everything happens so fast. If you don't become an instinctual player, you'll soon become a former player. The game will pass you by.

Isn't parenting something like that? A lot of men confess to the guilt-inducing struggle of trying to become established in their career at the same time their kids most want to spend time with them. The natural chronology of life seems to work against us, and we constantly have to make choices that resemble lose-lose propositions. If we work hard at our jobs, we feel guilty that our children miss out on time with their dad. If we cut corners at work, we fear that we'll lose our jobs and won't be able to provide for our kids.

Men and women, fathers and mothers — almost all of us wish we could just slow things down a bit. Even vacations can make us feel rushed! One mother lamented how exhausted she became while trying to get her family ready for a weeklong trip. "We spent months making sure the kids had the right clothes, the right suitcases, the proper identification for international travel, and about a million other details — all for a week of 'rest.' I'm so tired, it'll be a long time before I ever agree to go on another vacation."

It dawned on me that not only am I not fully qualified to parent, I also have to admit that sometimes — out of weariness, distraction, or whatever — I don't even live up to my own capabilities. I'm less than *my* best, even though I realize my best isn't good enough!

The Samuel Syndrome

As a child, I loved to read about the prophet Samuel. From birth God called him to be a prophet and spoke to him as a boy. When Samuel grew up to become a mature man, he set up both Saul and David as kings — but don't think of him as a royal brownnoser. When the time came, he rebuked Saul for offering an improper sacrifice and then courageously committed what could have been considered an act of treason by anointing David king while Saul was still alive.

In Samuel's hands, Israel transformed itself from a tribe ruled by a judge to a people ruled by a king. Truly he was a seminal figure in Israel's history and, by all accounts, a faithful servant of God (see 1 Samuel 2:35 and 12:1–5). Yet both his kids rebelled against God:

> When Samuel grew old, he appointed his sons as judges for Israel. The name of his firstborn was Joel and the name of his second was Abijah, and they served at Beersheba. But his sons did not walk in his ways. They turned aside after dishonest gain and accepted bribes and perverted justice.
>
> 1 Samuel 8:1–3

I've read some good Christian books that put the blame on Samuel. The authors assume that Samuel failed as a father; but nowhere does Scripture even hint at this. It just says that Samuel's sons went bad. Eli — whom Samuel succeeded — is specifically charged with not restraining his sons (1 Samuel 3:13), so the fact that the Bible remains silent about Samuel's alleged failure leads me to conclude that Samuel should not be faulted for his kids' choice to lead ungodly lives.

Yet here's the hard truth: Ultimately we wear our kid's failure and guilt as though it were our own. I'm not saying we *should;* I'm just saying we usually *do* — and others tend to reinforce our shouldering of this burden. We live in an era of linear thinking: do good, we're told, and God will bless you, and all your children will become godly believers. Mess up, and God will curse you financially, relationally, and vocationally, and your kids will destroy their lives.

But to maintain a strictly linear train of thought is to diminish the nature of being human. We are not raising robots; *we are shepherding image bearers of the Creator God* who live with freedom of choice, their own wills, and a personal responsibility of their own. It seems to me that we tend to take too much credit for kids who turn out good, and too much blame for kids who turn out bad.

You want to hear a severe truth? None of us can be such good parents that God becomes obligated to save our children's souls. On the more encouraging end, none of us can mess up so badly that our children somehow extend beyond the reach of God's mercy.

Judah's King Asa began his reign as a God-fearing king, but he fell from the Lord's favor when he relied on foreign powers rather than on God to defeat his enemies. When challenged about this, Asa actually imprisoned the prophet who spoke God's truth to him! Yet his son Jehoshaphat was a different story: "The LORD was with Jehoshaphat because in his early years he walked in the ways his father David had followed" (2 Chronicles 17:3). Asa's poor example, mercifully, did not pollute his son.

The Bible records instances of faithful servants of God who raise ungodly children (Samuel), and servants who abandon God but who yet have faithful, God-fearing offspring (Asa). It even records egregiously wicked kings (Ahaz) with heroic, God-following sons (Hezekiah).

Even if I *were* a perfect and wise parent always at his best, *I have no guarantee that my children would always choose wisely.* And just because I have many weaknesses doesn't necessarily mean my kids will suffer.

I realized a truth that had lain hidden for so long. Though I had wonderful, godly parents, I still grew up with certain disappointments that I wanted to rectify as a parent. It finally dawned on me that I had asked something of my parents that they could never be: I had wanted them to love me as only God can love me. And now *I* wanted to love my kids as only God can love them.

In short, either I was setting up rivals for God or I was trying to compete with God — both are efforts doomed to failure. I finally came to a major crossroads: instead of competing *with* God, I realized God had called me to focus my efforts on introducing my kids *to* God, even using my own failures and inadequacies as compelling causes for my children to find their refuge *in him.*

What will it be for you? Will you try to compete with God, or will you work to introduce your children to the one true God? May the Lord have mercy on your soul if you're a legalistic parent! You're going to be fearful, miserable, exhausted, and frequently frustrated — but more than that, you'll bury yourself under guilt.

All of us can look back and see lost opportunities in our parenting, as well as seeing our character flaws reproduced and even enlarged in our children. We assume that these lost opportunities and character flaws are to blame when our children rebel — and sometimes, we have to admit that our failings *have* assaulted our children.

If you're a divorced mom and you see your son acting up, *of course* you're going to think things would be different if Dad still lived at home. I would be less than honest if I suggested things probably wouldn't be different. Yet perhaps as a result of your divorce you've taken personal inventory and addressed some areas in your life that needed to change — and your son has watched it take place and is benefiting from it.

Hear the Samuel Syndrome: *It is possible to be a faithful servant of God who has one or more kids go bad.* And consider the Ahaz Syndrome as well: *It's possible to be a wicked parent with very godly offspring.*

I am *not* saying that children can't be led astray and even damaged by deficiencies in our parenting. Scripture clearly says that having unruly children may limit what roles we can play in the church (1 Timothy 3:4–5). But the failure of kids does not necessarily mean we have failed as parents, even though it does probably mean we'll *feel* as though we've failed as parents. Guilt is a given for a fallen parent called to raise sinful kids; none of us will be perfect mothers or fathers.

We find our only refuge in God's grace and mercy. It's not possible to be a parent without occasionally feeling guilty — but that's a good thing, as we'll see momentarily.

Gold-Plated Guilt

Not so long ago, the word *polio* struck fear into the heart of every parent. Today, the effects of polio seem little more than a very bad memory. Why the difference? Doctors have learned how to beat the disease. Similarly, one or two generations ago, a diagnosis of cancer meant a likely death sentence. Today, according to an oncologist friend of mine, doctors routinely cure more than seventy percent of cancer patients.

Guilt is a fierce reality, an eternal judgment of damnation — but God has provided a cure in the death and resurrection of Jesus Christ. What once was deadly can now play a positive role in our lives and hearts and souls. Just as former Olympic runner Marty Liquori talks about the "gifts that cancer can give,"[4] so we Christian parents can talk about several positive roles that guilt can play in our lives.

1. Guilt Can Point Us to God

Sometimes we parents need to remind ourselves of a few basic facts. First, we're not God. We're going to miss some cues. We're going to feel tired. We're going to occasionally get distracted by our own temptations and failings. Sometimes our parental vision will be impaired by our own health needs, vocational concerns, or even ministry obligations. Since we are finite human beings with limited understanding who require a certain amount of sleep, we can't be God to our kids.

Others of us (though I don't include myself in this; God blessed me with wonderful, godly parents) have to recognize that maybe Mom and Dad never taught us how to raise children. Maybe you didn't have nurturing parents who demonstrated for you what it meant to be a father or a mother. You never saw spiritual training modeled, so you entered parenting as a rookie without a coach. If this is you, *of course* you're going to make mistakes! How could you not?

You need to know that God has different expectations for different parents. Jesus makes it very clear (in Luke 12:48) that, while all of us are guilty, God does consider our background when deciding the *degree* of guilt: "From everyone who has been given much, much will be demanded; and from the one who has been entrusted with much, much more will be asked."

The positive side of our limitations is this: *weakness on our part can actually become a strength when we use it to transfer our kids' allegiance from us to God.* We need a Savior, just as they do. We can love them — but God alone has loved, is loving, and will love them with a perfect love. Our children need to know that even if Mom and Dad let them down, there is One who will always "be there" for them.

My desire to be "the very best daddy in the whole wide world" cloaked a desire to be treated like a god in my own house. What enormous pressure this put on me! How much more freeing to admit to my children, "Do you see, kids, why Daddy needs a Savior, just as you do? All of us are helpless apart from God's grace." I can't be God to my kids, but I can model my need for God. Guilt has given me this gift.

What is better for the kingdom of God? That my son and daughters would say, "I can never serve God like Dad did" or "If God can use my dad, he can use me"? There is no question — the latter statement is the reality that most serves God's purposes long term. It is my job as my children's parent to model my own need for God's mercy and to demonstrate how God can use even sinful people to accomplish his aims.

In this sense, we shouldn't look at guilt as a parking lot but as a car wash. When guilt feelings keep us self-absorbed, destroy our motivation, and make us discouraged, guilt has become a parking lot — not a good thing. But when guilt reminds us that we are insufficient, and when this insufficiency points us to God — his forgiveness, his empowering Spirit, and his provision of grace — then guilt becomes a spiritual car wash. You don't camp out in a car wash; you just go there to get clean! You drive through the car wash and come out on the other end with an entirely new outlook. That's one of the *healthy* roles that guilt can play for parents: pointing us and our children to God.

2. Guilt Can Motivate Us to Do Better

Sacred parenting is a very long journey. It's hard to focus on a task for eight hours, much less eighteen years. The length of parenting means that there will be highs and lows, good days and bad days. Yes, we're going to miss some things. *All* of us could do better. All of us could do more.

As parents, we need to cultivate the attitude that seventy-five-year-old John has toward golf. I met John while playing on a public golf course. John plays golf seven days a week, weather permitting. As one player missed a putt, someone else offered his consolations, and John said, "When you play every day, you don't worry too much about all that because you know there's always tomorrow."

That's not a bad motto for parenting: *There's always tomorrow.* Of course, there's never a *guarantee* of tomorrow, but even so, for most of us, parenting lasts decades, not days. We'll have good days and bad days. When we see parenting as a long journey, we don't drown ourselves in guilt on days that rate less than an A+. We won't always be at our best, but we'll usually have another go at it the next day.

Don't look at your failings apart from God's grace and God's provision. Guilt becomes deadweight when you become consumed by your failings, past or present. But guilt can become positive motivation when you hear our Lord say, "Then neither do I condemn you. . . . Go now and leave your life of sin" (John 8:11).

Recognizing that I become deadweight after 9:00 p.m., guilt can motivate me to get more involved at 7:30 p.m., before my brain turns to mush. It means I spend more time with my kids on personal lunch dates, when I'm more alert and available to them. Whatever your own scenario, let your guilt lead you to become more involved instead of causing you to pull back in frustration.

Because of the breadth of God's mercy, we get another day, another chance. Because of the depth of God's mercy, we can't exhaust his grace! We can look forward with confidence, use our failings as teachable moments, and wake up with cleansed souls and fresh hearts, knowing we've learned some valuable lessons for the next day.

3. Guilt Can Remind Us of God's Providence

Parental guilt can actually encourage us to rest in God's providence. It's no accident that we have the children we have; God made them and placed them in our care. When he did so, he knew our limitations, but he still entrusted us with these children. I like Carolyn Mahaney's thoughts on this topic:

> We can deduce that if God in his divine wisdom chose to give sinful children to sinful parents, then our children are not so weak that they are unable to endure our sinful behavior.... Our children are not that fragile. If they were, God would have waited until we were further along in the maturing process before he gave them to us. But he didn't.[5]

As people of faith, we need to trust God and let some of the responsibility fall back on him. This doesn't mean we become cavalier and fail to fully engage ourselves as parents to the best of our ability. But it does mean that we have a place of rest — it's called trusting in God's providence and in Christ's sufficiency. All of us come up short as parents — but Christ promises to make up for what we lack. How could you find yourself in a more secure state? If we expect ourselves to be perfect, we'll feel forever frustrated — and indirectly we'll call into question God's wisdom and ultimate purpose for our lives.

4. Guilt Can Teach Us to Love Mercy

One of my favorite phrases for meditation in all of Scripture comes from Micah 6:8, where we are told to "love mercy." Micah doesn't tell us to merely "demonstrate" mercy or to "discipline our-selves" toward mercy; he tells us to fall in love with it!

The Hebrew word for this love, *ʾāhab*, is used of a husband toward his wife and appears frequently in Song of Songs. To "love" mercy is to feel enthralled by mercy. When you love someone, you talk about that person. A parent who loves mercy feels so thankful for the mercy God has shown them that he or she frequently men-tions it to others. Such a mom or dad cherishes mercy; the mere thought of it warms her heart, brings a smile to his face. The person who truly loves mercy will have a childlike awe and wonder: "God has shown me *mercy!*"

Those people who love mercy are not thankful merely for the mercy *they* have received; those who love mercy are also eager to show mercy to *others*. Like God, they *want* to forgive, they feel *eager* to forgive. You don't have to convince them to show mercy; they love to show mercy. Mercy is the defining principle of their lives.

What does this have to do with guilt? Meditating on the won-derful reality of mercy led me to a jaw-dropping truth: God could baptize my guilt because without guilt there could, by definition, be no mercy! Guilt is a terrible reality, *but mercy is more wonderful than guilt is terrible* ("mercy triumphs over judgment" [James 2:13]). With-out acknowledging our own guilt, we would never sense the need for mercy, so we wouldn't appreciate this glorious gift of God. And with-out the guilt of others, we would never be able to apply mercy. Fac-ing the reality of guilt head-on, unflinching, we open ourselves to the even more beautiful reality of God's mercy.

What does this mean, practically? Turn guilt feelings into a call to worship! Acknowledge your guilt, and then thank God that he has made provision for your guilt. Confess that you have fallen short as a parent, but then expend just as much energy worshiping the God who forgives and who will show mercy to you in your failings. And then apply this same mercy to your children and your own parents. Can you accept that *your* parents weren't perfect? That *your* parents had limitations? That *your* parents, distracted and tired and harried, didn't always live up to their best?

It may sound crazy, but using guilt as a call to adoration can turn parental guilt into a pathway toward intimacy with God.

5. Guilt Has a Positive "Hidden Agenda"

I told one group of men that I wished I could start parenting now, at age forty-one. I feel more mature at this point, more settled in my career, with a better perspective to begin parenting than when Allison was born to me at the age of twenty-five.

But here's the rub: What helped me to become more mature? What has given me a better perspective? What has worked on my character over the past decade and a half?

Raising my kids!

I wouldn't be the man I am if I hadn't raised Allison, Graham, and Kelsey. Not that the "man I am" is particularly mature or wise, but he is more mature and, yes, wiser than the young man he was at twenty-five. To be sure, God can mature a soul in other ways, but in my own life, raising children has provided a major pathway to spiritual formation.

Yes, I've failed at parenting — again and again. I wasn't smart enough, attentive enough, or sensitive enough. I remained too self-centered. Sometimes I felt simply too tired or was just flat-out too immature.

Yet a simple truth has helped me face my guilt. God revolutionized my understanding when he seemed to drop this thought in my head: God cares just as much about *my own growth* as he does about Allison's, Graham's, and Kelsey's. From my perspective, I want to sacrifice for my kids, put them first, and consider their needs above my own. But from *God's* perspective, the Lord wants the process of parenting to change *all* of us — myself (and yourself) included.

It's not as though God thinks only our children need to be spiritually formed. God is working on all of us. As the parents, we're to sacrifice and show greater maturity; yet in God's eyes, the ground is level at the cross, and he wants all of us to grow toward him.

This is, in fact, the "gold behind the guilt," God's "hidden agenda" in parenting. God cares so much about you that he's willing to risk letting you raise one, two, three, or even more of his precious children. He knows ahead of time that you're going to make mistakes. He knows at the outset that you won't be a perfect parent — but he is so zealous for your own growth that *he is willing to take that risk.* Scripture clearly states how zealously God guards these small persons. Even so, he lets *you* take care of some of them!

I saw this from another perspective when I took my daughter and her best friend with me on my speaking trip to Orlando (see page 28). We were gone for six days, and I remember considering it the highest compliment that Laura's parents would entrust their then ten-year-old daughter to me for that length of time.

God entrusts *you* with one or more of his children for at least *eighteen* years.

When we look at parenting this way, instead of producing guilt, it gives us greater understanding. God has created an institution — the family — through which he can shape, mold, and form all of us, parents included. We come into the family as imperfect people, and we sin against each other every day; yet through rubbing shoulders and learning to ask for, and offer, forgiveness, we all come out the richer for taking part in this sometimes painful process.

God adores your kids, *but he is also crazy about you.* You're his much-loved son or daughter. He has a direct interest in your care and your spiritual growth, and he sees your kids as valuable teachers and prophets to that end.

So what can we say? Guilt has a place. When we fall short, we *should* feel guilty. But God has a remedy! To look at guilt without seeing God's remedy is as silly as worrying about polio without considering the vaccines through which doctors have eradicated it. Justified or unjustified guilt feelings can discourage, weaken, and frustrate us. But guilt forgiven, baptized, and even sanctified by Christ's work on the cross can motivate us, encourage us, and keep us focused. In this light, guilt can actually be our servant as we embrace the sacred task of parenting.

Imperfect Parents

A young father followed the same routine every evening: He went into the kitchen, opened a cupboard, and took out a glass.[6] He then walked over to a cupboard, pulled out a cookie jar, took out two or three cookies, and put them on a plate. Then he'd go to the refrigerator, get some milk, and pour himself a tall glass. Following that, he'd walk into the living room and enjoy his milk and cookies while sitting in his favorite chair.

One evening as he was heading into the kitchen for his nightly ritual, the father noticed his three-year-old son heading into the kitchen ahead of him. The boy had a determined look on his face. Instead of announcing his presence, the father decided to stay unobserved so that he could watch what his son seemed so determined to do.

The boy pulled out several drawers, essentially making steps so he could climb onto the counter — something he was forbidden to do. Next he walked across the counter (another no-no) and opened an upper cupboard door. He reached in and pulled out a glass, knocking over several other glasses in the process. The young boy placed his glass down, hopped off the counter, then picked up his glass, and put it on the floor. He marched to the refrigerator and pulled out the milk, then poured it into the glass. The flowing milk proved too strong for his little hands, and it spilled over the top of the glass. The little boy wiped up the spilled milk with his shirt.

Then he left his milk, walked over to another cupboard, and pulled out the cookie jar. This was strictly forbidden; the father's son knew he wasn't supposed to get cookies without permission. But he reached in and while doing so pulled several other cookies out of the jar. The boy put them back and wiped up the crumbs with his now milk-soaked shirt.

The father stepped out to intercept his son, only to be greeted by a huge smile. "Here are your cookies, Dad. I love you."

In this story, I want you to place yourself in the son's position, not the dad's. We're the little child, trying to serve our heavenly Father and yet making a lot of messes in the process. We can't reach as high as we'd like, so we make do with makeshift steps to reach the counter. We knock over a few glasses, and we spill the milk while we're trying to prepare a drink. Lacking all wisdom, we come up with the great idea of cleaning up the mess with our shirt instead of with a washcloth. But what dad wouldn't feel touched by such a display of service, however messy it might be?

We're not the best parents, not by far. We don't have all the wisdom we'd like. We don't understand how everything fits together. We make mistakes, we make messes, we can do everything wrong — but God looks at us with a Father's delighted eyes. Where we see weakness, God sees humility. Where we see messes, God sees intent. Where we see failings, God sees motives.

And he smiles. He takes us into his arms. And he laughs a delighted Father's laugh.

I stopped trying to run things the way I wanted many years ago. I started listening to God and letting Him have His way in everything. If men like you did that, you would find the answers, instead of spending your lives beaten by the problems you yourselves create.

Frank Buchman

Listen and understand.

Jesus, in Matthew 15:10

Chapter 4

Seizing Heaven

How Raising Children Teaches Us to Listen to God

My youngest daughter, Kelsey, is a talker. One of her friends once asked her, "Kelsey, do you *ever* stop talking?"

"Why would I?" Kelsey answered. "Talking is my spiritual gift!"

And she can do it fast. "Don'tyouthinkthatbeingatalkshowhost would be a good job for me?" Kelsey once asked me. "Talktalktalk-talktalk, that's all they do, andI'dbereallyreallygoodatit."

Years ago she inquired, "How come everybody always asks me if my jaw gets tired?" This happened shortly after a friend of ours gave Kelsey a ride home from church. I'll never forget opening the door and seeing the weary look on our friend's face as Kelsey marched right past the threshold.

"Wow," was all our friend could muster, a blank look betraying her exhaustion.

One time, I called Kelsey on my cell phone during a trip. When I feel tired, I particularly like to talk to Kelsey because she does most of the work. The signal faded on my cell phone, so I immediately called back but got a busy signal. I waited another couple of minutes, called again, and still, no luck. Kelsey didn't realize what had happened until "some lady" (as she put it) finally said, "If you'd like to make a call, please hang up and try again."

"Dad?" Kelsey yelled into the phone. "Aren't you there?"

When she finally hung up and I called her back, Kelsey asked, "Now what was the last thing you heard me say?"

When I told her, she lamented, "That was five minutes ago! I can't remember all that, but I've got lots more to say . . ."

One time I did something that I'll long regret. On a family drive, Kelsey kept all of us "company" with her chatter, but after a few hours, it can become difficult to keep up. My son was getting tired, and I was trying to concentrate on finding our destination. I could see my son beginning to lose his patience.

"Graham," I whispered, "all you have to do is say an occasional 'uh-huh' every couple of minutes and she'll never be the wiser."

Kelsey later found out what I said and felt deeply hurt — and rightly so. I felt terrible, asked for her forgiveness, and put it down as yet another parental failure.

Being around kids — admittedly some more than others — invites us to learn how to listen anew. Most people think of religion as a bunch of dos and don'ts, but I believe a relationship with God is distinguished first of all by *listening*. During the dramatic transfiguration, when Peter, James, and John got a firsthand look at Jesus' true glory, God the Father admonished the chosen three, "This is my Son, whom I love. *Listen to him!*" (Mark 9:7, emphasis added).

Like Father, like Son. Listening is a constant refrain in the teaching of Jesus:

- "Listen and understand" (Matthew 15:10).
- "He who has ears to hear, let him hear" (Mark 4:9).
- "Again Jesus called the crowd to him and said, 'Listen to me, everyone, and understand this'" (Mark 7:14).
- "Consider carefully how you listen" (Luke 8:18).
- "Listen carefully to what I am about to tell you" (Luke 9:44).
- "My sheep listen to my voice" (John 10:27).

What distinguishes a Christian from those who don't believe or from those who make no room for God in their lives? A Christian *listens* to God while the world ignores him. Sometimes we downplay the role of listening, insisting that listening alone comes up short; we have to obey, after all. But frankly, being flat-out ignored offends as much as anything. We know this as parents. Does anything feel more irritating than talking to kids who tune us out (even though I've admitted doing this very thing to my daughter)?

God remains active in our world — and he speaks to us if we'll only listen:

- "Surely the Sovereign LORD does nothing without revealing his plan to his servants the prophets" (Amos 3:7).
- "Call to me and I will answer you and tell you great and unsearchable things you do not know" (Jeremiah 33:3).
- "He who forms the mountains, creates the wind, and reveals his thoughts to man, . . . the LORD God Almighty is his name" (Amos 4:13).
- "The LORD confides in those who fear him" (Psalm 25:14).
- "Everyone who listens to the Father and learns from him comes to me" (John 6:45).
- "All your sons will be taught by the LORD" (Isaiah 54:13).

Many of us don't actively rebel against God. We don't shake our fist at him or malign his name — but we do ignore him. We get too busy to listen. And that offends him just as much as refusing to obey. We could call this lapse "practical atheism." We *say* we believe in God, but what good is our belief if it doesn't intersect with everyday living? The world can do without what I've called in another book "Christless Christianity."

The Israelites sinned in this manner during the time of Joshua. After a visit from the deceitful Gibeonites (who misled the Israelites into making a treaty, convincing them that the Gibeonites didn't live in the promised land God had commanded the Israelites to conquer), "the men of Israel sampled their provisions but did not inquire of the LORD" (Joshua 9:14). Like a prideful parent, they looked at the obvious signs — the Gibeonites said they were from far away and looked as though they had traveled a great distance — and arrogantly thought, *This is an easy one; we can handle this. We'll make the treaty.*

I'm ashamed to admit how many times, as a parent, I've done the same thing. Outward appearances have fooled me. An issue didn't seem serious enough or complex enough to bother God with, and consequently I made some foolish choices that were founded in ignorance. We are a prideful people by nature, and pride keeps telling us we don't need God to handle the situation at hand. Listening to God provides the true test of our humility. Humble people listen; prideful people never seem to have the time to wait on God.

That's why I think listening is a key component of Christian parenting and spirituality. It changes the nature of our faith, and it redirects what we do. It moves us from merely a human-centered faith of willful obedience and timeless principles, and ushers us into cooperating with God as he actively moves upon his world. It is one of the ways that we can "seize heaven" and invite God's presence into our lives.

Practical Help

Listening to God makes parenting *sacred*.

Catherine Marshall became a single mom when her husband, Peter Marshall, died unexpectedly. Peter was a spiritual giant — a nationally known author and the chaplain of the United States Senate — and his passing left a big void in the life of his son, an emptiness impossible to fill. Catherine found comfort in daily listening to God: "In my situation the best answers to the sense of helplessness and frustration came through my early morning quiet time when in prayer I would seek God's guidance for my son."[1] Catherine no longer had a husband with whom she could discuss her son's development, but she had a God — a God who speaks.

Listening to God has also deeply affected my own family. As I wrote this book, I spent time listening to God. Early one morning, I clearly sensed that I was to take a break from work and drive Allison to an appointment — a four-hour commitment. Lisa does this 90 percent of the time, but God seemed insistent. It was my turn to do this.

I mentioned it to Lisa at breakfast, and she seemed pretty blasé about it, which sparked in me some second thoughts. I had a good bit of work to do, after all, and if Lisa didn't really care ... Yet later in the day, Lisa got more and more tired, even taking a nap (something she rarely does). And then she got a call from her sister, who planned to stop by the next day. None of Lisa's siblings had ever visited our new house, so I knew Lisa would want to spend a good bit of time cleaning and organizing.

The thing is, neither Lisa nor I knew in the morning how tired she was getting — but God did. Neither Lisa nor I knew that her sister would call and say she'd like to come over — but God knew. And by listening to God, we managed to schedule our day so that we could actually prepare for a future as yet unknown to us (but completely known to God, who happens to care for my wife and who wanted to use me as an instrument of his concern). Admittedly, this is a pretty mundane example. It's not a dramatic event, a spectacular miracle — but these small directions can make a big difference over the course of a lifetime. And they can certainly occur more often for all believers if we would just take time each day to *listen* to the God who speaks.

I wonder: How would our marriages be transformed if we learned to listen to God on behalf of our spouses? How might husbands feel encouraged if wives learned from the mouth of God what kind of day their husband was having and made appropriate preparations for his return home? How might wives feel uplifted and strengthened if husbands would take time out of their day to ask, "Lord, what do I need to do today to better love my wife?" How might kids find strength and warning and guidance and inspiration if their parents would glean insights from the God who created them, from the God who knows their thoughts, from the God who knows their inner struggles and who hears every conversation they have with their friends?

An Inspired Life

True listening is an *active* discipline. Failing to listen is not so much a sin as it is a choice to live a powerless, uninspired Christian life. Just as we have to choose to hear what our children are truly saying, so we have to choose to hear those quiet whispers of divine love and guidance.

The great challenge, of course, is that listening to our children and our God can be difficult. Sometimes we misunderstand our children, and sometimes we will mistake our own fears for the voice of God. But the fact that we aren't perfect hearers provides no excuse to throw out the discipline of listening; it simply means that we need to build safeguards into our application of that listening. We know, for instance, that God won't speak contrary to his Word. We know that in the majority of cases, God follows common sense. And we know that God has given us his church — other believers — to help us discern his words.

God is eager to speak, and he can get through to us despite our imperfections. As long as we remain *humble* listeners — willing to subject our hearing to wise correction — the discipline of listening can change our families, our lives, and our relationships.

One of the most powerful times of intimacy with my Lord occurs when God reveals to me some challenge in the life of one of my children, urging me to address a particular issue or concern. In those seasons, I feel like a co-laborer with God, as though the two of us are working together to complete a dynamic work in a human soul.

Even more important is what the recipient receives. I remember once asking a man a question that stopped him in his tracks. "Why did you ask me that question?" he demanded.

"Well, I prayed about our meeting today and thought this was something I should bring up."

"That's exactly what my wife and I have been fighting about for *two weeks!*" This led to a long conversation, but it occurred in the context of this man coming to understand that *God* saw into his heart and read his needs. In the end, this reality alone far outstripped any advice I could give.

If we ask our heavenly Father — and just as important, patiently wait for an answer — God will often tip us off to what is really going on in our kids' hearts. My own insecurities and immaturity usually prompt me to focus on things in my kids that God could care less about while neglecting the very things God is most concerned about. For me, listening has provided vital corrections.

What Kind of Diaper Is That?

Lisa's ability to hear the difference in Allison's cries amazed me as a young father. She could clearly distinguish between a "wet diaper" cry, an "I'm hungry; feed me now or I'll die" cry, and an "I'm in pain" cry. To her credit, Lisa used this special gift to its fullest extent during those long nights when an infant's piercing wail sliced into the quiet of our sleep. I'd often try that old husband standby, "Honey, the baby needs to breast-feed, and I don't have breasts, so I guess you have to be the one to get up and take care of her."

"That's not a hungry cry," Lisa insisted. "That's a messy diaper cry, and last time I checked it doesn't take a pair of breasts to clean up a baby's bottom. But nice try."

Skeptical, I'd get up and check, and sure enough, that earthy smell enveloped me as soon as I entered the room. Lisa never erred. After getting a clean diaper, the baby dropped right back to sleep.

One time our doctor thought Lisa had become too good a listener. "Babies need to learn to communicate," he explained, "and if you always anticipate everything, you can actually hold them back from learning how to do that more effectively." But God has invented an effective method of humbling the parent who was a great listener of babies. It's called adolescence. During this stage, you have to learn a whole new language. Grunts, groans, icy stares, bursts of irritated breaths — these traits represent a teenager's fervid quest to keep parents guessing about what's really going on inside. One mother confided how she had asked her fifteen-year-old daughter if she had finished her homework. A seemingly simple question — but it made her daughter explode and run to her room in tears.

If a parent truly wants to relate to his child, he's going to have to learn how to listen, to pick up on verbal as well as nonverbal cues. A mom will soon learn that child number two speaks with a different voice than does child number one or child number three. She'll have to adjust her listening skills to tune in to the speaker. Some children seem so quiet and compliant that we have to actively approach them to discern what they want to communicate; others blurt it right out. It's no exaggeration to suggest that half of parenting is — or should be — listening.

Yet it's so tempting to give up on listening when our kids make it painfully difficult. Because listening is an active choice of love, its greatest enemies are apathy and busyness. Most of us would never intentionally abuse our children, but all of us are tempted at times to stop listening to them, even though listening is the active force of love. Let me be blunt: *to stop listening is to stop loving.* Love is not about what you *don't* do; it's about your movement *toward* someone. The opposite of love is not hatred; it's apathy.

Thankfully, this discipline of listening, so crucial to the art of parenting, provides great spiritual training for the practice of prayer. Yes, that's right. Raising kids can teach us how to pray.

Entering the Interior Castle

When Graham was quite young we talked one day about heaven.

"There's no better place, Graham," I told him as he snuggled close. "No crying, no sickness, no bullies; the girls there don't have cooties; there aren't any under-the-bed monsters — plus, we'll all be together."

Graham nodded. "I can't wait to sit on God's lap," he said, "and your lap, too."

There may be no safer place in the world, spiritually, than a parent's lap. Take the most frightened child; take a little girl who skinned her knee or a boy who was picked on by a bully. Let their hearts race at a hundred beats a minute, tears cascading from their eyes — then place this child in the all-encompassing lap of a parent. Suddenly, the heartbeat drops in half and the tears slow to a trickle. The child is safe.

A parent's lap is the most secure refuge ever invented by God. Even as adults, we secretly harbor the desire to lose ourselves in a lap — the spiritual lap of God. In fact, one Hebrew name for God is "the Place." Mystics throughout the ages have sought to reach this destination, a quiet spiritual refuge in a rushed world. The task of raising children points the way there. True spiritual listening is about climbing into God's lap, restful and secure, and hearing his soft words of love, affirmation, correction, and challenge.

The biggest change in my prayer life probably occurred as the result of reading about two different people: Teresa of Avila and Frank Buchman. I once treated prayer in the same way I treated my mileage charts as a long-distance runner in high school: always wanting to set new records and run a little bit further than before. If I wanted to become a better runner, I thought, I'd have to run sixty miles a week instead of fifty, and then seventy, and so on.

In the same way, I thought that in order to improve my prayer time, I'd have to pray *longer*. I needed to engage in one-hour, then two-hour, and then three-hour times of prayer. And then I'd have to kick in a few all-night vigils, as well as the twice-yearly weekend prayer retreat.

Teresa of Avila didn't define prayer by time or frequency but by *intimacy*. Though this may sound elementary to many of you, it revolutionized my prayer life. Teresa's book *The Interior Castle* charts the soul's progress in terms of intimate attachment — beginning with the prayer of meditation, moving on to the prayer of recollection, the prayer of the quiet, the prayer of union, and, ultimately, the "interior castle," which she describes as the "fullness of spiritual marriage."

My testosterone-trained technique could take me only so far; I benefited from an insightful woman who taught me how to approach God a little more softly and who pointed out that much of prayer is about climbing into God's lap and resting. Then I read a number of books about Frank Buchman (he died in 1961, the year of my birth), who founded a powerful movement known as "Moral Re-Armament," or the Oxford Group. Buchman urged believers to spend time every day listening for God to speak. In a 1935 address to ten thousand people who met at Hamlet's Castle at Elsinore in Denmark, Buchman made this declaration:

> We accept as commonplace a man's voice carried by radio to the uttermost parts of the earth. Why not the voice of the living God as an active, creative force in every home, every business, every parliament? ...
>
> The Holy Spirit is the most intelligent source of information in the world today. He has the answer to every problem. Everywhere when men will let him, he is teaching them how to live. . . . Divine guidance must become the normal experience of ordinary men and women. Any man can pick up divine messages if he will put his receiving set in order. Definite, accurate, adequate information can come from the Mind of God to the minds of men. This is normal prayer.[2]

This practice of listening to God influenced the highest levels of many national governments, and it made a major impact on millions of individual lives. Christianity, Buchman insisted, begins with listening. To a group of twenty-five thousand people in Birmingham (Great Britain), Buchman proclaimed, "The lesson the world most needs is the art of listening to God. . . . God gave a man two ears and one mouth. Why don't you listen twice as much as you talk? This is a daily possibility for everyone — to listen to God and get his program for the day."[3]

Many of us would enjoy far more effectiveness in our ministries if we would *do* less and *listen* more. This lesson, frankly, I continue to learn. My five previous books were perhaps most marked by study. This book, more than any of my others, was literally birthed in prayer. The chapters wouldn't come together until I sat before God, asking him to show me the main point of each one. A pleasant change — and one I should have learned years ago!

We stand on dangerous ground if we ever let service to God crowd out our time of listening to God. Gordon Smith, in his fine book *On the Way*, writes quite bluntly, "It is inconceivable to think that God would give us so much to do that we can no longer spend extended time with Him."[4] Listening doesn't detract from our service; it empowers it.

One time, I was speaking at a "Sacred Marriage" seminar on the East Coast. I had covered the material many times before, but I like to pray beforehand to see if God would like me to customize it for the particular audience. That weekend I focused — for the first time ever — on the idea that the participants' marriages were very precious to God, even if they were no longer precious to them. The word *precious* kept coming up time and time again. The word didn't appear in my notes; I simply felt that God wanted me to make such an emphasis.

Afterwards a young wife came up to me with tears in her eyes. "What you said," she began, "about our marriage being precious to God ..." She paused, composed herself, and added, "My *name* is Precious. I can't tell you how much that spoke to me."

What are the odds? How many people have *you* met named Precious?

But that's the point. I wasn't playing the odds. I was listening, and God spoke, hitting at least one woman at a very deep level.

This kind of thing happened to Frank Buchman all the time. One evening, while walking down the street, he clearly had the thought to speak to the man strolling in front of him. At first Buchman hesitated, but God seemed insistent. Finally Frank called out, "I felt I ought to speak to you. I thought you might need something."

"Of course I'm in need," the man replied. "God must have sent you to me."

The man's mother was dying in the hospital. His brothers and sisters had remained at the bedside, and he had stepped out to clear his head, not at all certain what to do. Frank returned with him to the hospital and had a powerful time of ministry. But because the ministry resulted from an act of listening, he was never tempted to take credit. A Japanese prime minister, impressed with Frank's achievements, once told him, "You must feel very proud of all this," to which

Frank replied, "I do not feel that way at all. I have had nothing to do with it. God does everything. I only obey and do what He says."[5]

A parent who listens to God for their children's welfare will gain this same humility. At times God has tipped me off to something I missed in one of my kids. The last thing these revelations do is make me feel proud; on the contrary, I feel humbled that I missed what now seems so obvious. Listening reminds me of how completely I depend on God to carry out the task of parenting. I'd be absolutely lost without his insight.

Sometimes listening can feel painful — in a good way. I've found that many times God will gently correct me with a question. On one occasion, the question went something like this: "Are you spending more emotional energy this summer getting to know what's going on in your adolescent daughter's heart or in trying to lower your golf scores?" He didn't say "time"; he didn't say "money" (both of which I could defend). God wanted me to consider the focus of my emotional energy — what did I find myself thinking and talking about?

Ironically, I find this gentle challenge a source of great comfort. You gain a calm assurance when you walk in the confidence that God will quietly let you know when you start to stray. You don't feel alone, unprotected, or unwarned. It's a very secure place to be, as you rest in God's shepherding care and listen to his voice.

My friend Annie Carlson, who has four children (one of whom she and her husband adopted), has an admirable perspective on this. "We're usually so concerned about finding God's will in major life decisions," she said, "but if we are constantly checking in with God on a daily basis, we get used to listening and then don't panic when big decisions come along." In other words, we learn to discern God's voice for major life choices by constantly seeking his guidance in the day-to-day decisions as we make listening to God a regular part of our experience. Raising kids means we need God's guidance on a daily, if not hourly, basis!

More than anything else, having kids forces me into the posture of listening. In my parental pride, I'm tempted to talk more than to listen, but I've found that talking without listening is a lousy way to build relationships with children. Raising kids has thus reoriented my entire approach to relationships, both with God and other people: listen, listen, listen!

While we still need to make our needs known to God, a mature pray-er will spend about twice as much time listening and waiting as she does talking. And you want to know a fascinating thing about spiritual listening? God changes languages. Sometimes he speaks through the Bible. A single verse can rip open your heart, shine its truth into your darkest places, and scrub you with an astonishing spiritual intensity. Other times the sight of a tree will force you to your knees as its branches and leaves unleash a thousand sermons at once. Still other times the silence of God will shut you down and do its work on your spiritual roots. God's silence can grow louder than a howling blizzard as he takes you through a cold spiritual winter. On occasion God speaks through dreams, the rantings of a child (Augustine had his life changed by hearing a child cry out, "Take up and read!"), a great work of art, a majestic piece of music, or a particular circumstance in life.

In any case, the very skills we need to hear children as they go through their various stages in life — as babies, toddlers, adolescents, and then adults — are the same skills that sharpen our spiritual sensibilities toward God.

An Extraordinary, Ordinary Day

I wrote *Sacred Pathways* when Graham was just five or six years old. One day I was working on the contemplatives chapter. While I'm not much of a mystic myself, I admire those brothers and sisters who take an austere room and spiritually decorate it into a corner of heaven; they take an ordinary, tired minute and infuse it with eternity. The most amazing thing to me about Christian prayer mystics is that they do just what they want to do, and what they will be doing five billion years from now — holding hands with their Beloved in loving adoration.

Maybe Graham is a mystic — or at least on that particular day he played a mystic's role in my life. "This has been the best day of my life," he blurted out.

Up until that moment, I had considered the day a bit of a downer. For starters, I felt preoccupied. A couple of weeks before then, I had sent a children's book manuscript to an agent. For various reasons, the manuscript mattered very much to me — but I received only silence, the biggest insult a writer can get. An empty post office box to a writer is like a deserted concert hall to a pianist, a silent store to a small business owner, or a vacant church to a pastor.

Like a narcissistic fool, I colored the day with my own disappointment. Meanwhile, my son filled it with promise.

The best day in his entire life? I looked at the previous eight hours and tried to see it through his eyes.

The day had begun with Graham and me visiting the athletic fields in Manassas, Virginia, to sign him up for fall soccer. Graham hadn't yet played in an organized sport — this would be his first season — so we stopped to watch a game. When we came home, I laid down with Graham as he took his nap. Once he fell asleep, I got up and read a book. When he woke up, he came right over to me, and I held him for a few minutes before we ate lunch.

Lisa had to take Allison to a birthday party, so Graham, Kelsey, and I were on our own in the afternoon. While Kelsey slept, Graham and I covered the outside of our house with ant crystals, fixed a shelf under the sink, and, while doing these chores, talked about whether one arrow could kill five cowboys. I had my doubts, but Graham assured me that one of his plastic Indians had accomplished the feat that very day.

When Kelsey woke up, the lunch I had prepared amused her for about two minutes, then she and Graham kept quiet with a jar of peanut butter and a bag of pretzels for about thirty minutes. I cleaned up the damage, and we all got ready to run some errands.

Our first stop was the post office, where my mailbox remained maddeningly empty. At that point, the empty mailbox unwisely defined my day.

Next we headed to Baskin-Robbins. I had some coupons that allowed me to get one cone and two sundaes for the price of one sundae. I gave Kelsey the cone so she could sit down, while the young woman with the sugar-encrusted wrists prepared the sundaes for Graham and me. When I came back with the sundaes, Kelsey handed me a smashed cone and promptly took the fresh sundae out of my hands.

The Baskin-Robbins store sat right next to Blockbuster video, so I told Graham he could run in and rent a *Speed Racer* video. He ran around the corner, and by the time Kelsey and I caught up with him, the coveted prize already lay snugly in his hands.

While we drove home under an unusually (for Virginia) gray June sky, Graham let out with his, "This has been the best day of my whole life."

His comment so startled me, I almost drove off the side of the road. Before Graham's evaluation, I might have given the day a C-, and yet here he was, grading it an A+. *What is so special,* I mused, *about running errands, receiving no news on the new book project, and getting ordinary stuff done around the house?*

But Graham the mystic saw the previous eight hours in an entirely different light. He looked at the soccer sign-up as a future promise, nap time next to his dad as a sacred moment, spreading ant crystals as "a whole lot of fun"; he could eat the ice cream sundae without freaking out about the calories or the fat content. And he could teach me that a gentle but firm hug between a father and a son as they walked out of a video store means more than all the full post office boxes in the world.

His ears could hear a song that I had grown too busy to hear — until I truly listened to that joy-filled assessment of what once seemed just an ordinary day.

One of the most important things the church can do for young people is to help them laugh. Our churches and our homes can be places of joy, and they will be if we ourselves learn the secret of joy.

Rev. John Yates

As a bridegroom rejoices over his bride,
    so will your God rejoice over you.

Isaiah 62:5

Chapter 5

Joy!

How Raising Children Helps Us
Embrace God's Joy

February 2002.

Sixteen-year-old Sarah Hughes felt nervous. From the time she was five years old, Sarah had dreamed of winning a gold medal at the Winter Olympics, but a fourth-place finish in the short program at Salt Lake City meant she would now happily settle for a medal of any sort.

In two hours Sarah was to skate the most important routine of her life. She couldn't shake the butterflies, so she called her older brother Matt. Matt plays the role of the family clown in the Hughes household.

"Matty," Sarah said, "tell me a joke."

Without hesitation, big brother talked about a grasshopper that walked into a bar. The bartender looked at the grasshopper and said, "Hey, we've got a drink named after you" — to which the grasshopper responded, "You got a drink named Irving?"

Sarah laughed. She relaxed, and then she skated the routine of her lifetime. Not only did she get a medal, she came from behind in one of the sport's most improbable scenarios to win the gold — to which Matt, who shares a bathroom with Sarah, responded, "Now that she's Olympic champion, do I have to leave the toilet seat down?"[1]

Sportswriter Rick Reilly called Sarah Hughes's Olympic gold medal "the sweetest story in sports this century." Sarah's parents certainly took the road less traveled to get there. Four years earlier, in

Nagano, Japan, another young teenager also won the gold, but at a steep cost: in order to train with a top coach, Tara Lipinski hadn't lived with her dad since she turned ten. Tim Goebel, who took a bronze medal in Salt Lake, left his dad at the ripe old age of eleven to pursue his training. Skating is far from the only sport where prodigies leave for distant lands. Future tennis stars routinely get shipped south to train with Nick Bollettieri. And David Leadbetter's academy charges a mere $40,000 to $45,000 a year to house, train, and feed budding golf stars.

But Sarah's parents kept their daughter home and their family intact, and they were blessed for doing so. Sarah's mom, Amy Hughes, once called her daughter "Dr. Sarah" for the effect she had on her as she was enduring breast cancer treatments. The chemotherapy, radiation, and stem-cell transplants understandably wore this mother of six down, but the kids stepped in. The oldest daughter, Rebecca, was attending Harvard, but she flew home on weekends to look after the younger kids. The oldest boy, David, contributed his own blood platelets to his mom. Brother John traveled with Sarah to the skating competitions — the ones Amy couldn't get to because she lay sick in bed, recovering — and he'd hold up his cell phone so Amy could listen to the music as Sarah skated, and then hear the sustained applause. Funny thing — on those days Amy seemed to be able to take more platelets than usual.[2]

What Amy and her husband, John, experienced is unusual in one respect: few of us will ever know the thrill of watching a son or daughter win Olympic gold. But oh, the joy when your children come together in a difficult situation and everybody pulls through! Few highs on this earth can compare to a family's joy.

Yes, kids can suck us dry. Certainly, excruciatingly painful moments can mark the parents' journey. Exhaustion can seem like a constant companion. On some days I feel like an abject failure as a dad. But let's not forget the times when even troublesome kids can reach up, unzip the veil that hides heaven, and show us what true love and sheer happiness are all about.

For most of us, these glimpses of heaven will seem far more subtle than winning an Olympic event. Outsiders could never hope to understand them. I remember watching my son put his arm around his younger sister to help her through a difficult time, gently guiding her and helping her and comforting her. I elbowed Lisa so she wouldn't miss it, and her face broke into one of the biggest smiles I've ever seen. If another family had walked by, they wouldn't have realized the miracle that had just taken place — when it's not your own kids, you don't even notice it, much less feel it — but that night Lisa and I went to sleep with very satisfied souls.

Other times, it's just plain fun being a parent. Recently, Kelsey asked to have a friend spend Saturday night with us. This friend's family doesn't attend church, and Kelsey felt eager to introduce her to Sunday school. Because Kelsey seemed tired, we said no, to which Kelsey protested, "But, Mom, this is a *spiritual* issue!"

Kelsey still didn't get her way, but we certainly had a good laugh about that one. We make sacrifices as parents, but we also reap a transcendent joy. How good God is to let us know this powerful pleasure!

Merry Mary

Parenting an infant is replete with promise and has been for centuries. It was particularly so at the time of Jesus' birth, inasmuch as many a Jewish mother hoped that her son would grow up to be the Messiah.

We don't have to imagine the joy Mary must have felt when she heard the good news that her son really was the Messiah, for Scripture tells us pretty clearly. Mary bursts forth in exultation:

> My soul glorifies the Lord
>   and my spirit rejoices in God my Savior,
>   for he has been mindful
>   of the humble state of his servant.
> From now on all generations will call me blessed,
>   for the Mighty One has done great things for me —
>   holy is his name.
>
> Luke 1:46–49

Jesus' conception and birth understandably brought great joy to Mary, despite the dark warnings given to her (see Luke 2:34–35). That joy continued for many years, and I think it may have hit another high point near Jesus' thirtieth birthday. Mary helped run a wedding celebration in which an embarrassing situation arose: the host ran out of wine (see John 2:1–11).

During your children's younger years you give and you give to them, but when they get older you learn you can depend on them, too. That's what happened here. Mary didn't fret about the lack of wine; she simply walked up to her son and said, "They have no more wine."

At first, Jesus seemed reluctant. He reminded Mary, "My time has not yet come." But Mary had a mother's optimism. She instructed the servants, "Do whatever he tells you."

And Jesus took care of it.

Mary provides a good example because her journey as a mother involved unparalleled heights of joy as well as excruciating bouts of pain. She went from the pinnacle event of giving birth to the Savior of all who would believe, and three decades later she plunged to the depths, personally witnessing each flinch of her son's body as the nails pierced his flesh, watching as the blood and water flowed when a sword slashed into his side. Times of agony lay ahead, but here, at this wedding in Cana, Mary could look with a mother's satisfaction and pride as her son "came through."

But joy also can mean sheer fun, and sometimes nothing says fun like having kids around. Carol Lynn Pearson became a single mom when her husband began struggling with his sexual orientation. Sometime after divorcing her, he died of AIDS. Certainly, she and her kids have seen their share of sorrows, but Carol seems mostly to remember the joys. In her warm memoir, *On the Seesaw*, Carol recounts the time she was having coffee with some friends when her ten-year-old son, John, walked into the room and announced, "Mom, it is my duty to inform you that a policeman will be arriving here in two minutes."

"Who called them?" Carol asked.

"I did," John replied.

Apparently John felt that his brother Aaron was "destroying the environment" by jumping off six-foot water pipes and into a creek, especially since Aaron had placed boards over the reeds to cushion his fall. John felt mortified over this act of "atrocity" and felt duty-bound to notify the legal authorities. The policeman showed up, had a good laugh, then explained to John when one truly needs to call in the law.[3]

Several years later, John knew his mom really wanted to attend a Liza Minnelli concert with her friend, so he scraped together fifty bucks to buy two tickets. This single mom felt touched more than you could know by her son's thoughtfulness and sacrifice. While we can't all raise messiahs, even regular boys can occasionally bring an angelic smile to a tired mom's face.

Biblical joy is the shared joy of fellowship. Jesus said, "I have told you this so that my joy may be in you and that your joy may be complete" (John 15:11). The apostle John wrote his first epistle to those he loved in order "to make our joy complete" (1 John 1:4). He tells the "chosen lady" (which may well have been a female personification of a specific church) of his second epistle that "I hope to visit you and talk with you face to face, so that our joy may be complete" (2 John 12). In his third epistle, John couldn't get any clearer: "I have no greater joy than to hear that my children are walking in the truth" (3 John 4).

While neither Jesus nor John addressed blood relatives when they talked about joy, the relationships they referred to certainly do, from a spiritual perspective, pertain to family. Numerous studies have shown that, on average, married people feel happier than singles. God shaped our souls in such a way that we become more complete in fellowship. Sin usually leads to isolation — whether it's the sin of substance abuse (picture a lonely drug addict escaping to get her fix), pornography (imagine a man alone in front of a computer), or even the most dramatic of sins — murder (the ultimate denial of fellowship). The Spirit of God, by contrast, moves us *toward* others, and this movement — though often painful — has the potential to release joy otherwise unknown in human experience. Even an introvert such as myself finds his truest happiness and satisfaction in shared living.

Joyfully Loving Sinners

Most parents have a two-prayer approach to their children. I still catch myself regularly falling into this trap. Our first prayer is usually, "God, protect them"; our next prayer is, "God, *change* them."

Isn't this so? Don't most parental prayers fall under the two umbrellas of "God, keep them from doing something stupid" and "God, keep stupid people from them"?

There's nothing wrong with these two prayers, but I found increased joy in my parenting when God introduced me to yet a third prayer, gently urging that I offer it at least as often as the other two prayers combined. The third prayer goes like this: "God, thank you for the way you're working in my daughter's life. Thank you for how I see you sanctifying my son. Thank you for the joy of living with my children. Thank you for the privilege of getting to spend my life with them."

Prayers of thankfulness have added a new dimension to my parenting. I try to thank God for my kids more than I ask God to change them. I pray with gratitude for the evidence of God's grace in their lives, and I list the qualities he's given them for which I feel grateful.

This practice has given me a new perspective. When I prayed only for their protection, I had to fight off fear. When I prayed merely for God to change them, I lost sight of their strengths. Thanking God for them and specifically meditating on those qualities in their lives for which I am grateful has given me a much greater appreciation for the privilege of living with these children.

It has also affected the way I parent. My son recently celebrated his thirteenth birthday. On Friday of that week, we spent the morning playing golf, then went out to lunch at a restaurant of his choice. During one stretch of conversation, I recounted to Graham the many specific ways I saw God moving in his life. "You asked Jesus into your heart," I reminded Graham, "and he took you at your word. Just look at how he's changing you."

There was one issue that Lisa and I desired Graham to grow in, however, so I seized on the corresponding virtue that would empty the negative behavior. I talked about how we see this virtue in Jesus, how it had affected my own life, and how I thought it would benefit his. Having essentially offered this commercial, I said, "Graham, seize that virtue this year! With God's help, make it your own!"

If I had prayed only about Graham's weaknesses, I wouldn't have thought of all the positive things God was doing in his life. Instead of recounting all the signs of God's favor, I might have listed all the "resolutions" he should adopt in the coming year (Graham's birthday is in December), thereby emphasizing his shortcomings. Praying prayers of thankfulness regularly reminds me of how faithfully God cares for my children, who have put their trust in him. It not only gives me increased joy in them, but it also gives me increased joy *in God;* like the apostle John, I truly have "no greater joy than to hear that my children are walking in the truth."

Praying prayers of thankfulness has also given me a more stable foundation on which to build a relationship with my children, particularly as they grow older. Think about it: if every time you prayed to God he seemed neurotically fearful for your safety, and then spent the entire time nitpicking over every possible flaw and absence of manners in your life, how often would you want to pray? Not very! If our heavenly Father doesn't model his care by showing obsessive fear for us and constantly harping over our failures, why should we build our relationship with our children on such a worthless foundation? How much better to follow our heavenly Father's model and rejoice in our children!

I want my children to think of me as their chief encourager, apart from the Holy Spirit. I desire that, regardless of how the world receives them, they will know that at least two people — their mother and father — will always delight in them. I pray that they believe without a single doubt that raising them has been one of the greatest blessings God could ever have given to us.

I learned this attitude from the apostle Paul, who experienced tremendous joy while loving followers who could be very difficult at times. These may have been his "spiritual children," but his love for them grew as hot and intense as anyone could feel for their own flesh and blood. Listen to the way Paul spoke to his sons and daughters in the Lord:

- "I am full of joy over you" (Romans 16:19).
- "I have great confidence in you; I take great pride in you. I am greatly encouraged; in all our troubles my joy knows no bounds" (2 Corinthians 7:4).
- "I thank my God every time I remember you. In all my prayers for all of you, I always pray with joy" (Philippians 1:3–4).
- "Indeed, you are our glory and joy" (1 Thessalonians 2:20).
- "Your love has given me great joy" (Philemon 7).

I wonder: If someone were to interview our kids and ask them, "Do your parents find great joy in loving you?" what would they say? Would our kids have the sense of cherished affection that Paul's spiritual children felt, or would they feel more like a burden than a blessing? One of the greatest gifts a parent can give to his or her children is to enjoy them, to cherish them, to laugh with them, to give them the satisfaction that we feel so very thankful to walk this life with them.

Keep in mind that the groups of people Paul cared for were not easy to love. The Corinthians fought about everything. They committed incest. Some were swindlers, and a few brought lawsuits against one another. The Galatians were leaving the gospel of grace and flirting with legalism. Among the Philippians, Paul had to settle personal disputes (Euodia and Syntyche), much like a parent referees a fight between two siblings. A number of the Thessalonians apparently grew quite lazy, and this long-suffering apostle had to admonish them several times to leave idleness behind. Yet, in spite of these churches' struggles and failings, *Paul found great joy in loving them.*

With true love comes true joy. No matter how difficult a person or church may seem, when God gives us a biblical compassion for them, he also provides a biblical joy. You don't see one without the other, at least not in Scripture.

Doesn't this exemplify the beauty of life in Christ? God could tell us to sacrifice for our kids, and we would do it. God could tell us to discipline ourselves on behalf of our offspring, and we would obey. But how blessed we are that God also says we are to *enjoy* our children. What a rich commandment!

Here's a challenging thought: If our children grasp more clearly where they fall short of our expectations than they see how God's grace is transforming them, if they think we feel more burdened by them than thankful for them, it may be because they're being raised by a Pharisee. They can also challenge our tendency to be what Søren Kierkegaard referred to as "stupidly serious."[4]

Stupidly Serious

According to a recent Barna study, evangelicals aren't very popular. When pollsters asked respondents to register their approval of various groups, evangelical Christians came in tenth out of eleven possibilities — trailing lesbians and lawyers, but beating out prostitutes! Pollster George Barna states that only one-third of those with no connection to Christianity have a favorable impression of born-again Christians; just over one-fifth feel positively toward evangelicals.[5]

In no way am I trying to suggest that we should concern ourselves with winning a popularity contest — but it's always wise to remain open to fair critiques. It's one thing to turn people away because we carry an unpopular message; it's another thing altogether to turn people away because we deliver that message in an obnoxious manner. In all our desire to "get things right," Kierkegaard's warning about becoming stupidly serious is the one charge most likely to correctly target evangelical Christians.

I once attended a gathering of believers when the meeting grew very tense. Then someone said something funny, and we all started to laugh, which had the wonderful effect of breaking the tension — that is, until an overly religious woman stopped herself and said, out loud, "I bind the spirit of laughter." This Christian apparently considered laughter the handmaiden of the devil, whereas in that situation I'm convinced it amounted to a grace from God. Some think God is always serious, and thus they deem laughter to be a result of the Fall.

True, incessant laughter and joking can speak of shallowness, but it can also reveal a profound depth. In his classic work titled *Orthodoxy*, G. K. Chesterton argues that Christianity fits humankind's deepest needs because it makes us concentrate on joys that do not pass away rather than on inevitable but superficial and transitory grief.[6] Instead of getting buried by the seriousness of a fallen world, faith in Jesus Christ offers us the ability to laugh and enjoy ourselves, resting in God's promised eternal joys and pleasures.

Throughout history, even the most devout and missions-minded Christians have lived with exuberance. Saint Francis of Assisi and his followers got rebuked in church for being so happy as they worshiped God. The first generation of Methodists received constant criticism for being "too enthusiastic." And the early leaders of the Salvation Army knew such joy that they could scarcely contain themselves. When someone told a drummer not to hit his drums quite so hard, he said, "Oh, sir, I'm so happy I could burst the blessed drum!"[7]

One of my favorite writers, Elton Trueblood, goes so far as to make this declaration:

> Any alleged Christianity which fails to express itself in gaiety, at some point, is clearly spurious. The Christian is [joyful] not because he is blind to injustice and suffering, but because he is convinced that these, in the light of the divine

sovereignty, are never *ultimate*. . . . Though he can be sad, and often is perplexed, he is never really worried. The well-known humor of the Christian is not a way of denying the tears, but rather a way of affirming something which is deeper than tears.[8]

In other words, being stupidly serious is a mark of being stupidly forgetful. We concentrate on temporal struggles and problems at the risk of forgetting eternal blessings. Even when I've fallen into temptation, after repentance I can find great joy in knowing that God doesn't treat me as my sins deserve. From first to last, the gospel is joy-producing good news.

In fact, being stupidly serious is a mark of disobedience. The New Testament commands us (no less than *seventy* times) to rejoice! Joyless Christians have lost sight of the good news of the gospel: that God created us, loves us, is redeeming us from our sins, and is preparing a place of unimaginable glory for us to enjoy throughout eternity.

Yet just look around you — observe people on an airplane, at the mall, or even at Disneyland, and see how few seem to exhibit even the smallest sign of joy. Children can help to awaken in us this God-given penchant toward joy. Particularly in the difficult times of life, children can be a source of profound encouragement.

Tiny Tonic for Hurting Souls

At the time of Allison's birth, I was suffering through a tough time. I worked for a public utility company reading electric meters, while trying to finish my master's thesis at Regent College. I felt jealous of a classmate who not only could attend school full-time to finish his master's degree but who also had applied for a Ph.D. program, something I desperately wanted to do. Dr. J. I. Packer had offered to write a letter to help get me into Cambridge University, but with the birth of a new baby, the finances just wouldn't allow me to pursue full-time studies in England.

Instead, I continued working as a meter reader in Lynden, Washington — home to dozens of dairies. I spent a good bit of my day hunting down irrigation meters in fields just fertilized or wading through the muck pens of yet another dairy. The first day I showed up for one particular route, a coworker said, "I thought I told you to wear boots."

"These *are* boots," I said, pointing to my ankle-high shoes.

"Well, *those* boots will be full in half an hour on this route."

She was right. I had no idea that slop pens in dairies could reach shin-high.

Because I'd often travel into the boonies, I had to bring my lunch with me and leave it in my truck. I don't know how many sickeningly warm peanut butter sandwiches I ate with the smell of fertilizer filling my nostrils, but I do remember telling Lisa, "When I get another job, I'm never going to eat a peanut butter sandwich again."

I felt so disheartened; I wanted to become an academic and a teacher, and instead I found myself running from dogs and slogging in the rain through farms, smelling manure all day long, with no intellectual stimulation — and then trying to finish my master's thesis at night and on weekends. It dawned on me one day that I had read meters the summer before I graduated from high school. I had read meters *after* graduating from high school. I had read meters during the summers while I was getting a college education. I had read meters *after* I graduated from college. And I was *still* reading meters after finishing my course work for a master's degree. Something just seemed radically wrong with that equation!

I'd come home from work, and I'd feel like crying — *nothing* seemed to be going my way — and the one light in my day was to take six-month-old Allison (to date, still the most beautiful baby I have ever seen) and lay down, her head resting on my chest. I remember praying, "Lord, I don't deserve to have a baby this beautiful." And I meant it. Allison seemed much too good for me; I had a pretty low view of myself, and it almost seemed as though God had somehow dropped Ally off at the wrong address.

Allison was my joy at the end of the day. Please don't misunderstand. I'm not equating beauty with worth. It is a true joy to love a quantifiably "homely" baby (and we've all seen our share!). But there was something about Ally that seemed almost otherworldly. Hugging her made so many of my disappointments melt away, and the sheer joy of holding her helped me continue in a situation that felt insufferable at times.

Even today, my kids provide a wonderful tonic in a busy schedule. A daughter like Kelsey forces me to slow down because she feels the need to talk through *everything*. I've learned that a five-word question can elicit a three-thousand-word response, and I'll marvel that she can keep going for so long without even taking a breath. I'll never forget the November 1 when then nine-year-old Kelsey looked at me with a grave seriousness.

"Daddy," she asked, "what should I be for the next Halloween? I thought I could be a pioneer girl but I was that two years ago and I know for the harvest party it has to be a positive character so maybe I should look at someone in the Bible but I — "

"Kelsey," I interrupted — it felt much too early in the morning for me to go *here*. "Halloween was just *twelve hours ago.* You've got 364 days to worry about your costume for next year. Do you really think you need to plan it out now?"

Just this morning, as I worked on this chapter, Kelsey came into my office to inquire if I kept a secret stash of balloons in my desk because she needed to borrow one.

"Why in the world would I keep balloons in my office?" I asked.

"Because they're your favorite things," she laughed, then corrected herself. "After ten-year-old girls, of course." (As I write, Kelsey is ten.)

While we may be tempted to think of such interludes as interruptions, they more closely resemble spiritual vacations. There's nothing like having children to fall back on when work gets tough. Our children can also teach us to become a little less busy and enjoy life a whole lot more.

Listening to Little Voices

Back when I worked in an office away from home, I got my daily post-lunch phone call from Lisa. She usually gave me about three updates on what was happening at home.

"Boy, I wish you could see your son right now!" Lisa said. Our then four-year-old boy was keeping himself busy. I had just given him a Baltimore Orioles hat, and Graham, even at four, really got into baseball. The second time I took him to a baseball game at Camden Yards, he looked out the window, saw the ballpark in the distance, and exclaimed, "Oh! My love!"

On this particular day in northern Virginia, well before baseball season, it was snowing — but Graham had on his Orioles hat, was hitting a ball at the top of a small hill, sledding down the hill to retrieve his ball, climbing back up, and starting the process all over again.

I wanted so badly to be home to watch him that it hurt. I thought, *The next time I get a call like that, I'm going home.*

A couple months later, that call came. When Lisa got me on the phone, she said, "Just a second. Graham wants to talk to you."

A tiny voice came on the line. "Papa?"

"Hi, champ."

"Hi. I was wondering, would you come home early and play football with me today?"

Graham had just gotten his first play football uniform, and he was eager to try it out. Thinking of the work still on my desk, I sighed. I'd have to leave work early, around 4:00 p.m., in order to make it home in time for there to be any light outside.

I took another deep breath. I had arrived at work by 7:00 a.m. but hadn't planned to leave until about 5:00 p.m. or so. Initially I viewed this as something I *should* do rather than something I really wanted to do. But then I remembered the call about him hitting his baseball and sliding down the hill to retrieve it. I had missed that event and regretted it.

"Yeah," I said. "Get your uniform ready."

"Can I tell you a secret?" Graham whispered.

"Sure. What is it?"

"I'm already wearing it!"

A couple hours later I felt transfixed by the sight of Graham in his football uniform, wearing a helmet two or three sizes too big, running down the field and looking back to make sure I was still chasing him.

Back then, I had a pretty utilitarian view of sports play. I wanted to teach Graham something, so we talked about how to hold the football so he wouldn't fumble when I tackled him. If I caught him getting sloppy carrying the ball, I'd knock it away so he fumbled. As I chased him on one play, I remembered thinking, *He probably won't remember this anyway. He's only four years old.*

But a second thought followed closely, overwhelming me in its power: *How cute Graham looks!* If you've never seen a four-year-old wear a football uniform, you're missing something. And then the thought hit me: *This is for you, Gary.* As I reached out to grab Graham, I realized there was nowhere else I'd rather be than here, with Allison cheering on the sideline, "Run, Grahammy, he's going to get you!" and Graham's head turning side to side, trying to figure out from which direction I was going to make my next attack. He could hardly see out of the oversized helmet, so he practically had to come to a stop to get his bearings. It was hilarious.

Only rarely do you find something so right and so fulfilling that you don't think you should be doing anything else. For an hour that day, I didn't feel like working, writing, or eating. I just wanted to chase a thirty-six-inch football player and watch him run.

During "halftime" we fell back on the grass. If I had stayed at work, I'd be fighting the traffic on I-66, the main roadway from Washington, D.C., into northern Virginia — one of the most congested highways in the nation. Instead of listening to traffic and weather reports "on the fives," I stretched out, a small step from heaven, in a place called contentment — not because of a call from a publisher, a job promotion, or a raise, but because a four-year-old had called with a simple question: "Dad, would you come home early and play football with me today?"

Families start to break down — and marriages often break down, for that matter — when we stop enjoying each other. There is a place for discipline, sacrifice, commitment, and perseverance; but an equally important place exists for enjoyment. Those who never take the time to truly enjoy their family miss out on one of the most profound wonders God offers. Such people may be all about serving, all about effort, all about sacrifice — but they are also stuck in a rut that makes them seem joyless, empty, and ultimately miserable. This type of life does not adequately represent the character of our Creator God. It seems far more inclined to the religion of the Pharisees than to the faith of Jesus Christ.

Joy in the Journey

During a long drive from Bellingham, Washington, to Portland, Oregon, I listened to one of the most extraordinary series of audiotapes

I've ever heard. The first tape replayed a sermon by C.J. Mahaney from Covenant Life Church in Gaithersburg, Maryland. (I could listen to C.J.'s tapes all day long.)

The second cassette featured Carolyn Mahaney, C.J.'s wife. She used some of the same verses that C.J. quoted in his message, but she approached parenting from the mother's perspective. It inspired and challenged me to hear how a husband and wife worked in tandem to connect their faith and their family.

But what made the series extraordinary was the third tape, made by C.J.'s three adult daughters (at the time of the taping, the youngest was twenty years old). The testimony of these young women about their godly upbringing and their parents' example could move even the most callous of listeners to tears.[9]

I turned off the tapes long enough to reflect on them, and in the silence noted one overriding thought: *This family managed to push back the chaos.* Our world suffers through an anarchy of rebellion, mixed roles, and missed opportunities. It urges people to choose their own lifestyle, without ever thinking about the ramifications of those choices. Couples get married without talking about the roles they plan to play. We don't want to offend, so we leave newlyweds to find their own way — and families often go adrift in the process.

But here was a family determined to live by a concrete biblical model — and the joy they shared because of following God's design became apparent to everyone who heard them speak. The daughters love being together, and all of them count their mother as the most influential person in their lives. C.J. has an unusually powerful and prophetic ministry with an ever-increasing international influence, but he got there without sacrificing his family on the altar of his vocation. I drank his family's joy as though it were my own — beauty is beauty, no matter what the frame.

Carolyn once had a sad conversation with a woman on an airplane. She noticed the woman addressing envelopes. The woman explained that she was sending out graduation invitations for one daughter and wedding invitations for the other. Carolyn was just about to congratulate her, when the woman said something that made Carolyn's heart sink: "It's so nice to be getting rid of both of them at the same time."

It's sad, but this is truly how some people look at their children — a burden to be borne, and then leeches to be kicked out of the house. Ironically, I've found that the parents who talk this way often have made the fewest sacrifices on their kids' behalf. It's a natural principle of life that the more time, effort, and energy we put into our family, the more we hold it dear.

Yes, parenting can be a lot of work. It absolutely asks a tremendous amount from us and calls us to make many sacrifices. But when we make these sacrifices and the work nears an end, few things are more lovely to behold than a godly family. The joy seeps over the family's experience to reach even a casual observer.

It's not as though the Mahaneys had no challenges. On the contrary, one daughter confessed how she once despised her mom's choices in life, an attitude this same daughter now calls her "greatest sin." But over time, love won out, the gospel-centered family built its foundation on the rock, and all its members are reaping a glorious reward.

There is no joy like God's joy. There is no family like God's family.

"We Will See Them in Heaven"

Brady Bobbink has served as a college pastor in the Pacific Northwest for more than thirty years. He has attended more regional Chi-Alpha conferences (called SALT — Student Activist Leadership Training) than he can count, but he enjoyed something special at a conference that took place in September 1995 — the first time that he and his wife, Shirley, and all four of their children attended together.

Their youngest son, three-year-old Seth, had finally left diapers behind, making traveling a bit easier. And their oldest daughter, Stefany, was engaged to be married the following summer, making this conference one of the final family vacations with just the kids. Brady couldn't wait.

He soon found, however, that traveling with the whole family provided a whole different experience than going by himself — and delightfully so. After concluding his lecture on worship, Brady was informed by his son Micah that they were going down to the river to throw rocks, then to play miniature golf, then to lunch, after which they were going to go swimming.

"Who decided all this?" Brady asked, feigning disappointment but secretly delighted with the day that lay ahead of him.

"Mom, Seth, and me voted on it," Micah explained. "Even if you vote differently, it's going to be three to one."

"Whatever happened to patriarchal rule, Micah?" Brady asked, trying to milk this one for all its worth. "You know, where the dad actually makes the decisions?"

"Come on, Dad," Micah said. "That was the seventies."

Brady had a lot of fun that day with his boys — but it was his daughters who brought him to tears later in the week.

Brady and Shirley participated in a worship service in which their two daughters, Stefany and Stacy, helped lead. Surrounded by all the people he loved most, worshiping the God he loved above all, Brady's heart practically burst. Does life get any better than this? Not for a gospel-centered dad, it doesn't.

Overwhelmed with joy and thankfulness that his once-little girls had grown up into godly women of faith, Brady drank in the deep assurance that their faith would remain throughout their lives. He turned to Shirley, pointed at the girls, and said with a choked-up voice, "We will see them in heaven!"

Shirley began to cry.

Character without courage is empty. Courage is what enables us to act on our convictions.

Susan Yates

Chapter 6

Vicious Vulnerability

How Parenting Confronts Cowardice and Builds Courage

Imagine passing through a desert, surrounded by hundreds of other people, in search of a better life. With each passing day, your water supply dips. Despite your best efforts at rationing each precious drop, eventually all the water vanishes. You can taste the sand in the back of your throat and it hurts to lick your lips — but not nearly as much as it hurts to look down at your little daughter, who, quite literally, is dying of thirst.

Her very face looks parched; her lips have cracked, and her tongue is swollen. She's so hot and thirsty that she can barely keep her eyes open as she shuffles through the sand.

How courageous do you feel right now? How adventurous? How hopeful? How trusting?

In my younger days, I always looked at the nation of Israel under Moses' leadership through a single man's eyes: they were a bunch of complaining, cowardly, thankless, and weak people. In the first five books of the Old Testament, it seems that God regularly threatens to wipe out his chosen people, but Moses intervenes and the nation of chronic complainers gets spared yet again.

As a dad, I look at their plight a little differently. It's one thing for *me* to get a bit thirsty; but now I try to imagine my response if I were to see one of my daughters shriveling up from a lack of water, her throat so dry that all she can do is choke out the parched words, "Daddy, water, *please* ..." If I couldn't answer her request by giving her a full cup, it's not difficult to imagine how I might join the complainers: "Hey, there was water in Egypt. My girls are *dying* here. We have to go back — now!"

Or if I heard Joshua and Caleb, after they returned from scouting the new land, boasting about its richness, but then heard the other ten scouts warn that its people looked like giants (Numbers 13:32–33) and that they would take wives and children as plunder (Numbers 14:3), I might soon join the wandering throng. Would I be so bold to engage in war if I knew defeat meant that another man (or worse, men) might ravage my wife and kidnap my kids and turn them into slaves?

It's easy to act brave when the stakes remain low. But the more you have to lose, the more courage comes at a premium price. That's why being a parent tempts all of us into becoming cowards.

The insidious thing about parental cowardice is that, in the name of protecting, it wounds. Upset with the Israelites for their lack of faith, God sends them back toward the Red Sea, saying, "As for your children that you said would be taken as plunder, I will bring them in to enjoy the land you have rejected. But you — your bodies will fall in this desert. Your children will be shepherds here for forty years, *suffering for your unfaithfulness*, until the last of your bodies lies in the desert" (Numbers 14:31–33, emphasis added).

Ironically and sadly, because the Israelite adults feared for their children's safety, those very children suffered at the hands of their parents rather than by the swords of a foreign nation.

Kids today suffer similar fates. We've all seen the kids who must endure an overprotective mom or dad who won't let them eat a hot dog (they might choke), climb a tree (they might fall), go to camp (they might be molested), or take up skiing (they might break a leg). In the name of protecting their children, these parents deprive and even harm them.

Cowardice is subtle. It hides behind legitimate concerns but pushes those concerns to such extremes that safety becomes the *absolute* priority. We have some wonderful friends who take my youngest daughter on a skiing trip every year. Kelsey loves these trips, but they terrify me. One year, I knew that Kelsey, then just nine years old, would be going up a ski lift with only her nine-year-old friend for company. Using a ski lift without a parent is the ultimate sign of becoming a "real" skier, so Kelsey and Laura were eager to take that step. And then, of course, Kelsey fully intended to ski down the mountain on a couple of flat sticks. I must have prayed ten times a day in her absence, and I jumped every time the phone rang, fearing the worst.

· To make matters worse, a serious earthquake rocked the Seattle area one year when Kelsey skied that mountain. The threat of an avalanche gripped me like a vise. I drove to the lodge to get her (we had decided in advance that I'd pick her up that day), trying not to think about the worst. When I arrived, I saw my little girl barreling down the slopes, hurtling over a small jump, and smiling like a Cheshire cat when she saw me.

I asked Tim, Laura's father, if he had felt the earthquake. "Earthquake? No. But that must be why they shut down the lifts for a short while to check them out."

It scared Lisa and me to think of Kelsey skiing down a mountain while Seattle suffered a serious earthquake. But if the fear of a potential earthquake ruled our lives (it's only a matter of *when*, not *if*, the Seattle area suffers from "the big one"), our kids would suffer from our fear more than they would from an actual earthquake. And frankly, the first person cowardice seeks to protect is the coward. Cowardice grows out of selfishness: "*I* don't want to lose my children." "*I* don't want to go through the pain of seeing something bad happen to them."

I believe that part of God's plan for parenting is designed to confront this self-centered tendency. Every stage of life presents new challenges to our courage. When our kids are babies, we worry about the threat of SIDS or the ill effects of a high fever. When they become toddlers, we worry about them swallowing something or wandering into the street, maybe falling down the stairs. Having elementary students, we don't want them to go into public restrooms alone or to be kidnapped if they should wander through a store or a street festival. As teens there's drug abuse, out-of-wedlock pregnancy, and juvenile-delinquent "friends." Charles Barkley, the fiery former basketball player turned television analyst, probably speaks for many when asked how he would handle his daughter's boyfriends now that she had reached her teen years. "I figure if I kill the first one," Barkley said, "the word will get out."[1]

And just when our children become adults and we think we're free from parental fear, along come grandchildren ...

Vulnerable

Parental cowardice is born in a curious amalgam of parental authority. The process of parenting does two simultaneous yet contradictory things: It gives us unparalleled power, while also making us nakedly vulnerable.

A young woman who finds out she is pregnant literally holds the power of life and death in her hands. The decisions she makes will have a major impact on her child's life span, development, education, and health. That's amazing power for a young woman.

But along with such power comes an immediate *vulnerability*. To suddenly have a child growing within you, knowing that you have a "date with destiny" in nine months, can create all sorts of new fears. Proudly independent women may for the first time in years look for someone to take care of them — at the very least, a doctor or a midwife. Childbearing and child raising were never meant to be solitary enterprises.

Take an Olympic athlete in her early twenties, put her in an earthquake, and she will probably find a way to come out okay. Now take that same woman in her late twenties, make her seven months pregnant — or pregnant with another toddler at her side — and she will face that same earthquake with vastly different emotions and fears. Jesus acknowledged this predicament when he talked about the destruction of Jerusalem, lamenting, "How dreadful it will be in those days for pregnant women and nursing mothers!" (Luke 21:23). To bring a child into your body, and then to bring that same child home, is to make yourself vulnerable in so many ways — emotionally, physically, and financially.

Author and speaker Iris Krasnow interviewed Barbara Bush in the early 1990s. During the interview, Barbara broke down in tears as she recounted losing a three-year-old daughter to leukemia — *in 1953*. Forty years had passed, but the sting and pain of that loss still felt heartbreakingly fresh. Even though she sat four decades removed, Barbara still had not shaken the soul-wrenching sadness that comes from losing a little girl. Krasnow realized what any parent who has lost a child could confirm: "I had yet to become a parent, but I knew then that when you lose a child you can never be totally happy again."[2]

I believe Iris Krasnow is right. Should any of my children precede me into heaven, I think I would always feel a touch of sadness, a wound in my soul, that in this life would never completely heal. Yes, I might have moments of laughter and fun — but every time I met someone with my child's name or came across something that reminded me of that child, I don't think the time would *ever* come when I would become callous and impervious to pain. Nor — and this may be the most significant statement yet — would I want to be.

In a talk titled "The Womb of Marriage," counselor Keith Yoder speaks of a high school buddy of his who very insightfully asked his mother, "Hey, Mom, what hurt more? The day you gave birth to me, or the day I left home for college?"

Without hesitation, the boy's mom said, "The day you left for college."

The pain, the vulnerability, will never completely leave a parent's soul. In many ways, it takes a tremendous act of courage to become a father or mother and expose yourself to such a threat.

Stepparents need the courage of warriors to face the difficult task of blending two families. They have to honestly acknowledge that the inevitable tension will wear on their new marriage during its earliest and most fragile season. Children of divorced parents are just as sinful as children whose parents have never divorced — and they may expertly play off their parents' fears, guilt, and hurt in an attempt to run roughshod over them. Taking on this challenge — raising someone else's biological child in the ruins of a previously failed marriage — and agreeing to negotiate the parenting process present an almost unbelievably daunting challenge.

Author and radio host Dennis Rainey points out the need for courage on the part of single parents: "I am impressed by the courage and tenacity of many single parents," he writes. "I believe some of the greatest rewards in heaven are being stored up for single-parent moms and dads who are facing steep obstacles but are fighting the fight of faith and finishing their parenting assignments well."[3]

I personally have all sorts of fears about how my children will handle living in a sinful, fallen world. I remember when our youngest daughter, Kelsey, was just eighteen months old. We were playing with blocks, trying to build a tower, and one of the words she kept using strangely challenged me.

"Good!" I said, as Kelsey balanced a yellow block on a red one.

"Good!" Kelsey squealed back as she reached for another block. For some reason, Kelsey's "goods" mesmerized me. Even though I was a young father, I knew enough to know that girls' "goods" soon turn into "bads." I'm not sure at what age this phenomenon kicks in — but I've heard plenty of girls and women express the "bads":

- "Bad hair!"
- "Bad body! I'm too fat!"
- "Bad drawing. I got it all wrong!"
- "I'm so stupid."
- "Bad, bad, bad."

I felt hungry to preserve Kelsey's "goods" as long as possible. I bore the fear that she would fall into the same trap, as well as the guilt that my own actions as a young man had undoubtedly contributed to other young women who took on the "bads."

"Good, Kelsey," I said, a little louder.

"Good!" she smiled back at me.

"Good!" I said once again, wishing with all my heart I could plant that word forever in her soul.

Fast-forward eighteen months. Kelsey was now three years old, and we had graduated to marbles. I placed one in the middle of the floor, and Kelsey threw about a dozen shots at that one marble, trying to hit it, but the marble remained surprisingly safe. Now so many marbles littered the floor, we could hardly identify the original marble.

"I like you, Kelsey," I say. I'm not sure why I say it; it just comes out.

"I'm precious," Kelsey answers, repeating my favorite pet name for her. "Tell me I'm precious."

"You're precious," I say.

Kelsey smiled, pitched a marble, and hit the one in the middle of the floor.

But fast-forward another seven years. Kelsey recently was crushed when a friend suggested that Kelsey's overalls looked "too wide." I'm not even sure what that means, but now ten-year-old Kelsey felt devastated to the point of tears. As a dad, I can't protect my kids from every hurt, every slight, every attack.

And that scares me.

In fact, some married couples use this fear as an excuse to not have kids at all, saying there's no way they want to bring a child into this world. But when I think of what Lisa and I would have lost — three human beings, each one precious in God's sight, eternally significant people — I realize I cannot let fear dictate my actions. The cost is just too great.

Had we taken this route, Kelsey never would have cried over her "too wide" pants — but the world would have missed her infectious laugh and unstoppable enthusiasm; it never would have known Graham's sensitive heart and sometimes exhaustingly penetrating mind; it would have forfeited Allison's poetic soul and quiet spirit.

See, that's the thing with fear: It makes us worry about the evil that might happen, and, when we're focused on that, we grow blind to the great good that can result. It's not just shortsightedness, it's pessimistic-sightedness — vision obscured by worry, blurred by fear.

While Scripture honestly admits the real threats we face in life, it remains equally forceful about not being driven by fear of them.

Don't Be Afraid

Just as cowardice remains a constant temptation for the spiritually aware parent, so it tempts anyone called into God's service. Just consider how many times God, Jesus, or an angel precedes a vocational call to service with the words, "Do not be afraid."

- To a man waiting on God to provide a son: "Do not be afraid, Abram. I am your shield, your very great reward" (Genesis 15:1).
- To a newly single mom, abandoned by her child's father: "The angel of God called to Hagar from heaven and said to her, 'What is the matter, Hagar? Do not be afraid'" (Genesis 21:17).
- To a father-to-be whose son was facing a life-threatening situation: "An angel of the Lord appeared to him in a dream and said, 'Joseph son of David, do not be afraid ...'" (Matthew 1:20).

Repeatedly God urges Bible characters not to fear:

- "That night the LORD appeared to [Isaac] and said, 'I am the God of your father Abraham. Do not be afraid ...'" (Genesis 26:24).

- "Then the LORD said to Joshua, 'Do not be afraid'" (Joshua 8:1).
- "But the LORD said to [Gideon], 'Peace! Do not be afraid'" (Judges 6:23).
- "The angel of the LORD said to Elijah, '. . . do not be afraid . . .'" (2 Kings 1:15).
- "But the LORD said to me [Jeremiah], . . . 'Do not be afraid . . .'" (Jeremiah 1:7–8).
- "And you [Ezekiel], . . . do not be afraid of them or their words. Do not be afraid, though briers and thorns are all around you and you live among scorpions" (Ezekiel 2:6).
- "Do not be afraid, Daniel. Since the first day that you set your mind to gain understanding and to humble yourself before your God, your words were heard, and I have come in response to them" (Daniel 10:12).
- "But Jesus immediately said to [his disciples], 'Take courage! It is I. Don't be afraid'" (Matthew 14:27).
- "The angel said to the women, 'Do not be afraid . . .'" (Matthew 28:5).
- "Then he placed his right hand on me [John] and said: 'Do not be afraid. I am the First and the Last'" (Revelation 1:17).

Do you see a pattern here? Just about everyone with whom God deals seemingly requires an initial "Now don't be afraid; this is what I'm going to do." In a how-to book, this is where I'd draw out "five principles to overcome fear in your life"—but you know what? Scripture doesn't provide those five principles, at least not in the passages just listed. In virtually every case, only one lesson emerges: Do what you know is right *regardless of how scared you feel.* As parents, we can't always control the fears that surround us, but we can choose whether we listen to them.

And if we can learn to do this with our kids, frankly, we'll be unstoppable when it comes to reaching out on behalf of God's kingdom. The greatest fear I have in life—without exception—is that something might happen to one of my children. Having faced down my greatest fear, what remains to stop me?

Just as some married couples choose not to have children because they fear what might happen to them, so many Christians choose to skate through life because they fear the consequences of stepping out. What if they try to start a ministry at their church and fail? Better not to even try. What if they mention their faith to a coworker and get laughed at? Better to let her perish in her sins. What if they pledge an amount of money they believe God wants them to pledge, but then a financial need comes up later that can't be met? Better not to listen to God.

I'm not saying we should act recklessly or toss discernment to the winds. But I am saying that the fear of what-ifs has stopped cold more good work than has moral failure. Fear doesn't create scandalous headlines, as moral failure does, but it does just as seriously injure God's work on this earth.

Here's the catch: Courage doesn't always get rewarded with success. Some fears do come true. I don't mind calculating the risk when it comes to my own safety, but when it comes to my children, I don't want to play the odds that thousands of kids Kelsey's age ski every year without serious incident; I want to *remove* the odds. I don't want *any* risk. But in a fallen world, that's asking more than God gives.

Through sacred parenting we learn to act courageously, regardless of how afraid we may feel. And when we step out in faith, we allow God to shape our souls in ways that will develop us far beyond the parenting part of our lives.

In this crossroads, sacred parenting builds in us the very character quality we need in order to fulfill God's call on our lives. Who finds it easy to step out into a ministry of any sort? We may run out of money. We may lack the necessary skills. We may do everything right but still fail. I well remember when I left a secure salaried position and started writing and speaking full-time. I was terrified. I came from a family that didn't do things that way. My dad took a job right out of college with a public utility, staying with the company until he retired. My oldest brother did the same thing; he's still with the same company, more than two decades later. Risking self-employment just isn't in my genes — but it was part of God's call to courage in my life.

What have you not done, simply because you lacked the courage? Who have you avoided talking to? What steps have you refused to take? At what point has fear rather than faith directed your steps? Parenting can help us learn how to overcome such fears. Let's be honest. Parents have plenty of things to fear: kidnappings, natural disasters, childhood diseases, physical injuries, poor moral choices — the list is never-ending. But none of these possibilities can ever compete with the providence of God. The author of this proverb is quite direct:

> Have no fear of sudden disaster
>> or of the ruin that overtakes the wicked,
> for the LORD will be your confidence
>> and will keep your foot from being snared.
>
> Proverbs 3:25–26

Of course, this *doesn't* mean repentant believers will never lose their children in a car accident or to a terrible disease. But it does mean their children will never perish apart from God's watchful eye or without God's covering grace. The world is not a big pit just waiting for an accident. It is governed by a good and generous God who remains in control and who repeatedly calls us to trust him:

"In God I trust; I will not be afraid" (Psalm 56:4).

"Surely God is my salvation;
  I will trust and not be afraid" (Isaiah 12:2).

"But now, this is what the Lord says —
  he who created you, O Jacob,
  he who formed you, O Israel:
'Fear not, for I have redeemed you;
  I have summoned you by name; you are mine.
When you pass through the waters,
  I will be with you;
and when you pass through the rivers,
  they will not sweep over you.
When you walk through the fire,
  you will not be burned;
  the flames will not set you ablaze. . . .
Do not be afraid, for I am with you;
  I will bring your children from the east
  and gather you from the west. . . .
Bring my sons from afar
  and my daughters from the ends
    of the earth'" (Isaiah 43:1–2, 5–6).

Capture these verses for the good of your soul. Instead of listening to your fears, talk to yourself! A pastor recommended the following exercise to me, which has helped greatly. Instead of *listening* to yourself, *talk* to yourself. Emotions can prey on us unless we mentally take charge and fight back. We don't have to let ourselves "tune in" to doubts and fears. We can talk back to ourselves; we can build our spirits with Scripture. Quote these verses to your cowering heart, and use this exercise as the pathway to choose courage. If you learn how to overcome fear as a parent, there will be no stopping what God can do through you on behalf of his kingdom.

I believe that, for the sake of the kingdom, we have to despise apathy more than we fear failure. I don't know of a single activist who hasn't embarrassed himself or herself by at least one instance of a serious lack of judgment or restraint. But their occasional failure looks glorious compared to the deafening silence of the masses who, out of fear, never leave their spiritual beds. While I don't consider myself an activist, I have embarrassed myself more times than I can count by the way I mix up words during a conference or seminar — but almost every week I get an email from someone God touched during one of those imperfect sessions.

To become a biological parent, we need only to contribute either spermatozoa or an egg. To become a sacred parent, we need courage — the kind of courage that kept Hagar from abandoning her child in the desert; the kind of courage that filled Joseph's soul as he defied Herod's edict and took the baby Jesus to Egypt; the kind of courage that leads women and men every day to boldly step out and take risks on behalf of God's kingdom.

"She Endured My Wrath"

Actor Al Pacino's mother and father split up in his very early years, so Al lived as an only child in a South Bronx tenement with just his mother and his grandparents. In his own words, "we were really poor."

One late evening, when Al was about ten years old, he sat freezing on the top floor of the tenement, where the heat never seemed to make its way up. He had school the next day, but a bunch of his friends were yelling at him from down below in the alley. They wanted to do some carousing and "have some real fun."

Of course, Al wanted to join them, but his mom said no. "My mother wouldn't let me. I remember being so angry with her."

Al wouldn't let the matter drop. He nagged, he pleaded, he threatened, he yelled. He tried his best to wear her down. "On and on I screamed at her," he admits, but *she endured my wrath. And she saved my life.*"

Her willingness to endure temporary wrath ended up protecting Al's future. He admits, "Those guys down in the alley — none of them are around right now. I don't think about it that much. But it touches me now as I'm talking about it. She didn't want me out in the streets late at night. I had to do my homework. And I'm sitting here right now because of it. It's so simple, isn't it?"[4]

Unfortunately, Al's mom died before she ever got to see her son's success. I keep thinking of this financially strapped, stressed-out, divorced mom, with a rebellious kid on her hands, her boy screaming at her, calling her names, demanding to know why he can't go out and cause trouble late at night like the other boys. Every word he utters cuts her deeply. It's not like she has a husband to support her; when her boy turns on her, she's alone. It must have been so painful to absorb his venom and hatred.

But she stayed tough even when he didn't understand her — and she saved her son's life in the process. Those carousing boys have all but disappeared. Al Pacino has achieved a high level of success, and he attributes it, at least in part, to a mom who had the courage to bear his youthful wrath. She was once misunderstood, but now she earns his highest praise.

This is the severe side of sacred parenting: giving to kids who can't see the benefits in what they're receiving, walking at times through the "valley of the shadow of death," being called all manner of names as we seek to raise godly children, crucifying our tendency to be people-pleasers. In the process, we get blessed, transformed, and invited into the very ministry of Christ himself. We join him in his own courageous confrontation of a broken and sinful world.

God designed and blessed anger in order to energize our passion to destroy sin.

Dan Allender and Tremper Longman III

Chapter 7

Burning Love

How Raising Children Teaches Us to Handle Anger

A pastor decided to preach a sermon on anger. After the sermon, he invited church members who needed special prayer with regard to their struggles with this emotion to come forward. Nineteen individuals responded.

Every one of them was the mother of small children.

Raising children often leads to certain spiritual hazards. On occasion, my children have caused me to laugh as hard as I've ever laughed; at other times, I've become so angry at them it frightened me, to the point where I almost didn't recognize myself.

The spiritual process of parenting means that we can no longer hide in the pleasant land of denial. Parenting brings real emotions to the surface — emotions too strong to ignore or deny. You can't become a parent without feeling, at various times, joy, sadness, anger, and a host of other human emotions. The process of parenting forces us to become more mature in handling some of the trickier emotions, particularly anger.

Contrary to popular opinion, anger itself cannot be a sin, because the Bible often portrays God as angry (Psalm 6:1; 38:1; Isaiah 12:1; Micah 7:9), and even his presence in a person can elicit anger: "When Saul heard their words, the Spirit of God came upon him in power, and he burned with anger" (1 Samuel 11:6).

Consider the forceful ways Scripture describes God's own anger: "See, the Name of the LORD comes from afar, with burning anger and dense clouds of smoke; his lips are full of wrath, and his tongue is a consuming fire" (Isaiah 30:27). This is no mere irritation; it is a very forceful and passionate wrath.

But God's anger differs from what most of us experience. His anger, in the words of Augustine, is not "such a disturbed feeling as exists in the mind of an angry man," but rather, "his just displeasure against sin."[1]

This means that motivation is everything when it comes to anger. The difference between righteous anger and unrighteous anger ultimately comes down to why we feel angry, what we feel angry about, and what we do with our anger.

Nehemiah provides a healthy example. When he heard that some of his own people were taking advantage of the poor, Nehemiah didn't shrug his shoulders, deliver an arrogant opinion on human nature, or ignore the situation. Instead, he became righteously white-hot: "When I heard their outcry and these charges, I was very angry. I pondered them in my mind and then accused the nobles and officials" (Nehemiah 5:6–7).

Nehemiah became angry, but he then paused to ponder his reasons for feeling angry. After thinking through the reasons and determining that he had good cause to be upset, he went into action, confronting the nobles and officials and demanding they make a change. He didn't deny, ignore, or repress his passion; instead, he used it as motivation, subjected it to wisdom and rational thinking, and then took action. Bravo, Nehemiah!

Moses is a complex man who was both commended and punished for the role anger played in his life. When Moses came down from Mount Sinai, toting the Ten Commandments, he saw the idolatrous revelry going on in the camp below as the people worshiped a golden calf. According to the book of Exodus, Moses' "anger burned" (Exodus 32:19).

When Aaron saw Moses fling down the tablets, he had an epiphany: *I'm in a lot of trouble.* I liken Aaron's reaction to that of a husband whose wife had just returned home after being gone all afternoon. The husband knew the house was getting messy and fully intended to clean it up — but he just never got around to it. After his wife returned, he began to see the house through *her* eyes and finally realized the extent of the mess. But too late!

Moses had left Aaron in charge. Certainly Aaron knew that worshiping a calf didn't follow Moses' directions. The raucous singing, the revelry, the "misbehavior," that followed was bad enough — but when his brother comes back after having sat in God's presence for several days, Aaron has the mother of all "aha" moments: *This must look* really *bad!*

A shocked Moses asks Aaron, "What did these people do to you, that you led them into such great sin?" (Exodus 32:21).

In what could be considered one of the more humorous passages in the Bible, Aaron feebly ekes out, "Do not be angry, my lord." (Exodus 32:22).

Don't be angry? *Don't be angry?!* How could Moses *not* be angry? That's sort of like a high school student who just wrapped the new family vehicle around a tree saying, "You're probably pretty mad, aren't you? Does this mean I can't go to the dance Friday night?"

Moses immediately recruited faithful Levites, who began punishing the worst unrepentant offenders with the sword, an act God later backed up by killing even more Israelites through a plague (Exodus 32:35). In this case, Moses' anger appropriately mirrored God's own response to sin.

On another occasion, however, Moses' anger got him in trouble. The Israelites complain about a lack of water, then begin moaning that they would have preferred to remain slaves in Egypt than to be thirsty and free in the desert. And Moses loses control of himself. He's had enough of their bickering, complaining, and ungratefulness, and so he cries out, "Listen, you rebels, must we bring you water out of this rock?" (Numbers 20:10). He then strikes the rock two times and water gushes out.

God immediately pronounces his judgment against Moses. He had instructed Moses to speak to the rock, but Moses struck it instead (as he had on a previous occasion recorded in Exodus 17:6) and in so doing didn't honor God as holy (see Numbers 20:12). Moses also made it seem as though he himself was going to provide the water: "Listen, you rebels, must *we* bring you water out of this rock?"

Why did Moses react like this? He felt angry — the right emotion — but in this case, he became angry for the wrong reason! It was all about him, not about God's righteous displeasure against sin. He used his authority and power to demonstrate his personal outrage. Moses had had enough of their grumbling and complaining, and he let his passion lead him to do *the right thing in the wrong way*. It cost him a ticket to the Promised Land.

Have you ever been there? Maybe your kid needed punishment — a rebuke, correction, perhaps even a spanking. You did the right thing, but *you did it in the wrong way*. You didn't take time to pause and pray, seeking God's wisdom in the matter. Like Moses, you used your parental authority to lash out at your kids for inconveniencing you, humiliating you, or frustrating you rather than to discipline and train them for their good and for God's glory. You slipped up and let sin rather than reverence for God drive your actions. Despite your best intentions, you had a "Moses moment" — and you realized just how frustrating the art of parenting can feel.

Walking Near the Dark Side

Author Rachel Cusk writes of her infant daughter, who cried for hours at a time. One morning, following a particularly long, loud, and sleepless night, Rachel fed her baby "for perhaps the twentieth time in ten hours." She put her daughter in the crib, hoping she'd finally go to sleep:

> I am not asking for a solid stretch: I merely require a few minutes to myself gluing parts of my face back on and saying things aloud in front of the mirror to see if I've actually gone mad. At this point I don't just *want* her to go to sleep. She *has* to go to sleep; otherwise I don't know what will happen. My position is at once reasonable, utterly desperate, and nonnegotiable.[2]

After placing her daughter in the crib, Rachel slips off into the bathroom for a few blessed moments of silence. Unfortunately, a very few. The baby soon cries, and Rachel — exhausted, weary, at her wit's end — begins to yell:

> I don't quite know what I am shouting, something about it being unfair, about it clearly being completely unreasonable that I should want FIVE MINUTES on my own. GO TO SLEEP! I shout, now standing directly over her crib. I shout not because I think she might obey me but because I am

aware of an urge to hurl her out of the window. She looks at me in utter terror. It is the first frankly emotional look she has given me in her life. It is not really what I was hoping for.[3]

Once her daughter drifts off to sleep, Rachel feels horrified at what just happened. She calls several friends. "*I shouted at her,* I confess. In the end I confess it to several different people, none of whom give me the absolution I am looking for. Oh dear, they say. Poor baby. They do not mean me."[4]

Having raised a colicky child myself, I can empathize with Rachel's story. A finicky child can wear you down. You swallow your anger for days on end, and then, in one terrible eruption, you blow. Even while you're doing it, something tells you, *This is terrible; this is horrible! What has gotten into me?* and so you vow never to be angry again — but that presents another problem later on.

Anger toward babies almost always relates to how we, the parents, are being inconvenienced. Later on in life, as our children grow older, anger is the natural response to moral transgression, creating moments in which we would have to be less than human, and certainly less than Christian, to *not* be angry. C. S. Lewis comments, "The absence of anger . . . can, in my opinion, be a most alarming symptom. . . . If the Jews cursed more bitterly than the Pagans, this was, I think, at least in part because they took right and wrong more seriously."[5] And yet to get angry is to walk such a fine line that Scripture often seems to discount it altogether:

- "Refrain from anger and turn from wrath" (Psalm 37:8).
- "Get rid of all . . . anger" (Ephesians 4:31).

Why the mixed signals? Part of the answer is that anger is not for the immature. It requires a certain spiritual sophistication to wield it appropriately. Perhaps that is why James warns us that we should be "slow to become angry" (James 1:19). All of us need anger to occasionally motivate us, but very few of us can make anger our ally without succumbing to its darker side. Although I don't think this fits every situation, in most circumstances our anger should be *reluctant.*

This two-headed reality of anger — occasionally necessary but always dangerous — leaves us with two options: (1) become hyper-religious and try to avoid anger altogether (becoming less than human and, ironically, less than religious in the process), or (2) learn to walk in the fields of anger, knowing that sometimes we will err as we learn to express appropriate anger.

I learned long ago that if I were going to make "sinless perfection" my highest goal, I'd better not get married. And if I did get married, I'd certainly better not have kids. There's no way we can walk in these intense relationships without stirring up sin, at least occasionally. Because of God's gracious and merciful provision through Jesus Christ, however, I can confidently enter these relationships, knowing that I'll sin and knowing that God will forgive my sin and even use my sin to refine my character and help me grow.

As blasphemous as this may sound to some, I no longer seek sinlessness; I seek maturity. I don't want to grow complacent about any conscious sin in my life, and I certainly don't take sin lightly. I readily agree with the great Puritan John Owen's warning: "Kill sin or it will kill you." But I also know that to grow in maturity, I have to enter and even embrace situations where, because of my fallen nature, sin seems virtually inevitable. I might cut down on certain sins if I literally gouged out my eyes and lived by myself in the desert, but in doing so I would also forsake the call to love — and, as I see it, commit an even graver sin, namely, the sin of pride.

To avoid anger altogether is to fall into the Buddhist trap of "annihilation of desire." The Bible makes one thing very clear: *God is anything but a stoic!* Only a grotesque and treacherous faith confuses tolerance and leniency with love. There is a time for anger and a time for wrath, but every time anger uncoils is a dangerous and fearful time we should accept only because we must, not because we can.

Parenting thus invites us into a very complex process of sanctification (spiritual growth). We'll mature, or we'll collapse — but we won't remain unchanged. C. S. Lewis makes this observation about the imprecatory psalms — those troublesome biblical passages where curses get uttered and violent wishes get spewed against the enemy:

> The Jews sinned in this matter worse than the Pagans not because they were further from God but because they were nearer to Him. For the Supernatural, entering a human soul, opens to it new possibilities both of good and evil. From that point the road branches: one way to sanctity, love, humility, the other to spiritual pride, self-righteousness, persecuting zeal. And no way back to the mere humdrum virtues and

vices of the unawakened soul. If the Divine call does not make us better, it will make us very much worse. Of all bad men religious bad men are the worst. Of all the created beings the wickedest is one who originally stood in the immediate presence of God. There seems no way out of this. It gives a new application to Our Lord's words about "counting the cost."[6]

Lewis's chilling words present us with a terrifying choice: Remain an "unawakened soul," or risk the vices that come from drawing nearer to God and entering the seductive world of religious insight and righteous anger. Parenting exacts a tremendous cost. It virtually ensures that we will grow stronger or weaker, but we will not and cannot remain the same.

Those who elect to become parents already have chosen to enter the more sacred world of religious insight and righteous anger. Even if we don't recognize parenting as a religious process, it becomes one. Suddenly, issues of fairness, provision, justice, and the future take on transcendent meaning. If you want to enjoy children without these challenging forces shaping your life, then visit a soccer game, rent a kids' video, or hand out treats on Halloween — but don't become a parent.

The Relationship behind the Wound

In the Old Testament, the wrath of God is best seen as "an expression of rejected and wounded love."[7] God gets angry *because he cares.* God gets angry *because the stakes are so high.* His is not a temper-laden coronary just waiting to explode; he feels deeply concerned because he knows the seriousness of our eternal destiny.

In the same way, we parents become most angry with those we love the most. The greater our emotional involvement, the greater our potential to get really angry, because we care so deeply about what happens to those we love and to our relationship with them.

Certainly we get angry when someone drives like an idiot on the road, cutting us off and all but removing our front bumper. We get angry, but we let it go. Why? We have nothing to hold on to. We don't have a name, a face, or a history. We have no one to confront, nothing that can be done, no issue of future interaction, so we *have* to let it go.

Ah, but when it's a spouse or a child, anger can use the triplicate past, present, and future against us. It recruits the past to make us feel betrayed: "After all I've done for you, *this* is how you treat me?" It uses the present to reveal our hurt: "I wanted this to be a special day, and now you've ruined it! How could you do this to me?" And it uses the future to sprinkle in a little fear: "What will happen to us? What will happen to *you?*"

We can't easily let go of this type of anger, because it is rooted in love, with all the expectations of love, the hope of love, and even the fear behind love. This helps to explain why relationships can feel so uncomfortable, particularly for men. The subtleties and layers of emotion demanded of us often go beyond our ability to manage them. Tell us to take a hill with a machine gun, and we can do it. Ask us to set a doorjamb, and we can get it done. Mention that the lawn needs mowing, and we can see a beginning and an end. But tell us to manage the conflicting emotions of anger, fear, love, relief, and thankfulness when a child comes home three hours after curfew? That's a lot tougher. This kind of scenario tempts us to shut down or to express *only* anger or perhaps some other one-sided emotion. We don't know how to wade through all the conflicting layers to accurately express how we feel.

Our friend Annie Carlson has worked through this issue with her husband. In the past, Annie had a tendency to use anger to express her hurt. "Sitting in the hurt feels too passive for me," Annie explains, "so if I skip the sad feelings and just get angry, then at least I feel in control." Now when Annie feels angry, she says she hears her husband's question ringing in her ears, "Are you mad or sad?" Annie's comments are particularly appropriate here, because we easily confuse hurt and anger, especially when one of our children causes our hurt. Acting out of woundedness can get us into all kinds of trouble.

Angry and hurt parents sometimes react to a wound by hurting the child they want to save. It is one of the great ironies of being a mother or father that in our frustrated relief over our child's physical safety, we can obliterate them verbally.

In God's provision, we have to become bigger than our wounds. That's why we parent "out of reverence for God" (2 Corinthians 7:1). When a child comes home late, the fact that he or she caused me to lose sleep, to worry, or to fear isn't the biggest issue. Emotionally, I want to make it the biggest issue, because that's how the episode affected *me*. That's the problem of acting out of our woundedness: It's all about *me*. But God calls me to act in such a way that it's all about *our children*, and their relationship to *him*.

So what do I do? I have to step back, as Nehemiah did, and take inventory. I have to put my emotions to the test and corral them with my intellect. I don't ignore them, but neither should I allow them to drive my reaction. They're just there, like the weather, making the situation more or less pleasant, but they must not determine what I do.

Handling anger this way is a fine art, crafted out of many and repeated failures. We can't learn to handle difficult emotions merely by reading about them. We have to walk through them. We have to experience them. And what invites us to do this more than raising children?

Yet the spiritual process of parenting does more than walk us through the minefield of expressing anger toward humans; it also invites us to enter the country of becoming angry with God. This is a particularly delicate emotion, in that whenever we have a disagreement with God, we can be sure God isn't the one to blame — but knowing this doesn't make the feelings any less intense, does it?

Anger at God

Many families have faced the traumatic ordeal of watching a son or daughter slowly die of a terminal illness. How could they *not* ask, "Lord, why won't you heal our child?" God certainly has the power to do it. Many times he does do it, but sometimes he doesn't. What then?

There seems to be no figuring out God's work in this area. One of the first books I helped write (*Out of the Silence*) told the story of Duane Miller, whom God miraculously healed of a throat ailment.[8] Focus on the Family featured Duane's story; the tape that recounts his healing makes the hair on the back of your neck rise. It truly is a miraculous tale. Yet Duane is the first to admit his astonishment that a young father, present in the same church on the same morning on which Duane got healed, died just a couple weeks later of a brain tumor. Duane's kids were adults; this young man's children were still very young and presumably needed him even more than Duane's kids needed him. Duane's ailment debilitated him, but didn't threaten his life; this man battled a terminal disease.

Why did God miraculously heal Duane and allow a man in the very same room, just three rows away, to die in his sickness? Duane would never suggest that his own healing resulted from faith or obedience. Rather, it happened by God's providential choice, offered without explanation or apology.

Here is where the Lord seems to beckon us to what the ancients called the spiritual discipline of surrender. Paganism seeks to manipulate divine forces to serve the human will: Do the right thing, and you obligate God to respond in a certain way. Authentic Christianity seeks to surrender the human will in order to serve and give glory to the divine God. At various points we will feel disappointed with God, frustrated with God, even angry with God — but what matters is that we make Joshua's famous declaration our own: "As for me and my household, we will serve the LORD" (Joshua 24:15).

- We may face unemployment, but we will serve the Lord.
- We may go to three funerals in one year, but we will serve the Lord.
- We may have two of our three children rebel, but we will serve the Lord.
- We may have cancer return after a time of remission, but we will serve the Lord.

As believers, we have the added hope — a divinely promised certainty — that ultimately, God will heal our children. The healing may not take place until heaven, but eventually it will come.

This is different from trying to "explain" God's ways, which often appear inexplicable. We can't even use character as a reason. While I've fervently taught and just as fervently believe that God uses trials to build character, to teach us lessons, and to do a deeper work in our souls, personally I'd rather die a little less mature if my child could be spared suffering! For good reason Paul tells the Romans to "mourn with those who mourn" (Romans 12:15). He's saying, "Don't offer easy answers; don't try to rid yourself of the burden of being around a grieving person by trying to make them forget it or to 'get over it.' All of that is self-centered religion. Instead, *mourn with them.* Take time to cry, to hurt, even to be angry — but don't lose faith."

It is natural and inevitable for parents to become angry, but in the process God invites us to step out of the human frailty that so easily feels aggrieved and don the Spirit-gifted attitude of humility, sacrifice, surrender, and love. Is this a flight into piety, using religious words to escape an ugly human reality? No, not at all! The Bible doesn't explain why God sometimes fails to act in the way we want him to act. Instead, it focuses on how *we* are supposed to act in the way God wants us to act. God, as our superior, has initiated our relationship, and as the revealer he can choose to explain — or not explain — whatever he wants. However much this may offend modern sensibilities, God reserves the right to keep us in the dark about some questions. One of the more practical teachings I ever received came from my theological mentor at Regent College, J. I. Packer, who noted, "The Bible doesn't answer every question that men and women ask of it." There is nothing to do about this truth except receive it.

I know in my heart of hearts that no one loves any child more than the God who created that child. Yes, you *would* die for that child, but *God already has*. No one feels that child's pain more than God himself. When you go to sleep, you forget about your child's ordeal, but God *never* sleeps. That child's predicament remains always before him, and the Lord never misses a single stab of pain. He hears every sigh, counts every tear, notices every wince.

At times it may not seem like it, but God cares and loves more than any parent has ever loved or cared. To suggest otherwise is both delusional and blasphemous. We have to recognize the subtle temptation that anger toward God slowly builds. If our subjective experiences go unchecked and unchallenged by absolute truth, they will destroy faith, foster resentment, and give birth to arrogant rebellion. As mentioned in the last chapter, we may need to stop listening to ourselves and start talking to ourselves, consciously calling to mind God's goodness and concern.

I've come to see that Satan is almost as patient as God. He'll cultivate in us a destructive attitude, thought, or habit, and then patiently wait for the dastardly fruit of that attitude, thought, or habit to destroy us. When we don't submit and surrender to God, we play into Satan's hands; we make it easy for Satan to blow all sorts of toxic spiritual poisons into our souls.

God is big enough and wise enough to handle our immediate, natural expressions of anger, but spiritually we must learn to submit —

as we admit that God knows more than we do and that he doesn't owe us an explanation just because we'd like one. This stretch of our sacred journey could be likened to driving through the fog: we may see no landmarks and get little assurance that we're even headed in the right direction, but the only way out of the fuzziness is to drive right through the uncertainty.

Where Angels Fear to Tread

So then, if we want to become mature, we have to learn to walk in a valley where sin appears inevitable but ought to be avoided. We are told, "In your anger do not sin" (Psalm 4:4; Ephesians 4:26), but for most of us this sounds fearfully similar to Jesus' seemingly impossible, "Be perfect, therefore, as your heavenly Father is perfect" (Matthew 5:48). We don't want to correct Jesus, because we know *that* can't be the right thing to do; but if we're honest, we ask ourselves, "Does he *really* mean that?"

He does, in the sense that Paul tells the Corinthians to "aim for perfection" (2 Corinthians 13:11) while readily admitting to another fellowship, "Not that I have already obtained all this, or have already been made perfect, but I press on to take hold of that for which Christ Jesus took hold of me" (Philippians 3:12). In the same way, we can "aim" to learn how to handle anger without falling into sin. But if we pursue it in the manner of a fearful, performance-oriented, legalistic Pharisee, we'll get beaten down within five minutes. Our kids will eat us for lunch and then have our guilt for dessert.

I believe we are to treat anger like a potentially toxic, yet highly potent and controlled, medicine. At times it must be prescribed, but we should handle it carefully and limit its use. For starters, if we use anger for too long, it becomes fatal; we're to get rid of it the same day that it is born ("Do not let the sun go down while you are still angry" [Ephesians 4:26]). Prolonged anger conceives resentment and bitterness. Resentment and bitterness will ultimately poison our souls if we give them a foothold. I don't think it's a coincidence that as soon as Paul urges us not to let the sun go down on our anger, he adds, "and do not give the devil a foothold" (verse 27).

Sometimes we need the force of anger to accomplish God's work. Our children need to see how offended we feel by their lack of respect and by actions that may endanger their lives or soil their character, or how passionate we become when we see injustice. Our kids will glean a rich harvest merely from watching what raises the ire of their parents and grandparents — provided we get angry about the right things! Who among us wants to raise apathetic individuals who don't give a rip about anything?

But once anger has aroused us, once it has led us to express our displeasure and motivated us to take the appropriate action, *then we have to let it go*. Otherwise it'll take us too far. We were right to hunt down Osama bin Laden after the terrorist attacks on September 11, 2001. We should have felt angry at the cruel, heartless deed he masterminded. But those who let their anger lead them to beat up, harass, or taunt anyone of Middle Eastern descent failed to put a hedge on their anger and allowed that anger to lead them into sin of their own.

What parameters should we draw for our anger? First, we should enter it reluctantly and fearfully. James tells us to be "slow to become angry" (James 1:19). Human anger, James observes, does not bring about the righteous life that God desires. It is not part of our original design. In a perfect world, anger would be unnecessary and inappropriate. God displays his anger at the fallen world and the fallen angels. The Fall foists anger on us, but it is like chemotherapy — an assaulting agent that becomes good only because the evil it attacks does more harm than any evil it can bring.

Second, we have to consciously limit our anger by not letting the sun go down on it. It would be simplistic to suggest twelve hours as the spiritual limit. If I'm talking to someone whose daughter has been murdered or raped, I'd never tell them that they have just ten more hours to be angry and then they need to "get over it." The sun going down is a metaphor: *We must contain anger within its proper season* and bring it to an end as soon as we can, lest it give birth to resentment and bitterness. The Bible means that as soon as we enter the neighborhood of anger, we should be eager to get out. It's no place to dwell. While we must occasionally pay it a visit, don't plan on buying property there. God graciously tells the Israelites of old, "I will heal their waywardness and love them freely, for my anger has turned away from them" (Hosea 14:4).

Third, we need to govern anger by reason, spiritual maturity, and patient wisdom. Love isn't "easily angered" (1 Corinthians 13:5), and an overseer — that is, a mature leader — isn't "quick-tempered" (Titus 1:7).

Anger becomes an element of our response, but a subservient one at best. We consider anger as one ingredient in the recipe of human relationships, but on its own, without a sprinkling of love, kindness, gentleness, patience, and a host of other godly ingredients, it remains bitter to the core.

Fourth, instead of running from anger, we need to remember that righteous anger is a double-edged sword. I ought to grow angry at injustice, but am I just as angry when *I* commit an act of injustice? Certainly I'm going to feel upset if my child does something foolish or immoral, but will I feel just as annoyed when *I* do something foolish or immoral? Anger becomes a problem when we use it only to chastise others and not ourselves. Two of my favorite contemporary writers, Dan Allender and Tremper Longman, give this important reminder:

> Jesus advised that we consider the log in our own eye before we deal with the speck in another's eye. Whatever failure or assault we hate in others, we must hate in ourselves as well. If we hate their sin more than our own, we will always be unrighteous. But if we hate the sin in our own hearts more than what we see in theirs, we will grow in the quiet, patient sorrow of true righteous anger.[9]

You see, when we parent out of reverence for God, we hate sin because *he* hates sin. We hate our sin, we hate our neighbor's sin, and we hate our children's sin, but we don't play favorites — just as God does not play favorites. To focus on my neighbor's (or children's) sin, but not my own, is to stop practicing the grace-based faith of Christianity and to start following the religion of the Pharisees. Remember, the verse that contains the words "out of reverence for God" begins with the words "Since we have these promises, dear friends, let us purify *ourselves* from everything that contaminates" (2 Corinthians 7:1, emphasis added).

Finally, we're told that love — not wrath, malice, or anger — constitutes the ultimate Christian response. When a child disobeys, God calls us to respond in love. Anger may become a servant of love, but it must never define it. Children need to see our total commitment to them, so they realize that our angry response does not reflect self-seeking (as though the greatest offense is the embarrassment brought on *us*) but rather shows a fierce and passionate concern for *their* well-being. Anger that mirrors God's own anger is thus a selfless anger. One element of self-interest remains — grief that a relationship has been betrayed and that trust has been broken — but the grief tilts toward what the offender has lost and toward our hope for their welfare.

In short, when children expose our impatience and self-centered frustration, they hold up a mirror to our hearts. Just as God's response to his children reveals his character, so parenting reveals our character. It exposes our sin and holds up to us a clear picture of what we feel most passionate about.

Although I teach a course called "Spirituality 101," I believe that learning to deal with anger could be called "Spirituality 601." It's graduate-level Christianity. Our children constitute our homework, our mixed emotions become our textbooks, and the character that results will reveal our final grade.

Uncomfortable Realities

On August 6, 1945, a dozen men walked somberly toward a sixty-five-ton bomber named the *Enola Gay*. Hours later, they dropped a bomb that delivered the destructive effect of twenty thousand tons of TNT, thereby unleashing the first terrifying instance of atomic combat. Five miles below, Hiroshima collapsed into ashes. One week and another bomb later, Japan finally surrendered.

When the twelve crew members of the *Enola Gay* returned home, they felt surprised to discover they had become famous. Each one of them grew familiar with flashing camera lights and enthusiastic backslaps. People paid for their dinners in restaurants, they were invited to lavish dinners and fancy homes, and their pictures appeared on the front pages of the nation's newspapers.

A leading Washington socialite gave what eventually became an infamous reception for one of the fliers. Dessert came in the form of a curiously shaped cake — baked, iced, and decorated to look like an atomic explosion. A news photographer caught the untoward scene. An Air Force man clearly looked uncomfortable while awkwardly holding a knife over the cake. Next to him stood the hostess, smiling as though her horse had just won the Kentucky Derby. Within days, the photo had covered the nation; everyone saw it, and almost everyone had the same reaction. Joy Davidman described it well:

Thereupon the conscience of America, already uneasily sparking and fizzing, reached critical mass and produced a very pretty little explosion of its own. No matter what we were — pacifist or militarist, civilian or soldier, Red or Red baiter — we all hated that cake. It was one of the few things the public opinion of this diverse and diffuse country has ever been able to agree on completely.... That cake was an obscenity. Christians differ as to whether or not they may in some circumstances kill; they do not differ about whether they may gloat over a fallen enemy. To this day the world has not been able to reach agreement on whether the bombing of Hiroshima was necessary. But one thing we'll all agree to: necessary or not, it wasn't funny.[10]

Anger, like war, is one of the uncomfortable realities of life. Living in a fallen world, raising fallen children, we are forced to confront disagreeable necessities. All of us wish we never needed to get angry, just as — I hope — we all wish our country never had to go to war. Sadly, sin sometimes demands a forceful response. Until Jesus returns, war will always erupt between nations, and anger will inevitably flare up between parents and their children. Some of us — weak ones like myself — enter into the arena of anger and adopt this emotion with great trepidation, regret, and almost always a large dose of self-recrimination. Others — the more forceful ones — grow all too familiar with the emotion. They revel in it, welcome it, and seem to enjoy it and even live for it. Both will be stained by it — one by their softness, the other by their thoughtlessness.

Unfortunately, we can't get around the fact that sacred parenting leads us into dirty spiritual realities. To avoid these realities is as much a sin as to glory in them. Ironically, most of us will probably fail from both perspectives! But we can't avoid them. We must face anger, knowing we will sin in our anger but also that God will forgive us while he uses the process to make us just a bit more like the Son who bore God's righteous anger on our behalf.

With the baby's birth, a lifetime of vanity vanished into thin air.
Rachel Cusk

Your attitude should be the same as that of Christ Jesus:

Who, being in very nature God,
    did not consider equality with God something to be
        grasped,
but made himself nothing,
    taking the very nature of a servant. . . .
Therefore God exalted him to the highest place.
Philippians 2:5–7, 9

Chapter 8

The Glory behind the Grime

How Raising Children Teaches Us to Look beyond Glamour and into Glory

Rabbi Nancy Fuchs-Kreimer confesses she never understood the Christian idea of God's incarnation until she had a child.

Nancy and her husband were nestled in their house on December 24, holding their six-day-old baby, when a Roman Catholic priest knocked on her door. Nancy was attending school at the time, and she assumed the priest had come to collect some chapters for her dissertation, so she explained that she hadn't done much in the past few weeks except produce the small bundle she held in her arms. The priest quickly assured Nancy that he hadn't come about the dissertation. "It is the Lord's birthday tomorrow," he said, "so I wanted to hold a baby in my arms."

The priest's comments kindled a moment of revelation for Nancy. "Having studied Christianity, I had read about incarnation, but for the first time I really 'got it.' In the Christian imagination, God was once a tiny body just like this!"[1]

What Nancy calls "the Christian imagination" we Christians call historical fact, but we can at least understand her wonder. The flesh of a baby seems a particularly unglamorous package to put a God in. Babies drool. They cry. They mess their diapers. They are everything a God is not supposed to be: frail, weak, and, most of all, utterly dependent. Yet our God came wrapped in just such an unglamorous package. What deep recesses of wisdom did he have to draw on to come up with *that* one?

Conceiving and raising children takes us through this same humbling process. A woman's body bloats, stretches, and swells as she prepares to welcome her baby into this world; the glamour of her youth gives way to water retention, ankles that may rival the width of her neck, and skin that gets stretched beyond repair. Not only do children bring about physical changes, they can also act like a tsunami in social situations, practically obliterating your once-alluring social life. Author Rachel Cusk's daughter had colic, which meant that she felt frequently embarrassed by her daughter's untimely wails:

> She has cried in her sling on walks, in her baby carriage when I am trying to shop, on the bus, on the subway, at the houses of friends and relations, in my and others' arms. . . . I have run home with her bawling in my arms, pulling the carriage crazily behind us while people stare. I have jumped off buses in the middle of nowhere. I have bolted from cafes. I have ended telephone conversations without explanation.[2]

Can anybody relate?

After several months the incessant crying became more "normal," and Rachel finally could see the spiritual benefit of those raucous weeks:

> With every cry she has tutored me in what is plain and hard: that my affection, my silly entertainments, my doting hours, the particular self I tried to bring to my care of her, have been as superfluous as my fury and despair. . . . That she has stopped crying I take as an indication that she judges my training to have been successful and the rank of mother attained; a signal that we can now, cautiously, get on with the business of living together.[3]

I remember the time a church invited me to speak following the publication of my first book. The staff had a lunch reception at one of the elder's homes following the service in order for people to talk to Lisa and me. Our baby had been saving up her digestive efforts for almost a week, and she chose to let loose the fruit of that work just fifteen minutes before we were scheduled to eat. Lisa was nursing her in a back room when the eruption — no other word does it justice — began. Lisa put a towel under the baby, but our daughter mimicked the Energizer bunny: She kept going and going and going. Soon the mess began to seep out under the diaper and even spread beyond the blanket. Another woman walked in to let Lisa know we'd be eating soon, and with a horrified gasp she asked Lisa, "What can I do to help?"

"Get Gary!" Lisa said.

Several people had surrounded me, asking various questions, when a woman told me that Lisa needed to see me *right away.* I walked into the room and couldn't believe my eyes. It didn't seem possible that such a small human being could make such an elephant-sized mess. "What am I going to do?" Lisa asked, horrified, her skirt beyond repair.

I slipped out and told our hostess that we would have to leave. When I tried to explain why, she said, "My daughter is the same size as your wife; she'll lend her a skirt."

I brought Lisa the clean skirt, thinking I had solved the problem. Lisa informed me otherwise. She had worn a very heavy skirt, so she hadn't bothered to put on a slip. In the sunlight, the daughter's flimsy skirt looked more than a bit revealing. But Lisa felt embarrassed to admit she hadn't been wearing a slip, so once again, a disconcerting dilemma engulfed us.

We had to laugh in spite of ourselves. We were at this reception to be *honored,* but we had never felt more embarrassed in our lives! We survived, though some church members may still be wondering why the author's wife never wanted to leave the table and, when she did, why she kept on her coat despite the hot spring sun.

Years later, my son, Graham, and the son of one of our pastors played on the same Little League baseball team. After the final game, we all headed to a buffet-style restaurant to celebrate. It was about 8:00 p.m., and Graham's friend — the pastor's son — bypassed the salads, took a little of the pizza, and went heavy on the ice cream and pudding. I commented to his dad, "Don't you remember the days when we could eat that much dessert and not pay for it?"

My son spent that night at our pastor's house. Graham woke up early the next morning when he heard some commotion and saw our minister, in his underwear, scrubbing vomit out of the carpet. Apparently Graham's friend didn't get away with eating all that ice cream after all. It came back to haunt him in a very physical and violent way. Graham was used to seeing his pastor dressed nicely in front of the whole congregation, so he understandably giggled at a rather different sight. As he recounted the story to me later, I retorted, "Well, that's one way to get to know your pastor."

Graham's little adventure provided a good lesson: No matter how exalted our position, if we have kids, the day will come when we'll wind up in some of the most undignified positions imaginable — including cleaning up vomit in our underwear at 2:00 a.m. The positive spiritual benefit is that it slowly transforms us from valuing the superficial allure of appearances and helps us focus instead on the influential aspect of meaningful relationships.

Acquaintances and networking — the playground of the seemingly powerful — allow us to move into and out of situations without care or consequences. The focus often rests on appearing competent or engaging or alluring and on leaving behind a positive impression. But real relationships aren't quite so sanitary. Things get messy; we see the sordid side of life, and we're asked to forgive and to love unconditionally. Real relationships take us into everything that casual social relationships allow us to avoid. If we embrace the real relationships over the superficial ones, our taste for intimacy will get trained in a positive spiritual direction. We'll begin to care less about image and more about substance. We'll understand that true intimacy exacts a price, calling us to a far deeper commitment than making an impression or putting on a false front does.

While there's nothing wrong with glamour per se, many important activities in life call us to get our hands dirty. Parenting in particular wakes us up from our self-indulgence and invites us to get involved in something bigger than adventure and even greater than glamour — the shaping of a human life and the destiny of an eternal soul. It's a messy business, but a highly important one.

Oh, What a Body!

Making this shift from valuing image to focusing on substance represents a crucial spiritual passage, particularly in a culture that values glamour more than just about anything else. How else to explain

People magazine's annual "50 Most Beautiful People" issue, with names most of us know, while scores of scientists, social health workers, and religious leaders labor in virtual obscurity?

The saddest part is how we've come to *define* glamour. The two words "sexy moms" don't normally go together, yet when you think about it, how do people expect that a woman *becomes* a mom? Sex and the single woman should be the oxymoron, not sex and the married wife and mother! Even so, lingerie stores glorify women who — based on the advertising — have never carried an extra pound or two of fat, much less a nine-pound baby. Sex gets portrayed as the playground of singles, resulting in a definition of "sexiness" that uses distinctly un-maternal terms.

This can start early. A close friend of ours felt horrified when she passed through a checkout at the grocery store and saw her young son's eyes grow wide as he gazed at the cover of *Cosmopolitan.* "Wow, look at that!" her four-year-old said, as she frantically grabbed the magazine to turn it over. "I wish she was *my* mom." Her four-year-old didn't understand that when a woman cares for babies and toddlers, she lacks the energy to work out at a gym three hours a day, wear the kind of clothes that would rip apart at the toddler's slightest grasp, or keep a hairstyle that requires regular touch-ups.

Adolescent males tend to be just as shortsighted, looking at women's bodies solely as objects of pleasure or sexuality. *Maxim, Details,* and other such magazines that feature lingerie- or swimsuit-wearing models in every issue are marketed toward males in their late teens and twenties. But as these men mature and watch their wives go through the process of birth, they can come to see those bodies — which once constituted mainly sources of pleasure in their minds — as miraculous instruments of nurture, life-giving care, and deeply significant nonsexual intimacy. This is a necessary milestone in every mature man's development.

Some women undoubtedly could feel offended by what I just said. I'm *not* saying that women are either sex objects or breeders. I'm trying to make a much more profound distinction. Both men and women must pass through the journey from centering on self (focusing on making an impression and getting what *I* want out of a relationship) to offering care to others — a highly significant, worldview-altering shift. Bearing and raising a child together represents the most striking point of this shift, and how we view our own and the other's bodies clearly indicates our understanding of this change. Where once the world seemed a place full of pleasure, a place where we were focused on and seasoned by pleasure, it now becomes a tapestry on which we can paint the experiences of selfless love. As we learn to give and receive love, we don't lose our taste for pleasure, but our spirits widen to look at pleasure in a new way. We find that giving care, providing nurture, and learning to sacrifice on behalf of another can provide even more meaning than the most intense pleasure imaginable.

The woman's body becomes a metaphor of this profound transformation. Giving birth to babies and then nurturing them can radically alter a couple's awareness of the body. Those beautiful breasts, almost overnight, temporarily become workhorses. They function no longer in a simply cosmetic or sexual fashion — they become essential nurturers, passing on the milk of life. Before nursing, women tend to think of their breasts almost exclusively in terms of their size and shape and perceived desirability by the other gender — but now something else rests between the often-romanticized clefts of a woman's body: a path to nurturing, life-giving care.

One woman told me that before she gave birth she considered her physical appearance her primary asset — pretty sad, but not uncommon in today's appearance-oriented culture. The great irony is that the process of birth may bloat a woman's body, but it can also *expand her soul* to free her from such superficial boundaries. A baby doesn't care if you look like a supermodel; he or she just wants to get fed and held.

Rachel Cusk summarizes this pull that women feel — looking good, offering care — when she writes about appearing outside in public with her baby daughter:

> When we go for a walk, I see young women in the street, beautiful and careless, and a pang of mourning for some oblique, lost self makes my heart clench. I look down at my daughter sleeping in her push-chair, the dark fringe of her lashes forming arcs on her pale skin, and a contrary wind of love gusts over me; and for some time this is how I am, blown this way and that, careening around like a crazy, febrile gauge trying to find north.[4]

As a young father, only a few years separated me from walking around a college campus and wanting to "look good." But one Sunday morning after our firstborn came along, it occurred to me on the way to church that I hadn't had time even to look in the mirror to see if my hair was combed! I had been so focused on getting the baby ready that I virtually forgot about myself. What a wonderful spiritual transformation!

The march to maturity is a meandering passage that abandons romanticized notions about beauty and worth based on appearances alone, but it's an essential one, a spiritual one, and a purposeful one. Not only does it affect how women view themselves, it also changes their view of their husband. If sexual intimacy were only about pleasure, that would be one thing. But when sexual intimacy leads to parenthood, an entirely different "application process" pertains. A woman might flirt with the "dark, dangerous" types of men just for fun, but as soon as she starts thinking of children, she may find herself gravitating toward someone a bit more stable.

Iris Krasnow writes about this in her book *Surrendering to Motherhood:* "Remember that stage when you wanted a child more than anything else and what you had instead was a chain of childish boyfriends? Thank God for the Chucks [her husband] of the world, the guys who finally come through for us."[5] This man may not look like Tom Cruise or have the biceps of Arnold Schwarzenegger, but he's there for you. He may not be able to bring an entire room to laughter, like Jay Leno can, but he can make *you* laugh. He may not have the bank account of Bill Gates, but everything he does have is yours. And you love him for it, in a way that you may never have appreciated in the past.

A child can make a woman look past a man's balding pate and paunchy stomach and fall in love with his heart, his stability, his support, and his strength. And a similar process can take place for men with regard to their view of women.

Bent Toward Care

Actress and director Rosanna Arquette screened a provocative documentary, *Searching for Debra Winger,* at the 2002 Cannes film festival. The idea for the documentary came about when Arquette discovered that Debra Winger, thrice-nominated for an Academy Award, had virtually retired at the age of thirty-nine because roles for "women that age" had all but dried up.

Winger knew early on in her career about the ridiculously short season for a leading woman in Hollywood. She recounts the time during her filming of *An Officer and a Gentleman* when a producer approached her off-camera with an envelope. Debra naturally assumed the letter to contain a word of encouragement or perhaps praise about how well the film was going.

Instead, the terse letter went like this: "You look a little bloated in the rushes." Inside the envelope the producer had tucked a water retention pill.

Winger was still in her twenties.

Society today has an obscene tendency to sexualize girls and desexualize women, completely reversing God's natural order. Britney Spears became the sex symbol of our age even before she could vote; and a woman of thirty-nine (Debra Winger) has to retire from Hollywood because she has grown "too old." In Arquette's documentary, actress Daryl Hannah talks of how, at the age of forty-one, she is often cast as a mother. Colleagues asked her, "Doesn't that bother you?" but Hannah insisted it didn't — until she visited wardrobe and saw the ugly, baggy clothes she was being asked to wear, along with an equally unattractive brown wig.

Something is wrong — profoundly wrong — when a girl defines sexual desirability and a woman is viewed as past her prime before she reaches her forties.

The lessons that childbearing and child raising teach men can change their lives in this respect: All of us guys need to move to a level of maturity that goes beyond looking at women as sex objects. Experiencing the miracle of birth with our wives and watching them nurse our children can train us to look at women in their totality, to respect them for the life-giving skills and the wonders of their anatomy apart from the aspect of sexual pleasure. Is anything more pathetic than a man in his forties or fifties who still looks at women only as sexual objects? Isn't this the very definition of an undeveloped man?

When I speak of an "undeveloped man," I speak of more than metaphor. Researchers have discovered three basic neuropathways in human sexual response: lust, attraction, and attachment.[6] The most primitive brain reaction is lust, but two of the higher chemical reactions in our brains include attraction and romance, followed by an attachment neuropathway that allows us to bond with others. Speaking of this latter pathway, researchers have found that "some of the most powerful neurochemicals in the brain are generated by this bonding process."[7]

Spiritually speaking, a man or woman stuck on lust *is* undeveloped; what's more, they miss out on one of the most powerful experiences in life, namely, loyal bonding. Loyal bonding brings a rush that is different from lust or romance, but its quieter undercurrent grows very strong, deeply meaningful, and is ultimately much more satisfying. It may lack the primitive edge of lust, but it carries the seasoned satisfaction of joy — a type of satisfaction never known by shallow men who think they are "trading up" by divorcing their wife and marrying a younger woman.

When a man has thoughtfully gone through a spiritual awakening, certain acts become unthinkable. How does a sensitive man even *contemplate* the thought of rape? A spiritually aware man would vomit at any inclination toward molesting or violating an innocent child. He has been bent decidedly toward offering care, protection, and nurture. He has become an enemy of exploitation, a fierce foe of violation.

Women inherently seem to know this. As a young man in my twenties, I unintentionally scared more than my share of women who had gone out for early-morning or late-evening runs. It felt so frustrating, because nothing I did helped. If I announced my presence from behind, they jumped. If I just passed them without saying anything, they jumped even higher. Whatever I did, I represented a potential threat. When I started jogging with my young daughter, that threat evaporated. If you're a woman, you know what I'm talking about. Imagine walking down a dark alley late at night, and you see a solitary man ahead. Your heart starts racing and your natural fears rise, but then you hear a light giggle and notice that the man is holding the hand of his little girl. Almost immediately your heartbeat settles down.

Once I even walked unbothered through the halls of my old elementary school. Had I been alone, I may well have been ushered out by a police escort. Hand in hand with my six-year-old, explaining that she wanted to see my old school, I had free rein to roam all over.

Why? At that moment I was a "nurturing" man — and nurturing men pose no threat.

A man or woman bent toward care and nurture no longer lives for himself or herself; they live for others. This is the spirit of Jesus, who even while being led away to the cross consoled those who mourned on his behalf: "Daughters of Jerusalem, do not weep for me; weep for yourselves and for your children" (Luke 23:28). Even in his darkest moment, Jesus looked after others. He had no interest in trying to make an impression! His body was bloody, dirty, disfigured, and bruised. He was too busy loving us, sacrificing for us, taking care of us, to worry about his appearance. In his glorious state, the Son was beauty beyond compare; in his incarnation, he was despised, broken, and bruised.

The world becomes a far different place when we learn to care instead of just to desire. Being glamorous is all about appearances and desire; giving care is all about substance and love. Desire is not bad, of course, but desire needs a context and boundaries. Certainly it needs to be channeled and occasionally rechanneled in the right direction. Childbearing and child raising provide all that and more.

Parenting leads us to turn a vital bend in the road toward adulthood. It helps us explore new truths and gain new respect — men for their wives in particular and for women in general, and women for their own astonishing capabilities and spiritual insight, as well as to alter the things they value most about men. That's why I believe that when a baby suckles at her mother's breasts, more than one is being nursed. The small one receives milk, but both husband and wife receive spiritual insights and life-altering awareness. Indeed, spiritually aware parents nurse their own souls. They will never look at their own or the other's body in the same way.

Masked Glory

When the kids were very young and still in diapers, I had what I considered the worst household job in the world — emptying the diaper buckets. As a young mother, Lisa was convinced that our kids would be emotionally, physically, and spiritually scarred for life if we ever let a disposable diaper *with all those chemicals* touch their precious bottoms. This meant we used cloth diapers, which, of course, stink, and which you soak in a huge bucket of soapy water that somebody has to dump out every few days. That somebody, unfortunately, was *me*.

I worked for a small Christian ministry at the time, so we couldn't afford diaper service. This was do-it-yourself diaper cleaning, the same way parents had done it since the Middle Ages, before all those "life-shortening chemicals" and "child-eating substances" such as plastic diapers and ready-to-use wipes gained such prominence.

One evening, knowing I had to leave the next day on a business trip, I started emptying the diaper bucket so Lisa wouldn't have to do it in my absence. I can still remember the smell. Even though it's been a good decade since that day, that pungent odor worked its way right past my nostrils and immediately lodged itself forever into my brain. The heaviness of the bucket presented quite a challenge for controlling the initial water flow so that you didn't splash yourself with the filthy water as you dumped the liquid contents into the utility sink. You also had to be careful not to let the diapers slip out of the bucket — which would mean having to pick them up *with your hands*.

As I was in the middle of hoisting that heavy bucket, balancing it on the edge of the sink, six-year-old Allison walked up behind me. At that age, when Allison wanted to talk to you, she knew no other context; it mattered nothing what you happened to be doing. So she yanked on my pants leg and handed me a picture she wanted me to take on my business trip, oblivious to the heavy, stinking bucket teetering precariously on the sink's edge.

"See, it's two hearts," she said. "This one says, 'I love you,' and this one says, 'I'll miss you and want you to come back right away.'"

I felt so touched I didn't know what to say. I *hated* emptying those diaper buckets — absolutely hated it. But at that moment, Allison's sweet note made me practically weep as I dumped that stinky mess into the sink.

Was the messy work a good trade for such a relationship with my daughter? A thousand times yes! I'd empty a hundred diaper buckets to earn one note like that. In a very real way, that putrid, filthy job cleansed my soul.

A profound spiritual truth lies behind the unglamorous lives and roles we adopt as parents. In heaven, Jesus was exalted as God, worshiped as the worthy divine being he is and was. To come to earth, he clothed himself in a body, and a very unglamorous body at that.

Scripture seems to portray Jesus as less than average appearance-wise (see Isaiah 53:2). In that body, no one could recognize Jesus as God. People didn't instinctively fall down on their faces saying, "I'm a dead man, for I've seen the face of a holy God!" Yet Jesus, encased in that plain human flesh, was no less God.

Looking glamorous has nothing to do with true importance and impact. Though Jesus looked earthy in his human body, his work took on unparalleled importance. He left the glamour of heaven to get dirty, and even occasionally smelly, on our behalf. He chose a relationship with us over a spotless appearance and heavenly comfort.

Parenting calls us to the same place. Iris Krasnow writes about the shift in her life when she traded in her bikini for a gray bathrobe that she wore virtually nonstop for the first six weeks of her baby's life. Later, when she returned to writing articles for various magazines, she got an assignment to write a profile on Ethel Kennedy. After weeks of making various attempts to reach Ethel, Iris finally got the esteemed mother on the phone, and at just that moment, her boy started shrieking into the receiver. Iris felt horrified; she had never faced a situation like this when childless! But Ethel Kennedy, no stranger to the process of parenting, consoled Iris with the words, "We can do this later. You go do what's really important."[8]

The Bible couldn't be clearer. Looks can deceive:

> But God chose the foolish things of the world to shame the wise; God chose the weak things of the world to shame the strong. He chose the lowly things of this world and the despised things — and the things that are not — to nullify the things that are, so that no one may boast before him.
>
> 1 Corinthians 1:27–29

This sobering message means that if we lived in the first century and felt motivated by glamour alone, we would have missed Jesus Christ. And if glitz motivates us today, we will miss the wisdom and genius of the gospel.

Having experienced our own lack of glamour as parents, we can take with us outside our homes a new understanding of what really matters. On a recent holiday I was picking up a few groceries. As the young man behind the cash register handed me my change, I said, "Thanks, Kurt. Have a great Fourth of July." Kurt's head jerked back as though I had yanked it with a steel chain. Though Kurt wears a name tag, few people ever read it, and even fewer use it to treat him like a person. What a rarity that a customer would use his actual name! Now we always share a few words whenever I go through his line.

Having been in lowly situations and having done less than glamorous work ourselves (changing diapers, mopping up vomit, and so on), we are set free to notice those whom others ignore. We've awakened to the fact that glamour misleads and that worldly "significance" isn't all it's cracked up to be.

In this sense, kids can teach us what truly matters and what is, in the words of Ethel Kennedy, "really important." Indeed, children actually help us grow up, put away our own childish things, and see in the mirror more clearly who God wants us to be (1 Corinthians 13:11–12). We act out of reverence for God instead of what *Vogue* or *GQ* tells us is the latest hot trend in glamour.

If you're a new stay-at-home mom, don't you dare look down on yourself because you've traded spaghetti-strap dresses for sweats, extra-large shirts, and towels draped over your shoulder to catch your baby's spit-up. In time, you'll be able to go back to those dresses (though you may have to upgrade to a couple sizes larger). If you're a dad who traded in his Trans Am for a minivan with a bumper sticker that reads "Baby On Board," good for you (between you and me, though, it wouldn't hurt to lose the sticker). Hold your head high as you add parenting to your résumé. Though the superficial around you might look down on you, the process to which you've given yourself closely mirrors the most profound movement of all:

Your attitude should be the same as that of Christ Jesus:

Who, being in very nature God,
    did not consider equality with God something to be
      grasped,
but made himself nothing,
    taking on the very nature of a servant,
    being made in human likeness.
And being found in appearance as a man,
    he humbled himself
    and became obedient to death —
      even death on a cross!

Therefore God exalted him to the highest place
    and gave him the name that is above every name,
that at the name of Jesus every knee should bow,
    in heaven and on earth and under the earth,
and every tongue confess that Jesus Christ is Lord,
    to the glory of God the Father.

Philippians 2:5–11

The Beauty of Small Things

Because we lived in Virginia at the time, it had been two years since we had seen my sister's home on Puget Sound. Linda and her husband, Dan, had bought a neglected house on a piece of property that had a breathtaking view of the Sound — a view that fills your soul as completely as a Thanksgiving dinner fills your stomach. Dan had done much to capitalize on the picturesque scenery. He's the type who looks at a house and doesn't see what's there, but what *could* be there. As such, he had practically torn the house down and rebuilt it.

We parked in full view of the water and ascended the stairs toward the side door. We could see the backyard, and Graham's eyes lit up at the soccer net; Kelsey jumped at the sight of the swing set.

We walked into a kitchen that had new cabinets, a tile-counter bar, and a living room with no need for pictures. Windows seemed quite sufficient. I wandered around, looked at the staircase that had been moved (mechanically challenged guys like me can't even *imagine* how to move a staircase), made my way downstairs, listened to Lisa's dad say, "Wow!" when he saw the master bathroom (I had thought the same thing and uttered the same word the first time I saw it), and overall felt very impressed with the work of my brother-in-law.

My meditations dissolved with an urgent "Uncle Gary, Uncle Gary, come quick!"

I turned and spotted Colby, my then three-year-old nephew, jumping up and down. "I want to show you a *spider.* A big, hairy spider!"

"Where is he?" I asked.

"Come here! I'll show you!"

Colby is now a teenager, but as a little boy he was the type of kid who screamed "life." Full of motion, energy oozed out of every pore in his body. Even when his arms and legs remained stationary — a rarity, to be sure — his eyes danced with light.

His sense of wonder made me smile. Here we were, several adults, marveling at the great workmanship of a home remodeler, appreciating the fine atmosphere created through months of hard labor — but Colby had no time for new tile floors, a customized kitchen, or a repositioned staircase. He felt transfixed by a spider. A big, *hairy* spider.

"It's in here somewhere," he squealed, crawling over a stack of tiles. "I saw it just a moment ago."

It borders on a cliché to talk about the simplicity of children. Simplicity is often an overly sentimentalized fact of childhood — but isn't it still a wonderful one? Colby didn't need a glamorous home with a breathtaking view of Puget Sound. An ordinary spider — the kind you could find in any abandoned warehouse or vacant lot — now *that* was something to get excited about.

May God grant us all the grace to become a little more like Colby.

Children today are tyrants. They contradict their parents, gobble their food, and tyrannize their teachers.

Socrates (470–399 BC)

But God demonstrates his own love for us in this: While we were still sinners, Christ died for us.

Romans 5:8

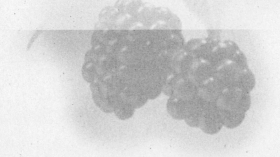

Chapter 9

Walking on the Wild Side of Parenting: The Gift of Extremely Demanding Children

How Raising Kids Teaches Patience, Long-suffering, and Perseverance

Should we have kids now, or wait?"

The young woman, who had been married just a few months, asked an honest question. The Christian who replied to her sounded very scriptural: "The Bible calls children a blessing from the Lord. Why would I want to regulate my blessings? Why would I ask God not to keep blessing me financially, or not to bless me now? Why would you not try to have as many children as you can? Don't you want God's blessing?"

This line of thinking took root in the late 1980s and early 1990s, an intense time for the pro-life movement. Understandably abhorred by the tragic waste of preborn life, the church wanted to recapture a broader view of the blessing that children can be. I can't tell you how many times I heard Psalm 127 quoted:

> Sons are a heritage from the LORD,
> children a reward from him.

> Like arrows in the hands of a warrior
>   are sons born in one's youth.
> Blessed is the man
>   whose quiver is full of them.
>
> Psalm 127:3–5

But Psalms isn't the only book in the Bible. Yes, children can be a tremendous blessing, but children-as-a-blessing is not the *only* biblical truth. As we'll see in just a moment, Proverbs also suggests that, in some instances, children can also feel like a *curse*.

In our enthusiasm to celebrate children (a good thing), we are sometimes tempted to overlook the key Christian doctrine of original sin. A child can be raised by godly parents, yet still choose to live an ungodly life: "A wise son heeds his father's instruction, but a mocker does not listen to rebuke" (Proverbs 13:1). Some sons can bring great honor to their home and their parents; others choose to bring shame: "He who gathers crops in summer is a wise son, but he who sleeps during harvest is a disgraceful son" (10:5). Some children will bring anguish rather than joy: "A wise son brings joy to his father, but a foolish man despises his mother" (15:20). At times children can even steal from their parents (28:24) or drive their mother from her own house (19:26).

In this regard, the Bible is more honest than many contemporary Christians. In the Old Testament, God gives us accounts of children who do all sorts of heinous acts. Abimelech, the son of Gideon, provides one such example. We don't know a lot about Gideon and his parenting style, but we do know that God's hand was with Gideon as he used him to free Israel from the control of the Midianites. After Gideon's great exploits, the people tried to make Gideon king: "Rule over us — you, your son and your grandson — because you have saved us out of the hand of Midian" (Judges 8:22). Gideon refused, demonstrating a noble and humble character: "I will not rule over you, nor will my son rule over you. The LORD will rule over you" (Judges 8:23).

Gideon lived a post-military life of blessing and had many children. After Gideon's death, one of his sons, Abimelech, burned with ambition to rule the nation. Desperate to establish himself as ruler and remove all pretenders, Abimelech murdered all his brothers, except for one. By the providential judgment of God, Abimelech died when a woman dropped a millstone on his head. The Bible tells us that God lay behind this attack: "Thus God repaid the wickedness that Abimelech had done to his father by murdering his seventy brothers" (Judges 9:56). God apparently didn't have a problem considering this child a curse. In his providential plan, he sought the death of this wickedly ambitious son.

Sometimes a wayward son or daughter results from a poor upbringing; the parents may indeed have to assume some of the blame (Proverbs 29:15). But a child can receive many spiritual advantages and still choose, with the freedom God gives him, to become a wayward son. Jesus loved Judas as a son, yet the betrayer still opted to turn against him. Adam and Eve had a godly son (Abel) and a murderous son (Cain). Was their parenting the *only* factor leading Abel to offer worthy sacrifices and Cain to turn into a selfish, jealous, and bloodthirsty sibling?

President John Adams had one son — John Quincy — who followed him into the presidency and enjoyed a prosperous career. Two other sons had shameful lifestyles. Charles Adams became an alcoholic — his mother described him as a "poor, unhappy, wretched man."[1] One relative described Thomas Adams as "one of the most unpleasant characters in this world . . . a brute in manners and a bully to his family."[2] John and Abigail raised one remarkable son and two disgraceful ones. Was their parenting the only factor that determined each boy's character?

I suspect I've probably raised more than a few eyebrows by now. I can even imagine some condemnations: "How *dare* you suggest children aren't a blessing? I bet you also favor abortion, don't you?"

No, I definitely do not. In the early to mid-1990s, I worked for Care Net, a Christian ministry that develops and does the training for pro-life pregnancy resource centers. Since then, I've spoken at nearly a hundred benefit banquets, helping crisis pregnancy centers to raise millions of desperately needed dollars. I am ardently, passionately, and unequivocally pro-life. But I've also had enough life experience to know that parenting — even sacred parenting — comes with no guarantees, and I grieve for the good, decent, and godly parents who get treated like pariahs because a kid of theirs goes bad. They weren't "perfect" parents, of course, and in that sense they may share some of the blame. But tell me — just who *is* a perfect parent?

Show me one father or one mother who didn't, at times, spoil their child, just a little. Who didn't, out of fear or weariness or ignorance or overcommitment, fail to confront something that needed to be faced, at least one time? I'll let that parent cast the first stone.

Some of us got away with it; some of us didn't. In my travels I've met far too many godly parents who live with a gaping wound. Not only do they face the pain of watching their deeply loved child self-destruct, but they also live with a judgment that the child's abhorrent way of life stems from *their* failure as parents.

Godly children are a tremendous blessing; this is a precious biblical truth. But Scripture is honest, and we should be as well. Wayward children can, at the very least, *feel* like a fierce curse.

Cut Twice

The Bible couldn't be more clear that wayward children will pay for their treachery: "The eye that mocks a father, that scorns obedience to a mother, will be pecked out by the ravens of the valley, will be eaten by the vultures" (Proverbs 30:17). The even harder truth for the parents, however, is that while the ravens peck out a difficult child's eye, *the parents will feel their own eye sockets burning.*

A wayward child wounds a parent in two ways. First, the child wounds the mother by despising her, cheating her, robbing her, or even hitting her. But then, almost inexplicably, he tears his mother's heart in two once again when she grieves over her profligate child's misfortune as he inevitably marches toward his own ruin. When he falls, her heart gets bruised! When he bleeds, she hemorrhages! She does not rejoice that her child "gets what's coming to him"; she mourns, even if that justice means the child will no longer be able to actively hurt her.

Is this schizophrenic? From a secular perspective, yes — but nobody ever said that parenting was easy or that love, or even grace for that matter, makes sense. We remain deeply vulnerable as parents, risking the pain of betrayal and then grieving over our betrayer's demise.

King David experienced this as a parent. His son Absalom plotted to steal David's throne by cunningly winning the favor of the people. He then hatched a well-executed plan to have himself declared king. Worse, he recruited some of David's closest advisers, publicly slept with his father's concubines, and then sought to kill his dad! In every way possible, Absalom humiliated and challenged his father, even hunting him like an animal.

David had to defend himself, but in doing so he gave strict orders to his men: "Protect the young man Absalom *for my sake*" (2 Samuel 18:12, emphasis added). In spite of everything, David essentially told his men, "Don't treat Absalom like the traitor he is; treat him like my son." The casual reader might well ask how David could look at Absalom as anything other than a bloodthirsty, ambitious rival who must be crushed — the casual reader, maybe, but not a parent.

David's forces routed Absalom's men, but as the messenger bearing the somber news approached David, the deposed king's first question shows what *really* concerned him: "Is the young man Absalom safe?" (2 Samuel 18:29).

You might think David would feel anxious about the fate of his reign, or at least inquire about whether his forces had defeated the enemy; after all, his very life was in peril. Instead, he inquired about the welfare of the man trying to kill him. When told of Absalom's death, David broke down emotionally: "O my son Absalom! My son, my son Absalom! If only I had died instead of you — O Absalom, my son, my son!" (2 Samuel 18:33).

David grieved for the son who sought to kill him as though this child had been the most faithful and loving offspring a parent could ever want. He mourned his loss; his heart truly broke in two. In this David displays the grace-filled love of a parent, mirroring the love of the God who loved us and who died for us while we yet remained his enemies: "But God demonstrates his own love for us in this: While we were still sinners, Christ died for us" (Romans 5:8).

How sobering to face the vulnerability that someone could make our lives absolutely miserable — and yet we would lay down our lives on his or her behalf without thinking about it. Just such an amazing spiritual transformation takes place in the journey of parenting. Once again, Paul models our call to this ministry when he writes, "Who is weak, and I do not feel weak? Who is led into sin, and I do not inwardly burn?" (2 Corinthians 11:29).

For many of us, however, the difficulty of parenting comes not in facing betrayal but in enduring a very tiring occupation.

A Complex Call

There's no getting around the fact that parenting occasionally can suck you dry. It will take you beyond your own strength until you want to weep from weariness, but then you watch, amazed that you still get up and give some more.

As a cross-country and long-distance runner in high school, I often teased some of the other track members, "When the going gets tough, sprinters stop." Yet parenting goes far beyond any endurance race I ever ran or ever will run. When you have a sick child, or a mentally ill child, or a difficult child, or perhaps just a normal, moody child, what wears you down isn't usually one catastrophic event; it's the daily grind of the same plodding steps — without end. And then doing it again. And again.

And again.

A young mother might understandably look back with a certain fondness to that time when she had her husband all to herself. I can understand this, because life seems a lot simpler when your home life consists of one relationship — you and your spouse. As soon as children enter the picture, it gets easy to choke on the complexity of family life. Not only must you navigate your relationship with your husband, but now you must factor in your husband's relationship with your oldest daughter, your husband's relationship with your middle son, and your husband's relationship with your youngest daughter. And then you must constantly negotiate the relationship between daughter to daughter, oldest daughter to middle son, and middle son to youngest daughter — not to mention your own relationship with each one. A family of five represents *ten distinct relationships*. Tension or disagreement in just *one* of those relationships can affect the entire family.

Even the most joyous moments with one child can get undercut by the expression of jealousy or anger in another child. As a young man, I read the parable of the prodigal son (Luke 15:11–32) from the perspective of the boys. I could understand the younger son's joy at his welcome home and also, to be honest, the oldest son's irritation that this prodigal received the royal treatment. But today when I read this story, I feel empathy most deeply for the father. What elation he must have felt at seeing a wayward son come back to his senses! I'm sure his emotions reeled, overflowing with relief and thankfulness and happiness. His face no doubt wore the biggest smile in all of Israel! Then, after the feelings of exhaustion from getting everything ready for the celebration, how his heart must have sank when the older son approached him, upset about the lavish and "unfair" treatment given the prodigal.

The dad just has to be thinking, *Can't you let me enjoy your brother's return without having to deal with your jealousy and bitterness? Is it too much to ask that I could have, after years of mourning, one moment of unpolluted happiness?* The most joyful moment of his life was undermined and marred by the resentment of his other son.

Yet every parent lives in this world, particularly mothers. Even when one child has a good day or has had a tremendous accomplishment, the mom may have to console a sibling who becomes jealous or resentful. With multiple kids in the family, it's a rare day indeed when some sort of conflict or disappointment doesn't have to be addressed.

And then there's the daily burden of multitasking. In addition to jobs outside the home, at various times within the home you'll get asked to sew something, cook something, clean something, schedule something, or answer some esoteric question. When my youngest daughter tried out for a choir, the director asked her, "Can't your mom work with you on these scales?" My wife can do a lot of things, but singing on key isn't one of them. The breadth of things a woman is asked to do — contribute to the family income, decorate, drive, schedule, cook and clean in her spare time, be a good lover, be a faithful member of the church, et cetera, et cetera — simply boggles the imagination.

In her memoirs, author Madeleine L'Engle refers to the thirties as "the tired years." Raising kids can leave you feeling exhausted — and there's no letup. I get frustrated when I look at some of the child-raising manuals whose authors act as though you can "take care of" a problem with three easy steps and then forget about it. Not in my house! Rarely does one response ever bring a matter to an end. Behavioral issues act like pernicious viruses — they mutate and adapt, and the wise parent has to keep coming up with newer and better approaches to address the same issues.

It's exhausting.

And it's really no single issue that drags us down or sends us over the edge. We blanch at the ever-present weight of all the issues put together — day in, day out, morning, noon, and night. A 2:00 a.m. wakeup call is as much of a reality as trying to wake up an adolescent who seems addicted to his bed. Eventually, we can feel crushed under the monotonous sense of duty and sacrifice. Parenting can surely be an exhausting profession, but it's also a complex calling — one that can have a profound impact on our spiritual development.

Bundles

Have you ever noticed that most trials come in batches and bundles? This past year, my pastor — a godly man with a powerful ministry — suffered through the loss of his father, an attack of kidney stones (perhaps the most painful ordeal any man can go through), and then a diagnosis of prostate cancer. Later that year, a staff member resigned due to a moral failure. This four-pronged attack just about took my breath away — and I wasn't even the one feeling the pain!

During the same year, a good friend of mine from Tennessee watched his daughter fight off a serious infection, found out that his mother had Alzheimer's, and then had one of the most difficult business years of any self-employed person I know. His business entirely depends on two items: the phone and his computer. Another company misappropriated his toll-free number, and he had to fight for weeks to get it back. His phone system crashed two times, as did the hard drive on his computer; though he religiously ran backups, a glitch resulted in the loss of vital information. To make matters even worse (as if all this wasn't enough), he discovered that an allegedly Christian client had cheated him out of tens of thousands of dollars — and then the man accused my friend of cheating *him!* I spoke to my friend at the end of the year, and just by his dead voice I knew something very wrong had happened. Life had broken him, but he remained solid in his faith and in his commitment to God.

Why do these bundles of trials seem so common? Why do I not even feel surprised anymore when earnest believers lay out similar stories, desperately seeking direction?

We have only one way to become mature and complete in God: We must develop the difficult but crucial discipline of perseverance. Jesus said that only through perseverance do we bear fruit: "The seed on good soil stands for those with a noble and good heart, who hear the word, retain it, *and by persevering* produce a crop" (Luke 8:15, emphasis added).

Paul says that character grows out of learning to persevere through many trials (Romans 5:3–4). James tells us that we should consider it "pure joy" when we "face trials of many kinds [that is, bundles], because you know that the testing of your faith develops perseverance. *Perseverance must finish its work* so that you may be mature and complete, not lacking anything" (James 1:2–4, emphasis added). Without perseverance, James tells us, we remain immature and incomplete, half-baked Christians, if you will. Later in his letter James adds, "As you know, we consider blessed those who have persevered. You have heard of Job's perseverance and have seen what the Lord finally brought about" (5:11). Peter tells us to "make every effort" to add perseverance to our faith (2 Peter 1:5–6).

There's only one way to develop perseverance: We have to surrender to God as we feel pushed past the human breaking point. We have to reach the threshold of exhaustion, and then get pushed even further. One trial can help us deal with fear. Two trials can lead to wisdom. But perseverance? That takes a bundle of difficulties. All of which means that parenting extremely demanding children feeds a spiritual need in our soul — to participate in the crucial discipline of perseverance on which our fruitfulness as believers depends.

Take This Cup

Greg and Melissa, a couple from the Midwest, face this grind every day as they live with their multiply challenged daughter. After one particularly difficult evening with Christy, Melissa almost lost it. She immediately went to Greg and confessed, "I don't want to suggest that God made a mistake, but *in this one case* I think it's possible. I can't put up with this any longer. I know the Bible says I'll be given the strength I need, but honestly, if I'm alone with that child for another ten seconds, I may murder her!"

Melissa truly felt as though she were barely balancing on her last nerve, just ready to snap. But here's the amazing part. I asked Greg what happened next, and he said they took a time-out together, both of them silently prayed, and then they returned to the moment-by-moment realities of raising this difficult child. "What else could we do?" he asked me. They had no cure, no three-step answer. Perseverance was their only refuge.

Today's Christian usually prays for relief, for comfort, and for healing — but that's *not* always what Scripture teaches us to do. For example, the apostle Paul prayed that the Colossians would be "strengthened with all power according to [God's] glorious might so that you may have great endurance and patience" (Colossians 1:11).

Instead of immediately asking for their deliverance, Paul prayed that the believers in Colosse would grow in maturity. If you think about it, how do we grow in endurance and patience? Only one path exists, which we've already mentioned: to have both our endurance and patience sorely tried, even past the breaking point, until we learn to rest in God's "glorious might." You'll never develop your biceps if you lift just one-pound weights; you have to stress the muscle beyond its normal routine. The same principle holds true spiritually. *If God gives us situations we already have the strength to handle, we won't have to grow in order to deal with them.*

I think both Melissa and Greg reached that spiritual crossroad that our Lord faced on the Mount of Olives: "Father, if you are willing, take this cup from me; yet not my will, but yours be done." The Father didn't remove the cup; instead, "An angel from heaven appeared to him and strengthened him" (Luke 22:42–43). Melissa didn't want to drink from the bitter cup, but God in his wisdom didn't remove the cup or even make it sweeter. Instead, he strengthened Melissa. He used a trying situation to develop this mother's endurance and patience. Of course, our natural inclination is to pray that God would remove the burden instead of giving us the strength and endurance to persevere. But it's God's choice to decide how he will answer, not ours.

As Melissa reflected on her ordeal, she realized how much the birthing process mirrored the parenting process. When Melissa gave birth to Christy, it was far from being a sentimental experience. On the contrary, her travail lasted thirty hours. At one point Melissa felt as though she couldn't possibly go on; her body had no more strength for one last push. She felt exhausted. Couldn't somebody just reach in and pull the baby out?

But somewhere, from reserves that Melissa didn't know she had, she found the strength to push. She got Christy out of her body — and now, as a mother, she had to plunge into the depths again, finding a spiritual strength beyond what she knew she had in order to continue mothering this difficult child. Thirty hours of labor? Ha! Melissa had no idea that the real journey lay before her.

Family life teaches us that we do some things simply because they must be done. We may even grow to resent them, but duty calls us to remain faithful. If we lived merely by inclination or happiness, our lives — and our world — would become a ruin. G. K. Chesterton confesses, "In everything on this earth that is worth doing, there is a stage when no one would do it except for necessity or honor."[3]

It helps to know that every family — and I mean *every* family — faces times when weariness leads the parents to ask, "Why bother?" Elton Trueblood has this gentle counsel:

> The desire to escape family responsibilities is practically universal at some time or other and if mere inclination were followed every family would break to pieces. . . . Countless humble homes have been made scenes of enduring wonder by the fact that an *accepted bond* has held the members together in spite of hard work, poverty and much suffering.[4]

Many people run from the difficulties of marriage by seeking a divorce, but except in the most extreme circumstances, you can't divorce a child. In this sense parenting can get even more difficult than marriage — we have no way out. A blessing lies behind this seeming burden, however. The ease of divorce is actually an enemy of true marital happiness, for some seek the immediately easy way, which statistics show usually leads to even greater misery. By fulfilling God's call to keep our marriages and families intact, we will find the spiritual blessing that results from hanging in there despite the pain. Sacred parenting, which rejects socially approved exits, invites us to experience the benefits behind these trials to an even greater degree.

The crux of the issue is this: Our first and natural inclination in any trial is to pray for God to remove the difficulty. But God's first priority is often to strengthen us in the midst of the difficulty rather than to take us out of the difficulty. That's because he can see the treasure that lies at the end of the trail.

The Treasure at the End of the Trail

Maybe you have a Rob Takemura in your life. Rob is the father of four children and served as one of the two best men at my wedding (I know, I'm weird; I had *two* best men). This lifelong friend of mine is the type of guy with whom everybody likes to hang around. He knows a lot about a lot of things, so he can enter just about any conversation, but he keeps his ego under control and doesn't dominate the discussion. He's just an overall good guy. You respect him; he's not usually going to do anything stupid or cruel. On the other hand, he's not insufferably pious; you really enjoy your time with him. Rob's wife, Jill, is the same way. She easily makes friends, and probably half a dozen women think of her as their "best" friend.

I'm sure you can think of someone similar in your own circle of friends, the kind of couple that just about everybody likes to be around. If you're throwing a party or inviting a group to dinner, you ask these kind of people first so you can tell everyone, "Oh, by the way, Rob and Jill will be there, too."

I probably spend more time with Rob than any other adult male — but being around Rob doesn't challenge my patience, simply because he's such a healthy individual. He and I participate in an accountability group (we call it the Pacific Rim, because Rob is full-blooded Japanese, Len is full-blooded Chinese, and Steve is part-Filipino; I'm the token Caucasian), and we frequently golf together. I can learn from Rob by trying to emulate his character — but he doesn't try my patience, he doesn't stretch my ability to forgive, and he doesn't make me dig down deep to respond to cruelty with love.

On the other hand, I once knew a man who hated women and acted cruelly toward men. Putting up with his constant criticisms of others, his lust to be recognized as significant and powerful, and his malicious use of what little influence he did have stretched me like I've never been stretched. I discovered spiritual holes I never knew existed and had to develop spiritual muscles in places that had long lain dormant.

To become mature people, we need both kinds of relationships — and that's where difficult children come in. It takes God-forged *agapē* love to reach out to someone who spites you, who returns your kindness with hatred, who considers gestures of generosity to be threats, who seems hell-bent on bringing destruction and chaos and division into every moment of his or her life (and your life, too). It takes more than human inclination and natural goodwill to keep relating to someone who purposely offends, revels in creative cruelty, and strikes back with a vengeance. Even if you know they do so out of woundedness or feelings of insecurity or abandonment, being around them still hurts. It still sucks you dry.

But in the bottom of the dry creek bed lies spiritual life, the fossil of character formation. If we die to human potential, we can be resurrected to spiritual strength. Greg and Melissa could survive in no other way. God invites them (although at times it may feel as though he is forcing them) to lean on a foreign strength — to go further, love deeper, and learn to care in a way they never knew they could.

Many of us can relate. Our initial excitement over the journey into parenting may have transformed into feelings of frustration, as though we found ourselves on a pilgrimage through the desert with no sign of rest or relief in sight. Despite the effort we've put into this child — or children — we've received only grief in return. Elton Trueblood points the way toward an inspiring vision that can help us persevere through the ups and downs:

> [Family life] has no magic about it. The family can be the scene of wonderful affection and it can also be the scene of debasing friction. The family . . . is our fairest ideal, but it does not come without effort. Family solidarity takes hard work, much imagination, and constant self-criticism on the part of all the members of the sacred circle. A successful marriage is not one in which two people, beautifully matched, find each other and get along happily ever after because of this initial matching. It is, instead, a system by means of which persons who are sinful and contentious are so caught by a dream bigger than themselves that they work throughout the years, in spite of repeated disappointment, to make the dream come true.[5]

A Look in the Mirror

Before I conclude this chapter, I think it's only fair to look from an entirely different angle at the patience, perseverance, and long-suffering that parenting demands of us. What our children ask of us pales in comparison to what we ask of God. In our struggles and our weariness, may we never get to the place of self-righteousness, forgetting that God has forgiven us, is patient with us, and endures our own failings to an even greater extent than we do for our children. Most kids live with us for two, maybe two and a half, decades; God puts up with us for the full breadth of our lives. While our children may occasionally provoke us with offensive words, God sees every offensive inclination of our hearts. For every single offense for which we forgive our children, God forgives us many times over. He remains patient with us for many times longer than we must exercise patience with our children. He doesn't ask anything of us as parents that he hasn't delivered a hundred times over himself.

We need to use the most wearisome aspects of parenting as the occasion for thanking God for putting up with us. When we look through this lens, we find that raising a demanding child can actually become motivation for worshiping and adoring God. No spiritually aware parent can at the same time become self-righteous. Only the most forgetful and the most blind among us can act arrogantly before God, as though he had given us a heavier burden than we had given him. Sacred parenting reminds us that no matter how difficult a child may be, we still play in the minor leagues compared to God's great sacrifice.

Consider how many times you have broken your promises once offered fervently and earnestly to God. Consider on how many occasions you have said or thought or even done vile things in full sight of a holy and perfect God. Consider God's eagerness to forgive you, the persistence of his grace, the limitless supply of his understanding and patience and mercy — all offered without condition on your behalf. Without difficult children, we might take this patience and mercy and forgiveness for granted. That's where difficult children become a rare gift — they show us a side of God we might otherwise miss.

An ancient story tells of a monastery with a very difficult monk — a contentious, obnoxious, arrogant, and divisive man.[6] If an argument erupted, odds were good that he was somehow involved. Any group of murmuring brothers almost certainly had his name on their lips. This monk had no friends but many enemies, and finally even he grew tired of the animosity and left the order.

While the brothers rejoiced, the abbot quickly realized his loss. He pursued the contentious monk and tried to persuade him to return. When the monk asked why he should come back to a place where clearly he wasn't wanted, the abbot offered to pay him a salary if he would just rejoin the monastery.

Imagine the other monks' consternation when they saw this hapless fellow walk back into the compound! When they discovered that he would receive a salary to live there, they grew furious. One marched over to the abbot's office to ask for an explanation.

The wise abbot responded, "This brother, as troublesome as he may be, nevertheless teaches you patience, kindness, and compassion; that is why we need him here. No one else can teach you the lessons he teaches."

Here indeed is the treasure at the end of the trail. No matter how difficult our children may be, God can and will use them to shape our souls into his Son's image. No matter how many bumps we may hit or bends we may have to negotiate along the road to raising our children, God promises to guide our steps, strengthen our stride, and refresh our souls. He knows we are insufficient, but he points us to his Son's provision and his Spirit's comfort, guidance, and power, all of which more than meet our needs. Even if we don't see all the results we'd like to see, at least we're getting steady reminders of God's patience and long-suffering toward us.

Parenting may not be an easy journey, but in this it is truly a sacred one.

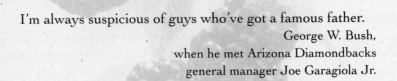

I'm always suspicious of guys who've got a famous father.

George W. Bush,
when he met Arizona Diamondbacks
general manager Joe Garagiola Jr.

You can't go home with the Rock and Roll Hall of Fame. You don't get hugged by the Rock and Roll Hall of Fame, and you don't have children with the Rock and Roll Hall of Fame. I want what everybody else wants: to love and be loved and to have a family.

Billy Joel

Chapter 10

A Very Boring Chapter in the Bible (That Can Change Your Life Forever)

How Raising Children Teaches Us What Really Matters in Life

As United States Marines stormed the beaches of Iwo Jima in 1945, corpsman Gregory Emery stopped to help a soldier lying flat on his back. Emery immediately noticed the red "M" drawn on the young Marine's forehead (signifying that he had already taken morphine) and the crimson-stained dressing that covered the man's stomach.

The wound and the treatment made one thing very clear: This man was going to die.

Literally speaking his last words, the wounded soldier asked Emery to get a photograph out of his pack. Emery reached in and pulled out a shrapnel-pitted photo of a woman and an infant. The dying Marine gratefully held the picture before his eyes.

Knowing the inevitability of the soldier's death, the corpsman moved on, intending to find someone whose life might yet be spared. But he felt compelled to look back. The wounded Marine heaved his last torturous breaths staring at the photo of his family. He died with their image before his eyes. Suddenly, in an instant, the woman and child in that photograph became all that was left of him.[1]

For millennia, people have died and others have replaced them. Some died in war; others died in peace. Some died in old age; many died in the prime of life. Some died happily married, surrounded by their children; others died estranged from their loved one, forgotten by their children. Some died poor; others died wealthy. But one thing we all have in common: we *will* die, and our descendants will carry on.

This is the message of one of the more boring chapters in the Bible. If you were writing a novel or any modern nonfiction book, you certainly wouldn't want to slow down your work with Genesis 5. Up to this point, the Bible has really moved fast. It starts off with a bang — creation — and moves from there to a tender love story, a little sex, jealousy, and then a shocking act of murder. I can hear a Hollywood director calling out, "We're rolling, baby!"

And then comes chapter 5. Any editor worth his salary would have interrupted Moses here and said, "Hey, Moses, this just isn't gonna fly. Everything goes flat at this point. The story is rolling right along, and then *wham!* All your momentum just hits a brick wall with this boring repetition."

Starting with verse 3, Genesis 5 collapses into nothing more than a litany of numbers and outdated names:

> When Adam had lived 130 years, he had a son in his own likeness, in his own image; and he named him Seth. After Seth was born, Adam lived 800 years and had other sons and daughters. Altogether, Adam lived 930 years, and then he died.
>
> When Seth had lived 105 years, he became the father of Enosh. And after he became the father of Enosh, Seth lived 807 years and had other sons and daughters. Altogether, Seth lived 912 years, and then he died.
>
> When Enosh had lived 90 years, he became the father of Kenan. And after he became the father of Kenan, Enosh lived 815 years and had other sons and daughters. . . .

From there, you plug in new names and different numbers, but that's pretty much the chapter. Some guy first becomes a father at an age well beyond qualifying for the AARP, and then he proceeds to produce more sons and daughters on his way to death's door.

In an era before political elections, athletic contests, and Fortune 500 lists of the most wealthy businesspeople in the world, people lived, had sons and daughters, and died. And that's pretty much all they were known for. We're not told if they preferred raising crops to raising cattle or even where they lived. We don't know how they spent their free time (if they had any), or what sort of property they owned, or lived on, or traveled over. We don't know if they were fat or thin, bald or hairy-chested, bowlegged or athletic. All we know is that they had kids, and then they died.

This simplistic view of life is shockingly honest. And many years from now, when most of us are a few generations removed from the land of the living, even our descendants probably won't know our vocation, our golf handicap, what houses we lived in, how good the garden looked, or whether we preferred Coke or Pepsi. Oh, our grandchildren, and maybe even the rare great-grandchild, may occasionally drum up a story or two about us — but after that, we're history. For all practical purposes, the only thing we did that will matter to them is that we chose to have sons and daughters, with the result that they're alive and they walk the face of the earth.

Even famous people like presidents must live with this reality. President Lyndon Baines Johnson called his biographer just two days before Johnson's death in 1973. Here was a man who, as president of the United States, would certainly be considered a "man of significance," vocationally speaking. Yet listen how futile it all seemed to him as he uttered some of his final words:

> I've been reading Carl Sandburg's biography on Lincoln and no matter how great the book's supposed to be, I can't bring Lincoln to life. And if that's true for me, one president reading about another, then there's no chance the ordinary person in the future will ever remember me. No chance. I'd have been better off looking for immortality through my wife and children and their children in turn instead of seeking all that love and affection from the American people.[2]

This stark, almost unmerciful truth certainly humbles the modern man or woman and challenges most of our modern aspirations.

What the majority of us spend the bulk of our time worrying about —
our 9:00 to 5:00 jobs, what houses we live in, how we're going to
spend the weekend, how physically fit we look, what vehicle we
drive — ultimately amounts to nothing and gets completely forgotten.
And what we often ignore in our pursuit of the above — that is, our
children and our families — are the only things we truly leave behind.

Keep in mind, we're talking about Genesis 5 — the Bible! This is
God's description of the world for the first few thousand years. And
God chooses to simplify these men's lives by mentioning their most
important work — having kids, dying, and then getting out of the
way. I wonder how we might simplify our own lives by recognizing
that eighty percent or more of what we spend our time on will ultimately be forgotten. Perhaps we might pay a little more attention to
the remaining twenty percent. Indeed, the effort we put into creating a lasting legacy through children and grandchildren might
increase significantly.

If you're still not convinced, take a test: Tell me the first name of
your paternal great-great-great-grandfather. That's just five generations removed. Can you name his wife? Where did the two of them
live? You probably can't answer that, but since there are always a
few genealogy buffs out there, let me dig a little deeper. Were these
ancestors of yours physically fit or out of shape? How did they spend
their free time? What caused them the most worry in life? What part
of their body hurt the most, and from what — arthritis, sinus trouble,
a backache? How many credit payments did they miss? How did
they come up with enough money to pay for their daughter's wedding? What was their favorite meal?

Almost none of us can even begin to answer these questions
about our ancient ancestors, yet these concerns often drive our own
existence. Now let's get a little more personal. If you can't answer
this about your great-great-great-grandparents, what makes you
think your great-great-great-grandchildren will be able to answer
these questions about you?

In short, when we're painfully honest, we have to admit that most
of what we fret over will, in the not-too-distant future, become
absolutely irrelevant, forgotten, and wiped away:

- How long do we have to wait before we remodel the kitchen?

- How will we scrape together enough money to get that down payment for the larger house or the new car?
- When am I ever going to get my hair to behave?
- How long can I endure a subpar marriage?

If my soul focuses on these concerns to the exclusion of loftier aims, I'm already living an antiquated life. In just two generations beyond — just two generations! — nobody will much care about the things that so greatly concern me now.

But you know what? Someday some kid is going to feel very grateful that a son I named Graham Thomas was born, got married, and had other kids — because that child wouldn't be alive if Graham hadn't been born, cared for, and guided into adulthood. The details — why Graham was conceived and when, how much money we had at the time of his birth, the nature of my occupation when Graham was ten years old, whether Graham's parents were happily married or just conveniently so — won't mean diddly-squat to these descendants. They'll just thank God that the Thomas line kept going long enough for them to join it.

Meditate on that a few times and see if it doesn't change your attitude toward the things that seem to matter the most to you right now. Who really cares — or will care — fifty or a hundred years from now? For me, Genesis 5 makes me want to enjoy and serve my God, enjoy my wife, invest a lot of time in my kids, and then welcome death as my part in getting out of the way so others can be born, live, and do the same.

Looking Into the Future

I was struck recently by a sight that may have given me a glimpse into the future. My youngest daughter, Kelsey, was riding her bike alongside me while I jogged. About midway through the run, we approached a couple taking up the entire sidewalk. I motioned to Kelsey that we needed to pass on the grass next to the sidewalk so they wouldn't have to move. As I got closer, I noticed that the younger of the two was a man in his fifties. He was gently helping a very feeble woman, probably in her eighties, who required a cane to shuffle along.

The thought hit me that, while I was now running and Kelsey needed a bike to keep up with me, the day would come soon enough when I might have to ride a bike to keep up with Kelsey as she ran. And the day wasn't that far off when Kelsey would become that eighty-five-year-old woman getting help from her fifty-five-year-old son — my grandson (who is not yet born). In that passing moment, I saw a generational glacier — the slow, steady, and unstoppable movement of time and family.

My great-great-great-grandkids won't care what size dress their great-great-great-grandmother wore. They won't give a rip about whether this book sold 35,000 copies or 350,000 copies (a book now enters the public domain seventy years after the death of an author, thus limiting royalties to descendants). They'll care about how much hair I had only because it reflects the sort of genes I passed down — but by then, I'm sure somebody will have discovered a cure for baldness. (I may be one of the last few bald men in the history of the world, for all I know.)

Even pop icons pass quickly into irrelevance. Does anybody honestly think that people will be talking about Tom Cruise or Britney Spears 150 years from now? As a member of the Authors Guild, I get a quarterly bulletin that usually includes about two pages of names of recently deceased members. One issue mentioned that Frank Slaughter, a hugely successful writer in the mid-twentieth century (perhaps the equivalent of a John Grisham today), died at the age of ninety-three. You think Slaughter stole the headline? Nope. You think he got at least a picture? After all, this is a *writer's publication,* and Frank Slaughter was one of the most popular writers of his day. No way. He got *one paragraph.* That was it. In that one paragraph, I learned that Frank was a physician whose novels became instant best-sellers in the 1940s and 1950s — but that happened many decades ago. Few people read his books today, and even fewer will read them tomorrow. In another fifty years or so, probably no one will read him, but he made headline material for a few glorious decades.

Our search for significance can become really pathetic, like two kids fighting over a broken toy. Now that his season home run record has been broken, how long will people remember Roger Maris? Who was the senior vice president of General Motors in 1975? In 1983? Who were the two senators from Virginia in 1910? Who pastored the largest church in America in 1935? What are the names of those who climbed Mount Everest in 1991? Who was the top fashion designer in 1954?

Few of us could answer more than one or two of these questions, and yet these sorts of people are the ones who most often earn profiles in *USA Today* and the most popular magazines and on television programs. Children teach us the profound and simple message that what popular society values most grows irrelevant and even comical when confronted by the inexorable weight of history. What often gets our least attention — a heritage of faith — is the only thing we actually leave behind.

Saved by Our Insignificance

I learn from Genesis 5 that I need to embrace my own insignificance. I know this sounds like a very countercultural idea, but I believe it represents biblical truth much more than the ambition-driven search for significance so popular today.

The truth is, only one out of ten billion of us will ever be remembered by history. There will always be the occasional Cleopatras and Napoleons recalled by later generations, but of the billions of people alive on the earth today, less than one-half of one percent will be remembered two hundred years from now. To organize your life around the off-chance that you'll be that one in ten million seems about as stupid as buying a lottery ticket and expecting to win. The odds are stacked so overwhelmingly against you that it makes no sense to base your life on such a foolish risk. Even those who do make a temporary mark often flame out. History is littered with kings and queens and even popes who now rate nothing more than an obscure footnote in obscure history books that nobody reads.

When I embrace my historical insignificance, I am set free to concentrate on very real — and eternal — relational significance. I matter to my wife. I am very important to my children. I have secure standing as an adopted son of the Most High God. These are the relationships on which I want to focus my life. This is where I want to spend my energy.

Some very close friends recently said something that surprised me. It was an offhand remark, but it stopped me cold. Of all their friends (and in spite of my travels), they said they believe I am more involved in my children's lives than any other father they know.

There's a reason for this. Even though I love what I do — writing books — I was recently sobered when I logged on to Amazon.com to look up the books of one of my favorite writers of all time, Elton Trueblood. His books are twice as insightful as my books, and better written. He was more intelligent than I am, wiser, and I believe a more powerful communicator. Even today, half a century after many of his books were written, I'm challenged by his thoughts. Yet almost all of his books are now out of print, and he died a scant two decades ago. I'm a fool if I believe it will be any different with me. Though out of obedience I want to serve God as he has called me to serve him, the most long-lasting way I can accomplish this is to pour my time into my kids.

A theological truth stands behind this reprioritizing. I get very nervous when I see highly visible Christian leaders talking about a particular anointing or special touch from God — creating what I call "spiritual castes." Scripture lauds just one hero, and that is God himself. In fact, the Bible goes out of its way to document how even major biblical characters had very noticeable flaws. Eve fell victim to the deception of the serpent. Abraham got ahead of God's plan and fathered a line of descendants that even today remains at war with Israel. Moses jumped the gun by killing an Egyptian, and later took credit for God's work and thus lost the right to enter the Promised Land. King David committed adultery and murder. Peter denied knowing Jesus three times. Paul persecuted the early church.

It's no accident that the Bible reveals such glaring flaws in our spiritual ancestors. God does not share his glory with anyone. No one can rival the Creator. It bears repeating: Scripture knows only one hero, and that hero is God. Our so-called search for significance is often a dangerous attempt to steal some of God's glory. We may make our lust for recognition sound angelic — wrapping our ambition in kingdom-building terms — but at root it becomes a demonic exercise to use God's gifting in order to make *ourselves* seem important.

Pastor, it's okay that not every one of your sermons will be remembered. Not every word you utter will be historically significant. Don't bury yourself under such a heavy weight! Go ahead and take that walk with your kids, even if your weekly sermon suffers. Businessman or woman, it's okay that your company may not outlive you. Don't wear the shackles that insist that your worth is wrapped up in how you build "something that lasts." Even the most successful businesses eventually collapse. Don't ignore those you love in a desperate attempt to beat the overwhelming odds that you are the one in ten million who will change business history.

I remember when my own ministry started to take off. Instead of begging publishers to publish my books, I actually began turning down several who wanted to woo me from my current publisher. Instead of calling pastors to see if there might be an opening to speak at their church, I started having to say no to many inquiries because my speaking schedule now routinely fills up about nine months in advance. In a very clear challenge, I sensed God telling me I had a choice to make: I could devote myself to becoming a strong and attractive tree that others would admire — "Look at those roots!" "Wow, look at all that fruit!" — or I could focus on planting a forest (that is, investing in others). God made it very clear to me what he would have me choose. And so I spend my days planting a forest.

It feels very freeing to accept your insignificance. Women and men who might be tempted to ignore their family in order to pursue society's view of what makes a person important can walk away from a temporal and ultimately false esteem that will rob them of a truly eternal impact.

Don't be fooled. Don't ignore what really matters, trying to play the one-in-ten-billion odds. Embrace your insignificance, and let it reestablish your focus. In God's delightful irony, embracing your temporal insignificance leads to the greatest eternal significance.

Definition of a Princess

Is there a little girl somewhere who *hasn't* dreamed about being a princess, at least once in her life? Maybe, but I've never met one.

When we think of a princess today, we think of luxury, servants, a palace, respect, power, and lots of money. When Sarah, Abraham's wife, hears that she will become a princess, the promise didn't include an opulent setting, a throne, or ruling power over a city. What made her a princess in God's eyes was that she would have countless descendants:

> God also said to Abraham, "As for Sarai your wife, you are no longer to call her Sarai; her name will be Sarah [Sarah means "princess"]. I will bless her and will surely give you a

son by her. I will bless her so that she will be the mother of nations; kings of peoples will come from her."

Genesis 17:15–16

Just as immature Christians think of their faith only individually (how God is blessing them, using them, building them up), apart from their role in the corporate church, so immature fathers and mothers think of themselves only individually, apart from their descendants (both spiritual and physical). When God makes a promise to Abraham, he extends it well beyond his own lifetime to that of his offspring: "All the land that you see I will give to you and your offspring forever" (Genesis 13:15).

Some time later, after God renews his promise to greatly bless Abraham, even to increase his ministry and influence, Abraham, surprisingly enough, seems far from pleased. Why? He still didn't have any children to pass that blessing on to: "O Sovereign LORD," he said, "what can you give me since I remain childless?" (Genesis 15:2). In a very practical way, Abraham is thinking, *You can give me all you want; but if it stops with me, what good is it? I already have all I need! Without children to pass it on to, what I have is useless!*

As a mature couple, Abraham and Sarah thought generationally, just as a mature Christian must learn to think corporately (of the church). It is our calling, and indeed, our glory, to look beyond ourselves to the good of God's church and toward the future of our children. This is God's own perspective. We're told that God chose Abraham, not just for the sake of Abraham, but for the generations to come: "For I have chosen him, so that he will direct his children and his household after him to keep the way of the LORD ..." (Genesis 18:19).

God told Moses that he had hardened Pharaoh's heart "so that I may perform these miraculous signs of mine among them *that you may tell your children and grandchildren* ..." (Exodus 10:1–2, emphasis added). God thought ahead several generations with regard to what he might demonstrate for the children and grandchildren. What would really matter for eternity?

This might sound petty, but this biblical truth is why the comment "Jesus would have died for me if I had been the only one" always rubs me the wrong way. It makes me want to crawl out of my skin, because that sense of self-centeredness so runs against the spirit of sacrifice, corporate responsibility, and other-centeredness to which the gospel calls us. I'm *not* the only one. And my generation *won't* be the last one. Until I understand this, I'll never begin to understand the kingdom of God.

Rabbi Nancy Fuchs-Kreimer recounts the true story of two Jewish parents who had never taken seriously their identity as Jews. But when their son was born, they had to make a decision about whether they would follow the ritual of circumcision. While their faith hadn't influenced their daily lives, they had qualms about breaking a three-thousand-year-old covenant. In the end, after much thought and deliberation, these essentially secular Jews decided to go through with the religious ritual. In an almost mystical way, the cut that separated a young boy from his foreskin launched his young mother into an even deeper plane of understanding. Immediately following the circumcision, she turned to her sister and said, "Now I am not only a descendant, I am an ancestor!"[3]

Viewing ourselves as ancestors as well as descendants represents a vitally important spiritual transformation. The sacred journey of parenting changes our perspective. We travel from "me" to "us," from individual to family, and we begin to understand the difference we can have on future generations. Rather than overdoing individual self-esteem, we could use a good dose of "family esteem," for sacred parenting makes us princes and princesses working on building God's kingdom!

Consider the case of a young man from long ago. Obed's mother had been a young, poor, foreign widow, and his father, Boaz, owned a field. Boaz wasn't unusually wealthy or abnormally poor; he wasn't particularly attractive or desirable. In fact, he had grown a little long in the tooth, but Ruth (Obed's mom) pursued him, they got married, and the couple gave birth to Obed — whose wife gave birth to Jesse, whose wife gave birth to David, the future king of Israel and arguably the man of his millennium.

Obed provided just one link in a historical chain of events — his worries, his joys, his greatest successes, and his greatest failures have long since been forgotten, but his offspring played a part in human history that has eternal significance. He lived, he died, and he got out of the way — but oh, what a destiny he left behind. Out of that link came the Savior of all who believe — Jesus Christ himself. It doesn't get much better than this when it comes to leaving a lasting legacy!

Sacred parenting calls us to focus our brief lives on what will create the most impact for future generations. We will soon be forgotten on earth, but we'll be remembered in heaven. Let us humbly accept this fact, and then embrace the sacred trust of children that God bestows on us. We must reprioritize our lives according to our own relative insignificance, finally learning to think as God thinks — generationally.

We are born, we die, and then we get out of the way. But those who hold parenting as a sacred journey, and treat it accordingly, will leave behind something wonderful and lasting.

There is a sense in which the family is made by the individuals which constitute it, but there is a far deeper sense in which the individuals are made by the family.

Elton Trueblood

There are plenty of parents very willing to be honored. The catch is that not so many of them are willing to be honorable.

Joy Davidman

Make every effort to add to your faith . . .

2 Peter 1:5

Chapter 11

Xerox R Us

How Raising Children Encourages Us to Improve Our Character

G eorge Gilder never got to know his father, a World War II bomber pilot killed in action while George still wore diapers. Though his dad had been a promising, Harvard-educated economist, George wouldn't allow people to talk about him for two reasons: one, he had a stepfather to whom he felt very close (he didn't want that stepfather to get hurt by too much talk about his biological father); and two, the topic embarrassed him: "I felt that when they described his extraordinary virtues, somehow by extension they were praising me."[1]

Even so, George followed in his biological father's footsteps by attending and graduating from Harvard. He also picked up his father's interest in economics, going so far as to write a manuscript titled *Wealth and Poverty*. On the very day George received the first bound pages of his book, he got a phone call from his uncle, who, to his great surprise, had discovered a big box filled with papers written by George's father.

Intrigued, George eagerly began combing through the papers, finally getting a firsthand introduction to his father's mind and beliefs. One item in particular caught George's eye: an unfinished, 175-page manuscript on economics. The contents nearly took George's breath away:

> One of its themes was the importance of what he called "intangible capital." It corresponded nearly perfectly with the key message of *Wealth and Poverty*: that the driving force

of a free economy was not material resources or even physical capital, but the metaphysical capital of family and faith. In fact, my father's work, if it had been completed, could very well have been titled *Wealth and Poverty*.

The manuscript seemed to confirm a deep sense I carried with me throughout my youth that I was linked in an almost mystical way to this man I never knew. Family was not some arbitrary accident of parental pressure and example that ended with departure from the household. Its influence did not flow only from genetic information or home education. It did not end with distance or even death.

My father taught me no economics, and Harvard taught me scarcely more in the one introductory course I took and barely passed. Yet discovering the literature of the subject in my fortieth year, I tapped a new source of creativity and intellectual power that I never imagined I possessed. I like to think some of that inspiration came from the young man in khaki who climbed into a Flying Fortress at the age of twenty-six in the war against the Nazis and left forever behind him a two-year-old boy and an unfinished text of economics back home in a box.[2]

To be a parent is to literally shape and influence another human life. This is hallowed ground, indeed — and a sacred call to consider carefully the mold we form with our own life. Indeed, this reality of so heavily influencing the next generation reminds us of the theme verse for this book: "Dear friends, let us purify ourselves from everything that contaminates body and spirit, perfecting holiness out of reverence for God" (2 Corinthians 7:1).

Why does parenting necessitate purifying ourselves? Because our children frequently follow the ruts we lay down.

Like Mother, Like Daughter

Lisa and I spent the last few months of our engagement at Western Washington University in Bellingham, Washington. We got married two days after my last final exam and the week before commencement exercises.

During our engagement, saying good-night was always the hardest part of the day. We were growing closer by the hour and had made a commitment to each other for life, but because the wedding hadn't yet taken place, we still had to keep a limit on the amount of time we spent together. Besides, we both had classes in the morning, Lisa's roommate needed to get her sleep, and I had to return to my own room.

These daily good-nights soon fell into a little ritual, repeated several times a week, with similar lines and identical action.

"Do you really have to go?" Lisa would ask.

"Yes," I'd say, knowing full well what would come next.

"Then leave your hand." Lisa would reach out and bring my palm to her cheek.

Fast-forward a dozen years. Lisa and I were married and had three children. Bedtime now featured kids and their own bedtime rituals. Kelsey stuffed her thumb in her mouth, her lambskin bunched up by her face, and dropped off to sleep in seconds. Graham flopped down on the bed, usually sleeping with a truck, a plastic sword, or a baseball mitt, and was out in minutes. Allison — well, Allison seemed allergic to bed at night and addicted to it in the morning — her mother's daughter if ever I saw one.

As I pulled the covers over Allison one night — knowing that no father ever performed a more futile act — Allison said, "Come closer." Her voice dripped with the devious tone that children mask so poorly. I bent down and Allison latched on to my arm. "Stay here," she said.

"I can't," I answered. "You need your sleep and it's time for me to turn the lights out."

"Then leave your hand." Her tiny fingers slipped down and pulled my hand to her face, cupping her cheek.

I almost fainted; it seemed so much like her mother in college. Both Allison and Lisa even picked the same cheek to press my palm against.

"Did your mother tell you to do this?" I asked.

"No."

"Did she ever mention anything about doing this herself?"

"No. Why?"

"Because your mom always did the same thing when she and I were back in college."

Allison's eyes sparkled. At night those eyes had more life than a South Carolina wetland.

"Give me your arm," Allison said, now gripping my elbow to keep my hand on her face. "You can go if you just leave your arm." Except for her gapped teeth and tiny body, I could have sworn I'd time-traveled into the past to those memorable college days.

I felt in a bit of a daze, leaving Allison's room. I could imagine a little girl, one hundred fifty years ago in Germany, lifting her father's large hands to her face. As a young woman, that same girl took a young man's hands and placed them against the same check. A few years later, she gripped those hands with a violent clasp as she expelled her first child; later still, perhaps she felt the now-shrunken hand of that same husband, cold with death, and one last time placed it to her cheek, moved it to her lips, then let it drop down in death.

That little girl became my wife's great-grandmother. Who knows how many generations have passed with that same fluid motion? Centuries of blood run through Allison; she takes her place as a part of women from faraway lands and generations.

I saw Allison in a new light — daughter of millennia, yet future mother of the ages. In such times I recognize a powerful holiness in others. Maybe holiness isn't the right word, but I know it makes me feel small, like I am touching something I have no business touching because it delves so deep and I am so coarse, so shallow, so unaware of the depth of ages in the women I so feebly love.

Like Father, Like Son

Spiritual impact is by no means directed solely by biology. On the contrary, many adoptive fathers and stepfathers have had far more impact on their children's lives than the child's biological father.

One mother told me of the time her husband and their adopted son went to a Promise Keeper's rally. One of the speakers asked all adoptive fathers to stand up. At first the father stayed seated. As his wife explained, he had all but forgotten that his son was adopted — they even physically resembled each other — but then he finally remembered and stood up. His son looked at him and thought, *Why is my dad standing up?* until he, too, remembered that he had been adopted. Afterwards, father and son had a good laugh about how both of them had made the same mistake. They could say with all sincerity, "Like father, like son."

Although we can reproduce children who look like us in a single act of sexual intimacy, the real reproduction is a spiritual one — living out our lives in front of children who will choose to imitate us in dramatic ways. This is a spiritual inheritance of a dramatic order.

Early one spring when Graham was just four years old, I was teaching him to play tennis. In Virginia the spring can get hot. I was mindful that swimming season would soon be upon us, so I thought I might take off my shirt to let myself tan a little. After a long winter, my skin gets roughly the color of fluorescent white. As a Christian courtesy to those who might forget to bring their sunglasses to the pool, I thought some bronzing might benefit everyone around me.

"Why are you taking off your shirt, Dad?" Graham asked.

"I'm just a little hot," came my simplified answer.

Instantly I heard his racket drop to the ground. "I'm hot, too," Graham said, and suddenly two fluorescent-white bodies graced the (fortunately, abandoned) courts.

The following Sunday, as Graham and I sat side by side in church, the pastor began reading from the book of Romans. I flipped open my Bible and followed along. When the pastor had finished reading, I laid the open Bible beside me and listened to the sermon. A few minutes later I glanced back down at the chair next to me and saw not one, but two open Bibles. Graham had carefully laid his Bible out, too, at the same angle as mine. Even though he couldn't yet read, Graham brought his Bible to church, just like Daddy did. And when Dad left the Bible open, Graham did, too.

The next day, Monday, was a holiday. I replaced a turn-signal bulb on our station wagon and, without thinking, cleared my throat and spit off to the side.

"Why'd you do that?" asked Graham, who was "helping" me.

"I don't really know," I said. "Sometimes a guy just needs to spit."

Less than five seconds later I heard Graham clear his throat, turn his head, and, you guessed it, spit off to the side.

Later that evening, we decided to conclude the weekend with a walk on a nearby battlefield (at the time we were living in Manassas, Virginia). Graham couldn't find his shoes.

"You look upstairs," I told him, "and I'll look downstairs."

As soon as I reached the landing and looked down, my heart skipped a beat. In the middle of the floor (just where my wife *loves* me to leave them), I had taken off my shoes and forgotten them. About six inches from my shoes lay Graham's little tennis shoes, placed right next to mine in the middle of the floor, mimicking the same angle my shoes had been dropped.

What a sobering weekend for me! I realized that *every move I made* was being watched. Every word I chose, every time I did something without even thinking about it, Graham was watching me and coming to the conclusion, *This is what I'm supposed to do, because that's what my daddy does.*

This phenomenon, of course, occurs universally. My friend Kevin Leman told me of a similar eye-opening incident with his own son. Dr. Leman happened to be driving a car when he cleared his throat and spit out the car window. His son immediately did the same thing, only he attempted to spit out the *driver's-side* window, hitting his dad square in the face!

Former National Football League quarterback Archie Manning remembers how his son Peyton — also an NFL quarterback — mimicked so many of his dad's mannerisms as he grew up that it felt almost eerie. Peyton listened to old broadcasts of Archie's playing days and would mutter them under his breath: "Manning of Drew rolls right — throws to Franks of Biloxi!" In the seventh grade, the first season Peyton started playing organized football, Archie was shocked to see his son walk bowlegged out of the huddle. Peyton wasn't naturally bowlegged; that funny walk was his imitation of his dad, garnered from watching so much film.

"It's natural for kids to idolize their dads," Archie admitted, "but Peyton was *studying* me." Later in life, when someone asked Peyton how he felt earning more for playing one game than his dad had earned for an entire season, Peyton replied with a clipped, "I don't compete with my father. I learn from him."[3]

To be a parent is to make an impression. There's no doubt that parenting, at least in the early stages, has a bit of a "Xerox" feel to it. The only difference — and what a huge difference — is that we don't reproduce paper; we reproduce human character, legacies, and destiny!

This is a serious call and challenge to all fathers and mothers. Because we feel secure in our trust in the finished work of Jesus

Christ, we sometimes take our continued growth in holiness for granted. Our unconscious thinking goes like this: *I know getting into heaven isn't a matter of my morality, and of course I'll repent of any major sin I fall into, so what's the big deal if I tolerate a few bad habits?*

Well, the Bible makes spiritual growth a *very* big deal. In fact, Peter tells us that we should "make every effort" to add to our faith "goodness; and to goodness, knowledge; and to knowledge, self-control; and to self-control, perseverance; and to perseverance, godliness; and to godliness, brotherly kindness; and to brotherly kindness, love" (2 Peter 1:5–7).

Think about that phrase "every effort." Every effort looks nothing like the casual trot of Barry Bonds as he ambles toward first base while "running out" a fly ball he knows will be caught. "Every effort," rather, recalls Ichiro Suzuki as he barrels toward first base trying to run out an infield single. That's the kind of exertion to which Peter calls us spiritually, as we add to our faith. According to him, laziness about increasing in these virtues is to be "nearsighted and blind" and to forget that we have been cleansed from our past sins (2 Peter 1:9).

If heaven doesn't give us the motivation to make every effort, perhaps having kids will. If we don't seek to add to our faith in this aggressive manner, Peter warns that we will be "ineffective and unproductive" in our "knowledge of our Lord Jesus Christ" (2 Peter 1:8). In other words, it's possible to become an unfruitful, unproductive Christian. We may get to heaven, but we'll arrive with an empty shopping basket, with no fruit to offer our King.

So often we parents decry the bad examples passed down by politicians, the lewd messages coming out of Hollywood, the destructive plot lines of popular television shows, and the obscene lyrics of modern music — but Peter challenges us to look not at Hollywood, New York, or Washington, D.C., but to the hearts of believers, to see if they are truly making "every effort" to add to their faith the virtues Scripture calls us to practice. If we are not, we have only ourselves to blame when the church seems ineffective and unproductive.

Christ's cross-won forgiveness doesn't mean God excuses us from growing in righteousness; it means he frees us from being self-centered as we do so! Growing in godliness is not about trying to achieve heaven but rather about leaving an authentic example for others to follow — beginning with our children.

The Sins of the Parents

Just over a century ago, Sonia Keppel believed her mother had a "brilliant, goddess-like quality," in part because of the flowers sent as "oblations to this goddess" by King Edward VII. Sonia's eyes filled with the orchids and ribbon-covered baskets delivered in horse-drawn vans by a coachman clothed in the king's finest. Though the gifts came through the channel of adultery, you can see how, in the mind of a young girl, Sonia must have thought her mom very special to receive such attention from no less a person than the king of England.

In the late nineteenth century, Mrs. Keppel's affair with the king did not destroy her marriage or her reputation — but times have changed. Sonia's granddaughter (and Mrs. Keppel's great-grand-daughter) grew up to be Camilla Parker-Bowles, long-standing mistress of Charles, the prince of Wales, and the *de facto* rival of the late Diana Spencer, princess of Wales. In this more recent incarnation, we saw just how destructive to an entire family — and even a country — adultery can be.

Most psychologists and counselors today are discovering that sins do, indeed, tend to be handed down generationally. One account by Patrick Carnes, a counselor who specializes in sexual addiction, shocked me. One of Dr. Carnes's patients felt deeply ashamed of his exhibitionist compulsion and entered therapy to confront this sin. With great embarrassment and shame, he assumed that only he struggled with this problem — until a little detective work disclosed that his father, two uncles, and two cousins were also exhibitionists.[4]

Dr. Carnes has found that, among his patients, "within the family, addictions would be like overlays whose reinforcing shadows simply deepened the patterns of family pathology."[5] A woman and man fighting their own personal temptations do not merely fight for themselves; they man the front lines in a generational war against evil. When we fall into sin, we open a gap that spiritually exposes our children and grandchildren. This reality alone should encourage us to stand strong against the temptations that test us.

God's provision in Jesus Christ means that we can never use "generational influence" to excuse our sin — but at the same time, it makes no sense to deny our family tendencies. As Dr. Carnes explains, "For the addict, part of therapy is to discover the role of the previous generation in the addiction."[6] What does this mean to me as a parent?

Sinning as a father is worse than sinning as a son, in that when I sin as a father, I risk perpetuating an evil for generations on end.

Though it may not seem fair, throughout history kids have often paid the price for the sins of their parents. A heartrending story from biblical times recounts how a father named Achan defied God's decree and stole some forbidden plunder. When Achan's sin came to light, he paid a severe price — but he wasn't alone. The nation stoned his entire family along with him. Achan's wife and kids suffered the ultimate punishment for Achan's greed (see Joshua 7).

Our children may not pay the kind of immediate price that Achan's family paid. It may take twenty or thirty years for our spiritual failures to show up in the lives of our descendants — but we can surely leave an easier or harder road for them to follow. If this doesn't motivate us to take our own spiritual formation more seriously, I don't know what will.

If you struggle with a tendency toward sin that you know has run in your family for generations, why not seek help now? Why not determine before God that you will break this chain? Peter assures us that "[God's] divine power has given us everything we need for life and godliness through our knowledge of him who called us by his own glory and goodness" (2 Peter 1:3). Lean on the pastors and counselors in God's church, glean from their insights and wisdom, but don't simply take a pass on a struggle that you know your children — and possibly your grandchildren and even great-grandchildren — may face if you don't call a halt to your sin.

A Positive Bent

Fortunately, *positive* generational influences also exist. One biblical story should encourage every mom who is married to a nonbeliever. Paul told Timothy to continue in the faith "because you know those from whom you learned it" (2 Timothy 3:14). We know from elsewhere that Paul refers here to Timothy's mother, Eunice, and his grandmother, Lois (see 2 Timothy 1:5). When Paul commends Timothy's family, he doesn't mention Timothy's father — a glaring omission. Acts 16:1 tells us that Timothy's father still lived, so most commentators assume he wasn't a believer.

Yet Paul believed that, through the influence of a believing mother and grandmother, Timothy had enough of an example to hold on to should any doubts arise about his faith. He urged Timothy to remember the examples of these women and to seize the power of their imprinting: *You've seen the difference it made in their lives, Timothy — now grab hold of it for yourself.* The sixteenth-century reformer John Calvin put it this way: "[Timothy] was raised in his infancy in such a way that he could suck in godliness along with his mother's milk."[7]

If you're a single mom, you can take great comfort from Timothy's life. Of course, the ideal is for a son to have a godly father as a role model; but lacking that, a believing mom can help point her son to other male role models (in Timothy's case, Paul), while she still serves as the primary role model. The task of single parenting certainly presents more difficulties, but never think of it as futile or without hope.

The Old Testament talks about a more traditional heritage, beginning with Aaron and his sons. After the consecration of Aaron as a priest, God directed Moses to consecrate Aaron's sons, "just as you anointed their father, so they may serve me as priests. Their anointing will be to a priesthood that will continue for all generations to come" (Exodus 40:15).

While today's kids typically don't follow their fathers into the same occupation (although my wife's family now has a fourth-generation auctioneer), we do pass down a spiritual heritage. Are we leaving an authentic example for our children to follow? Will what they've seen draw them to God, or will our hypocrisy create a road-block for faith? None of us can leave a perfect example, but we can provide a genuine example, an authentic picture of what it means to walk hand in hand with God.

The Right Kind of Reproduction

The question begs to be asked: Do our lifestyles leave something that our children must overcome, or are we blazing a godly path for them to follow? If children catch both some of our strengths and some of our weaknesses, the process of raising them calls us to get more serious about our own character growth. If we start to veer off course even fifteen degrees, and our kids maintain that direction, and their kids follow them, soon the entire family line will be radically off track.

My esteem for the apostle Paul only grows over time. The deeper I get into his writings, the more the depth of his faith humbles and challenges me, particularly in this issue of his leaving an example. Paul has the temerity to tell the Corinthians, "Therefore I urge you to imitate me" (1 Corinthians 4:16). In case they didn't get it, he repeats himself later in the letter: "Follow my example, as I follow the example of Christ" (1 Corinthians 11:1).

To the Thessalonians, Paul gives essentially the same advice:

> For you yourselves know how you ought to follow our example. We were not idle when we were with you, nor did we eat anyone's food without paying for it. On the contrary, we worked night and day, laboring and toiling so that we would not be a burden to any of you. We did this, not because we do not have the right to such help, *but in order to make ourselves a model for you to follow.*
>
> 2 Thessalonians 3:7–9, emphasis added

And to the Galatians, the great apostle says, "I plead with you, brothers, become like me ..." (Galatians 4:12).

Could he have made the implications any clearer? Paul lived in such a way that he set a plumb line for others to follow. He had to make sure that he stayed headed in the right direction, because he specifically told others to do what he did, and even to model themselves after him. This is the call of a parent times ten! Even without specifically requesting that our children follow us, they will do so, at least to some degree. They may try to imitate us, or they may push away from us and rebel, but they *will* react to us and to our way of life.

I remember one time praying for my son, Graham. The Lord seemed to interrupt my prayer with an intercession of his own: "You must become what you're praying for Graham to become." God seemed to be telling me that, while he felt eager to answer my prayers on Graham's behalf, he also intended to use me to bring about those answers. If I want Graham to be a man of prayer, I must first become a man of prayer myself.

I don't feel quite as confident as Paul did, telling others to "imitate me." I hope that Graham, Allison, and Kelsey will surpass me in some areas of character. But whether I feel as confident as Paul or not isn't the point — the reproduction already is taking place. So I must ask myself, *What am I going to do about it?*

We can't avoid leaving ruts. To have a child is to influence another life, perhaps even several generations. The only question is, in what direction will our ruts carry our children?

When I was about to become a father, my friend Burgess Meredith said, "You're gonna find something wonderful — someone you love more than yourself." For self-centered people, it's a great blessing.

Peter Boyle (actor)

He sacrificed for their sins once for all when he offered himself.

Hebrews 7:27

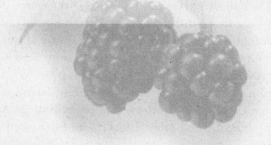

Chapter 12

Sacrifice

How Raising Children Teaches Us to Sacrifice

During a prolific career, Dick Schaap wrote more than two dozen books and hosted numerous television and radio sports shows. His son Jeremy followed him into the sports reporting business and has worked for ESPN since 1996.

When Dick suddenly and unexpectedly died following a seemingly routine surgical procedure in 2001, the sports world reeled in shock, having lost a recognizable and respected voice. In a column celebrating his father's life, Jeremy described how Dick had made perhaps the ultimate sacrifice on his behalf:

> My father saw Bill Mazeroski end the 1960 World Series with a home run, he saw Jerry Kramer throw the block that won the Ice Bowl, he saw Muhammad Ali and Joe Frazier pummel each other in Manila, and he saw Reggie Jackson hit one home run in Game 6 of the 1977 World Series. Jackson, of course, hit three home runs to help the Yankees beat the Dodgers in that game. My father saw him hit the first, off Burt Hooton. When Jackson hit his second, my father was at a concession stand buying me popcorn. When Jackson hit his third, my father was buying me a soda.
>
> Eventually, he forgave me. I think.[1]

Parents make legitimate claims on their children — respect and obedience, for starters. But children make many claims on their parents. The fact that they exist calls out for our nurture, our care, our love, our commitment, our time, and our financial support. This claim that children have on our time, money, energy, and thoughts can lead us into the spirit of sacrifice, the heart of authentic Christian faith.

Put Down That Fork

The first person on whom child raising places a massive claim is the mother. The father gets nine months to warm up to his responsibilities, but because the child resides in the mother's body, she faces an instantaneous — and severe — claim. British writer Rachel Cusk brings this reality to life in her book *A Life's Work:*

> Like a bad parent, the literature of pregnancy bristles with threats and the promise of reprisal, with ghoulish hints at the consequences of thoughtless actions. Eat pâté and your baby will get liver damage. Eat blue cheese and your baby will get listeria, a silent and symptomless disease that will nonetheless leave your baby hideously deformed. Stroke the cat and your baby will get toxoplasmosis.... A temperature of more than 104 degrees sustained for several days could damage your baby in the first seven weeks of gestation, so don't use saunas, have hot baths, or for that matter wear a jersey at any point in pregnancy.... Don't drink or smoke, you murderer. Don't take aspirin. Wear a seat belt when you travel in a car.... Anyone thinking that pregnancy is the one time in their life when they are allowed to be fat can think again. Don't eat cakes, biscuits, refined white flour, chocolate, sweets, fizzy drinks or chips. *When you raise your fork to your lips*, reads one book on this subject, *look at it and think, Is this the best bite I can give my baby? If the answer is no, put your fork down.*[2]

Rachel talks of the "curious role" an unborn child plays in the "culture of pregnancy": "It is at once victim and autocrat."[3]

Everything about the woman's lifestyle — what she eats, drinks, wears, enjoys for exercise and recreation — suddenly comes up for debate. Most people have their little vices — my daily Pepsi, C. S. Lewis's afternoon pipe, a young mother's five cups of coffee, a golfer's occasional cigar — but a pregnant woman is asked to withdraw cold turkey from virtually every vice overnight, or else she is made to feel that she plays a role in her unborn child's potential destruction and disfigurement.

In short, the woman's call to sacrifice begins as soon as she discovers she's pregnant. My wife, Lisa, was a hero in this regard. She took the nutritional guidelines as gospel and didn't even *think* about breaking them. Given my own poor eating habits, both of us gave thanks that my body never fed an unborn child.

A parent's willingness to make such sacrifices has great spiritual benefit. Christianity was birthed in sacrifice and calls us to many acts of sacrifice. Because we worship a generous and merciful and loving and giving God, we find it easy to slip into a "Christmas tree" view of the faith — that Christianity is all about continuously opening up present after present as we gather around the Lord's tree — instead of the metaphor given to us by the New Testament, an image centered around the cross. Jesus saw sacrifice at the heart of what his followers do: "If anyone would come after me, he must deny himself and take up his cross daily and follow me" (Luke 9:23). The apostle Paul underscores this when he says an attitude of sacrifice lies at the foundation of Christian worship: "Therefore I urge you, brothers, in view of God's mercy, to offer your bodies as living sacrifices, holy and pleasing to God — this is your spiritual act of worship" (Romans 12:1).

We love to talk about the blessings of our faith, about God's provision and the gifts he gives to us — but an immature believer can receive all of these. It doesn't take a lot of faith to accept God's generosity! But true spiritual maturity often reveals itself during those times God asks us to sacrifice. While we find it easy to "open up" a spiritual gift, it's not so easy to lay one down on God's behalf. We need training to be able to do that. Sometimes, we even have to be cajoled into doing it! In this sense, children can become tools in God's hands to teach us how to embrace the crucial spiritual discipline of sacrifice.

Rethink That Ambition

Deacon John Adams, a common farmer and shoemaker in the eighteenth century, lived by a simple axiom: The only truly sound investment is land. Once purchased, land should never be sold. Historians believe that Deacon John made just one exception to this rule: He sold ten acres to send his oldest son, John, to college. Although he broke a heartfelt principle, Deacon John willingly made that sacrifice in order to give his son the best chance at success.

John didn't waste his father's sacrifice. He eventually became the second president of the United States.

The act of raising children confronts our narcissistic selfishness and invites us to sacrifice our own welfare on behalf of another human being — which, of course, provides marvelous spiritual training. A man once forcefully told me that he would *never* incur debt to send one of his children to college, nor would he even think about reducing his retirement contribution just so they could get a bachelor's degree. He had his own dreams of retirement, and while I don't argue that men should not pursue their dreams, I do argue with the notion that we should be selfish in doing so. Paul sounds quite adamant about this: "If anyone does not provide for his relatives, and especially for his immediate family, he has denied the faith and is worse than an unbeliever" (1 Timothy 5:8). Sometimes responsibility, loyalty, and maturity call us to willingly lay down our dreams for the sake of those we love — and in the hope that those who come after us can accomplish even more than we could.

Wasn't this Jesus' own modus operandi? Didn't he willingly give up his life at the remarkably young age of thirty-three? Imagine how much more he could have done with another three or four decades on this earth! Yet Jesus told his disciples, "I tell you the truth, anyone who has faith in me will do what I have been doing. He will do even greater things than these, *because I am going to the Father*" (John 14:12, emphasis added).

How will we do greater things than Jesus? On the back of his sacrifice ("because I am going to the Father"), that's how. How could John Adams get an education and climb out of his lower-middle-class background to become one of the most influential men of his day? On the back of his dad's sacrifice, that's how. How do kids get nurtured with the active love, available counsel, and prayerful presence they so desperately need? On the backs of their mothers' sacrifices, that's how.

Kids' needs are rarely "convenient." What they require in order to succeed rarely comes cheaply. To raise them well will require daily sacrifice of many kinds, which has the wonderful spiritual effect of helping mold us into the character of Jesus Christ himself. God invites us to grow beyond ourselves and to stop acting as though our dreams begin and end with us. Once we have children, we cannot act and dream as though we had remained childless.

A few years ago, a man who may well be the most influential pastor in the United States invited me to address his staff and then afterwards shocked me to my core by offering me a position in his church. As a writer, I really couldn't have had a better platform to promote my books; even more important, I have the highest respect for him and his work and consider his ministry both strategic and richly blessed by God. But my family had settled in Bellingham. In fact, on the very day this pastor talked to me, we had just closed on a house, and my kids — who had moved with us from the East Coast four years prior — felt comfortably settled into their relationships with friends, their school situations, and their youth groups. I felt like a fool for letting the offer pass. Vocationally, there seemed little question about the choice I should make. But my dreams do not and cannot begin or end with me.

One year later, a seminary sent me a job description as a "writer in residence" that felt so inviting it made my wife laugh. As she read it, she said it seemed as though they had read my mind. "They couldn't have come up with something more inviting if they had tried!" she exclaimed. She was right.

Yet that job offer felt like a dagger through my heart because I eventually realized, kicking and screaming all the while, that I would have to let this opportunity pass, too. When we moved our kids to the state of Washington, I promised them, "This is it until you're out of the house. I won't disrupt your lives like this again." I would have had to move to take that "ideal" position. Yes, it represented a lifelong dream, a job description that couldn't suit me better — but I'm not just a man, I'm a father. And in this case I believed my fatherly responsibilities needed to count more than my personal ambition.

I believe that Elton Trueblood, at least, would agree with me — and I feel pretty safe in that man's company. He makes this observation:

> At the same time that a doctor was made president of the American Medical Association, his son was accepted in Phi Beta Kappa, and his friends noticed that he took far more satisfaction in the latter honor than the former. Indeed, the man who, after he has a family, is still putting his main

emphasis on his own personal ambition and advancement is revealing his own failure to mature. Personal ambition may be necessary for the young, but it is increasingly unlovely in those of older years.[4]

I understand why Deacon John sold ten precious acres of land for his son's future. I'd mortgage my house, I'd give whatever I have, to get our kids on a solid footing. In a letter that generations of Adamses have learned by heart, Deacon John's son, President John Adams wrote this:

> I must study politics and war that my sons may have liberty to study mathematics and philosophy. My sons ought to study mathematics and philosophy, geography, natural history, naval architecture, navigation, commerce, and agriculture in order to give their children a right to study paintings, poetry, music, architecture, statuary, tapestry, and porcelain.[5]

Part of carrying out our parental responsibilities requires adopting the Christian posture of humility. However "important" we may think we are, we should expect that God can do even more important things through our children. It is our duty to give them our full attention and our best effort, hoping that they can build on this to become influential Christians themselves. It is shortsighted at best, and the height of arrogance at worst, for fathers or mothers to become so busy with their own ministries and lives that they shortchange their children, forgetting that they have a responsibility to pass on to the next generation whatever advantages they have received.

A former seminary professor of mine, the late Klaus Bockmuehl, modeled this. As compelling a figure as he was, Dr. Bockmuehl told me that he aimed to lift his students onto his shoulders so that they could stand taller than he had. Though I doubted at the time — and still do today! — that I could ever match his depth or influence, his words present a compelling picture to me as a father hoping to lift *my* children onto *my* shoulders.

A Blanket of Sacrifice

Campus pastor Jim Schmotzer told me of a friend who had a daughter in eighth grade. In the first flush of adolescence, she felt increasingly embarrassed about the clothes her mom always wore. Finally, the mom couldn't take it anymore and explained something to her daughter: "Look, honey," she said, "I realize the clothes I wear are out of style, but you need to know something: I dress like this so you can dress like that. We can't afford for both of us to buy the latest fashions."

I think of the homeschool moms I've met — including my wife. Sometimes Lisa wishes that she, too, could work out at a fitness club four times a week, sip leisurely coffees at Starbucks with friends, and spend more time doing the things she enjoys doing; but homeschooling two children (our oldest now attends high school) is a full-time job.

God calls us as parents to lay down a blanket of sacrifice on behalf of the next generation. This is the way of Jesus. In many ways, sacrifice defines love. It was one thing for Jesus to tell the world, "I love you." It was another thing entirely when he demonstrated his love by dying on our behalf. Paul tells us, "For you know the grace of our Lord Jesus Christ, that though he was rich, yet for your sakes he became poor, so that you through his poverty might become rich" (2 Corinthians 8:9).

Don't move too quickly past this statement! Jesus made himself poor so that his spiritual children could become rich. Jesus allowed himself to be humiliated so that we could be glorified. He died so that we could live. Everything we have spiritually comes on the back of Jesus' sacrifice.

Without sacrifice, love becomes mere words and empty sentiment. Heavyweight boxer Mike Tyson captures the spirit of this age when he talks about how much he "loves" his children, even while admitting that he hardly ever sees them: "I don't have much of a relationship with [my children]," he told reporters one night before a fight. "We got problems in my household. But it's all good. I'm the best father in the world. They couldn't have a better father than me. If I never showed up another day in my life, they could never have a better father than me because no one could love them any more than I do."[6]

Despite Tyson's *feelings*, hard evidence would suggest otherwise. Court records revealed that from 1995 to 1997, Tyson spent almost twice as much feeding and housing his animals (including over a thousand pigeons and plenty of cats) as he had on child support.[7]

Words and feelings are the cheap currency of sentimentality; sacrifice is the backbone of true, biblical love: "Greater love has no one than this, that he lay down his life for his friends" (John 15:13).

Laying Down Legitimate Needs

Journalist Iris Krasnow talks about how she got all dressed up for a "delicious" afternoon and evening out. She really needed a break from parenting four young boys, and she was looking forward to it with every fiber of her being. First, she planned to get her hair done. Then she intended to teach a class on writing at American University. Then she hoped to meet a close friend at a restaurant to have some "grown-up conversation." It all sounded too good to be true.

Unfortunately, it was.

As Iris pulled on her black wool pantsuit with satin lapels, dreaming about what she would eat and drink in just a few short hours, one of her sons came into her bedroom and informed her that he had just thrown up and that his head was "on fire."

Iris took his temperature: 103.

Iris didn't just *want* this break from her kids; she felt she *needed* it. But her son needed her as well. Whose rights would prevail?

Krasnow relates, "As I held him in my lap, his sticky face burrowed into my black blazer. I picked up the telephone and called the pediatrician, then canceled the hair appointment . . . , the writing class, and the Cactus Cantina date with Becca."

"Mommy, will you hold me?" her son asked.

"Yes, honey," Iris replied.[8]

The way Iris responded reminds me of Jesus' response just after he heard the news of John the Baptist's execution. What a sobering moment in Jesus' life! He knew that the violence leveled on the neck of John the Baptist provided only a tame precursor of what would soon happen to him. He saw the clock moving forward; his own date with martyrdom drew ever nearer. Quite understandably, Jesus felt drawn to seek out a much-needed time of solitude with his Father. "When Jesus heard what had happened [John the Baptist's death]," Matthew writes, "he withdrew by boat privately to a solitary place" (Matthew 14:13). Jesus *needed* this time alone.

But when the crowds heard that Jesus was nearby, they followed in large numbers. Instead of getting some time alone, Jesus faced a huge group of people wanting yet another piece of him. Jesus could have legitimately sent the crowds away, explaining that he needed to pray; no one could have faulted him for that. But, according to Matthew, Jesus "had compassion on them and healed their sick" (Matthew 14:14). This went on *all day long.* And at the end of the day, Jesus fed the five thousand.

Now sometimes we make it sound as though Jesus accomplished his miracles merely by snapping his fingers. In reality, a work of that magnitude took great energy and strength. Jesus was fully God, but he was also fully human, subject to weariness. Imagine having such a challenging emotional day, then summoning the strength to heal scores of sick people, and then finding one last vestige of strength to feed a crowd of five thousand.

Jesus must have felt beyond exhaustion, in tremendous need of spiritual and physical renewal. We don't have to guess about this; Matthew's narrative depicts a clear urgency. Directly following the feeding of the five thousand, Matthew recounts, *"Immediately* Jesus *made* the disciples get into the boat and go on ahead of him to the other side, while he dismissed the crowd. After he had dismissed them, he went up on a mountainside by himself to pray" (Matthew 14:22–23, emphasis added). Jesus would do his duty, *but immediately after completing that duty,* he eagerly sought time for prayer.

How many parents have felt at their wits' end, eager for time alone, only to have to sacrifice it on behalf of their children? When God calls you into this arena, remember that you have one who understands. Jesus has been there. He knows exactly how you're feeling and invites you to turn this difficult moment of sacrifice into a profound place of intimacy and understanding with him. He knows what it feels like to need some time alone, some time to get refreshed and renewed, only to have that time stolen by the reality of tending to the needs of others.

Unhappily for us parents, children's needs rarely arrive when we feel at our best or when we're well rested. They come when we feel exhausted, when we're in our own time of crisis or in the midst of our own worries. Kids don't check our schedules before they get sick, have fights among themselves, or choose to rebel. This is the heart of a parent's sacrifice — putting our own needs beneath the more urgent calling of child raising.

Many of us won't be asked to make major sacrifices. Sacrifice and the corresponding virtue of humility aren't built on giant gestures as much as they are forged with consistent, thoughtful actions of an everyday nature: a dad choosing to play a board game with his little girl instead of turning on the television; a woman making sure she's home for dinner instead of staying late at the office; parents who enjoy a hobby far less frequently than they'd like for the sake of spending more time with their children. Elton Trueblood put it best:

> It is the right of little children to have individual love all day long and to have more than the tag ends of affection. But this situation will not change until the family is seen as an institution so precious that men and women will sacrifice something, even in excitement and personal expression, in order to maintain it.[9]

In 2 Corinthians 12:14, Paul admonishes, "After all, children should not have to save up for their parents, but parents for their children." Though Paul speaks in financial terms here, the principle goes much wider: the needs of children obligate us as adults to care for them, even if in doing so we must incur great sacrifice. He goes on to say, "So I will very gladly spend for you everything I have and expend myself as well" (verse 15).

The Practical Side of Sacrifice

Let's look at some of the practical ways we will be called to sacrifice as parents.

1. Time

One of the first great sacrifices we make for our kids involves giving up time. Weekends and evenings now are defined by family needs and desires, independent of our own individual wishes. For the parent who stays at home, the sacrifice grows even larger; just about every minute gets spoken for.

Rachel Cusk describes a scene I'm sure most mothers have personally experienced—the thrill of seeing an infant start to fall asleep, perhaps finally offering you a few moments to yourself:

> Her eyelids begin to droop. The sight of them reminds me of the possibility that she might go to sleep and stay that way

for two or three hours.... The prospect is exciting, for it is when the baby sleeps that I liaise, as if it were a lover, with my former life. These liaisons, though always thrilling, are often frantic. I dash about the house unable to decide what to do: to read, to work, to telephone my friends.... Watching her eyelids droop, my excitement at the prospect of freedom buzzes about my veins. I begin manically to list and consider things I might do, discarding some ideas, cherishing others. Her eyelids droop again and close altogether. In repose her face is as delicate, as tranquil as a shell.[10]

All children require loads of time. Since parents don't get any more hours in a day than childless couples, they have to crucify some activities in order to make way for the new demands. Nothing can substitute for time spent with kids, and this time frequently must come from something else we would prefer to do.

But isn't all ministry this way? Wouldn't all of us like to volunteer for Habitat for Humanity, help build a church in Guatemala, volunteer for a crisis pregnancy center, or do some other works of service *if only we had the time?* Those who do these things have no more time in their day than those who don't — just as fathers who talk to their children don't have twenty-eight hours as opposed to silent dads who have just twenty-four. Time is no respecter of persons. It's all about where we choose to spend our hours and what we will willingly sacrifice in order to free up some of those hours.

2. Sex

Having children is a good way to strengthen your abstinence skills. As soon as kids arrive on the scene, chastity takes on a whole new meaning.

One time after I had returned from a long speaking trip, Lisa and I understandably felt more than a little romantic. Both of us very much wanted to "get together," but an unlikely string of coincidences kept putting off any activity, night after night. Finally, after almost a week had passed, we determined to enjoy our Saturday night. Unfortunately, we forgot about the implications of telling our oldest daughter she could invite two of her friends to spend the night.

We didn't know that one of those kids has chronic insomnia. She stayed up past midnight, then read right outside our room until about

1:00 a.m. — a good two hours after I had fallen asleep. (Call us prudes, but we thought it rude to ask her to go downstairs in a strange house all by herself and read her book so that her friends' parents could have sex.) We lived in a rental house at the time, with thin walls and even thinner doors, which meant that the only action heard that night in our house was the heating system clicking on around midnight.

The next morning I woke up, looked at Lisa, and said, "Did we miss out *again*, or do I just have a really pathetic memory?"

Lisa laughed and said, "Don't even go there. I've forgotten how to do it, it's been so long."

Previous generations of believers sometimes looked down on married Christians because they didn't practice chastity. Only a single person or a couple without kids could think such a thing. We may not practice *perpetual* abstinence, but kids certainly have a way of making sure we become familiar with the idea!

An interesting aside: When my wife read an early draft of this book and came across the sentence at the beginning of this section ("Having children is a good way to strengthen your abstinence skills"), she wrote in the margin the question, "Is that good, within marriage? Seriously!"

I think it *is* good in that, while I believe passion and desire are healthy, holy, and God-created, all of us need to learn self-mastery, or what the Bible calls self-control. Just because it's "okay" to have sex as married people doesn't allow us to throw self-control out the window. Only a selfish spouse would demand sex, knowing that his or her partner feels exhausted. Paul made it very clear that mature Christians draw a distinction between what is *allowed* and what is governed by love (see 1 Corinthians 6:12). Sex is a powerful and very delightful marital reality, but I've spoken at enough marriage conferences to realize how very painful it can be as well.

What makes sex relationally painful? Selfish demands. Manipulation. Malicious denial. In short, everything that goes against the spirit of sacrifice. Though our children don't know it — and we'll probably never tell them! — by teaching us to sacrifice, they actually purify and strengthen our sexual relationship, even though we may not enjoy intimate relations quite as frequently as we used to.

3. Prayer

Parents of newborns, parents with multiple toddlers, and parents with busy teenagers need as much time for spiritual reflection and study as anyone else — perhaps more — but let's be realistic. The schedule of such a parent doesn't afford the same opportunity as that of a single college student or an empty nester. The irony is that just when we need prayer the most, we may have the least time available for it.

Even the classic writers recognized this. Thomas Kelly, in his renowned work *A Testament of Devotion*, admits as much when he writes the following:

> Do you want to live in such an amazing divine Presence that life is transformed and transfigured and transmuted into peace and power and glory and miracle? If you do, then you can. For, *except for spells of sickness in the family and when the children are small, when terrific pressure comes upon us*, we find time for what we really want to do.[11]

In a passage where he emphasizes that we do what we really want to do, Kelly admits that, in the case of young parents, sometimes our prayer times get cut short for legitimate reasons. To help us cope, he gives this word of counsel:

> I find that a life of little whispered words of adoration, of praise, of prayer, of worship can be breathed all through the day. One can have a very busy day, outwardly speaking, and yet be steadily in the holy Presence. We do need a half hour or an hour of quiet reading and relaxation. But I find that one can carry the re-creating silences within oneself well-nigh all the time.[12]

Francis de Sales, a well-known spiritual director in the seventeenth century, admits, "We must sometimes leave our Lord in order to please others for the love of him."[13] Francis also explains that God doesn't look down on us for doing this but rather sees such sacrifices as part of our devotion to him. To a woman frustrated that her pregnancy sapped her strength and thereby undermined her spiritual devotions, Francis gently offers this counsel:

My dearest daughter, we must not be unjust and require from ourselves what is not in ourselves.... The child who is taking shape in your womb will be a living image of the divine majesty; but while your soul, your strength, and your natural vigor is occupied with this work of pregnancy, it must grow weary and tired, and you cannot at the same time perform your ordinary [spiritual] exercises so actively and so gaily. But suffer lovingly this lassitude and heaviness, in consideration of the honor that God will receive from your work.[14]

In another letter, Francis urges a young pregnant woman to refrain from fasting. He explains that God will not be pleased if, as she seeks him, she robs a growing child of its needed nourishment in the process. Our spirituality must bend to our current station in life.

Elton Trueblood has helped many Christians face this tension between family life, service, and devotion by pointing out that we live our lives in chapters. No one chapter defines a complete story. There is the chapter of your singleness, the chapter of your first years as a married couple, the chapter of your years raising toddlers, the chapter of your years raising teens, the chapter of your years as empty nesters, and the chapter of your years as a grandparent. God won't judge our lives by one chapter in isolation but by the story these chapters, woven together, create. During some of these chapters certain things slide, including extended hours in personal prayer. But the heart of the matter is your overall attitude toward serving the Lord and those he loves. Over the course of your whole life, does your story reveal devotion and adoration?

Remember Jesus? He wanted to pray, but those who needed him captured his attention, and he had to put off his time of worship and reflection. He returned to prayer as soon as possible, but even he learned to bend his need for time with his heavenly Father around his earthly duties.

Time, sex, and prayer represent just a few of the areas that require parental sacrifice. We could talk about finances, sleep, peace and quiet, personal hobbies, and so much more. But once we adopt the *spirit* of sacrifice, the application usually becomes clear. As parents, we cannot and must not live as childless men and women. But even more than an obligation, we must consider this an invitation to experience a side of Christ that is at the heart of a truly authentic faith: biblical sacrifice.

Why Sacrifice Matters

The apostle Paul felt awed by God's sacrifice on his behalf. Through his writings, Paul reveals a man who could never get over his astonishment that Jesus had died so that he might live. Just consider how many times Paul seems stuck on this wonder:

- "He who did not spare his own Son, but gave him up for us all ..." (Romans 8:32).
- "the Lord Jesus Christ, who gave himself for our sins ..." (Galatians 1:3–4).
- "The life I live in the body, I live by faith in the Son of God, who loved me and gave himself for me" (Galatians 2:20).
- "Christ loved us and gave himself up for us ..." (Ephesians 5:2).
- "Christ Jesus, who gave himself as a ransom for all men ..." (1 Timothy 2:5–6).
- "the glorious appearing of our great God and Savior, Jesus Christ, who gave himself for us to redeem us ..." (Titus 2:13–14).

Even when discussing other issues, such as marriage, Paul can't get away from this theme: "Husbands, love your wives, just as Christ loved the church *and gave himself up for her* ..." (Ephesians 5:25, emphasis added).

You can tell a preacher's hot-button issues by how often he returns to the same topic, and this notion of Christ's sacrifice on our behalf is certainly one of Paul's — which leads us to ask, *why* does Paul seem so acutely sensitive with regard to Christ's sacrifice on his behalf? Or just as revealing, why do *we* seem so apathetic in comparison? I believe that Paul had a keen appreciation for Christ's sacrifice because he had "entered the game." He knew what sacrifice felt like. He had been stoned, beaten, and shipwrecked on behalf of the faith. He had gone hungry, cold, and tired. Because he had sacrificed, he knew firsthand what it takes to deny oneself on another's behalf, to bear the pain, to face the loss — which helped him appreciate the even greater sacrifice of Christ on our behalf.

It's like this: You can't really appreciate how good a golfer Tiger Woods is unless you've tried to play golf. That's why other professionals seem to be in even greater awe of him than the casual fan. Those professionals know how difficult the shots are that Tiger seems to consistently pull off. In the same way, if we live coddled Christian lives, never sacrificing ourselves, the cross becomes a sentimental fairy tale — a good story to tell once a year, but something that becomes so familiar we can't wait to move on to talk about the resurrection. But if we have suffered as Paul suffered, if we have sacrificed for someone as Paul sacrificed for those under his care, we look at the cross in awe because we realize that all our suffering, multiplied by a hundred, still can't compare with what Christ endured on our behalf. As a result we are in absolute awe of what God has done for us. The passion of the cross metamorphoses from an abstract concept to an astonishing reality.

All this leads to thankfulness and an appreciation for Christ's work that will never dim; its truth will always flood your soul. I can't prove it, but I think Paul broke up emotionally when he wrote Galatians 2:20. Clearly he knew sacrifice: "I have been crucified with Christ and I no longer live, but Christ lives in me." When he got to the words "who loved me and who gave himself for me," I believe the tears flowed freely. Paul comes back to this thought again and again. He can't get over it: Christ *died* for us! He *suffered* for us! He *bore the horror of our sins* on his shoulders!

If you look at the cross with the bored detachment of someone viewing a still-life painting, one of two realities are probably true: You're not a believer; or you're a believer who has never sacrificed on behalf of God. You've never truly taken up your cross and denied yourself to follow him. Without sacrificing ourselves, we can't really appreciate Christ's sacrifice — which means that children, with all the demands that they place on us, usher us into a deeper understanding of and even an astonishment at what God has done on our behalf.

This thought was in the forefront of my mind when I read of how one mother described a difficult cesarean section she underwent in order to give life to her second child. She was pushed into the operating room, which reminded her "uncannily of pictures I have seen of execution chambers." Surrounded by strangers wearing masks, she suddenly felt people crowding around her, grabbing her arms and legs, pushing up against her back. At one moment, someone injected a needle into her hand, while another person injected something else into her back. She looked to her side and saw "a giant, three-pronged valve" being stuffed "bloodily" into a vein. Her natural response was to fight back against this open assault, but how? "I don't know to which front to send my defenses, where to concentrate my powers of endurance, and so I give up and hang my head."[15]

As I read this account, I couldn't help but think of Aslan, slaughtered on that ancient stone table, pulled on and poked from all sides.[16] Every mother has walked this road. To offer life to another, she literally shares her body for nine months, and then even risks her life and health to bring this child safely into the world. Once the child is born, other sacrifices present themselves. Both men and women can rise to the demands and have their souls shaped accordingly. If we embrace these great and small tests with our spiritual eyes opened, we may even come to cherish the sacrifice required of us, so rewarding do we find the spiritual blessings that follow.

One Last Christmas

In 1918, a doctor told Billy Miske, a professional heavyweight boxer, that life had just handed him a knockout blow called Bright's disease. The doctor said that Billy's severely damaged kidneys made it unlikely that he would make it to thirty.

As it turned out, the doctor was right.

The doctor strongly recommended that Billy hang up his boxing gloves, right then and there, and retire to a softer job — and maybe his body would hold out a few years longer.

This physician didn't realize the mound of debt that already had buried Billy. In the words of sportswriter Rick Reilly, Billy's car distributorship didn't "distribute near enough cars," and he trusted people too much — friends took advantage of Billy and often didn't pay him for cars they drove off the lot.[17] He also had a family. They needed to eat, and since his business had failed, Billy knew only one way of putting bread on the table: Win it with his fists.

So the sick man kept fighting. In fact, he entered the ring thirty more times after his fateful diagnosis. Most top heavyweights today fight maybe twice a year; Billy kept mixing it up in the ring every other month or so. And he didn't fight marshmallows — three of those bouts came against the legendary Jack Dempsey, whose fists felt like wrecking balls. During one bout, Dempsey hit Billy so hard on the chest that Billy immediately developed a purple welt the size of a baseball. Looking at that ghoulish purple welt scared Dempsey half to death, but he didn't have time to feel sorry for Billy, because Billy kept trying to knock his head off.

But if one thing attacked more relentlessly than Billy Miske, it was Bright's disease. Eventually the disease took its toll. Billy fought his second-to-last fight in January 1923, and by that fall he had become a shrunken caricature of his former self, unable even to work out, much less box.

Billy hoped he'd get one last Christmas with his family. Yet he couldn't bear the thought of his wife and three children celebrating Jesus' birth around an empty table and a house without gifts — he was flat broke — so he decided to do the only thing he knew how to do. He returned to his manager and asked him to arrange one last fight.

If the manager and Billy hadn't gone back so far, the manager probably would have laughed in Billy's face. After all, Billy had become little more than a shrunken scarecrow. Instead, the manager laid it out straight: "Billy, I don't like to say this, but if you went in the ring now, in your condition, you might get killed."

"What's the difference?" Billy shot back. "It's better than waiting for it in a rocking chair."

Knowing the desperation of his ex-fighter, the manager said he'd consider it if Billy went back to the gym and got himself in shape. Billy knew he lacked anything close to the strength it took to complete a workout. He figured he could squeeze out one last fight, but no workouts. His body just didn't have the strength.

"Can't do the workouts," he admitted. "But I've got one more fight left in me. You've got to help me."

Knowing Billy's desperate straits, the manager gave in. He found a pretty tough opponent, a man named Bill Brennan, who himself had managed to survive ten rounds with Dempsey. If you can last ten with Dempsey, you're for real.

The manager scheduled the fight for November 7. Billy showed up that night looking even weaker than he had when he first approached his friend. As people expected, the fight lasted just four rounds, but Billy took home a check for $2,400 — a small fortune in the 1920s.

On Christmas morning, Billy Jr., Douglas, Donna, and their mom, Marie, woke up to a storybook Christmas. Around a veritable wall of presents, a toy train clanged around the tracks. Marie couldn't believe her eyes when she saw the baby grand piano of her dreams sitting in the living room. They ate like kings and queens, princes and princesses, laughing and singing and celebrating like you wouldn't believe. The kids couldn't wipe the smiles off their faces, but one person's smile outshone them all — Billy Miske knew the fight had been worth it.

The day after Christmas, Billy called his trainer one more time, but this conversation concerned an entirely different fight.

"Come and get me, Jack," he said. "I'm dying."

The trainer rushed Billy to the hospital, but back then, they could do nothing for him. Billy's kidneys failed, and he left this life, at the age of twenty-nine, on New Year's Day 1924.

Oh, yeah. I forgot to mention one thing. Remember that November 7 fight, the one that went just four rounds? It ended so quickly because the emaciated, deathly ill Billy Miske knocked out his opponent.

Never bet against a dad determined to make the ultimate sacrifice to give his family one last Christmas memory.

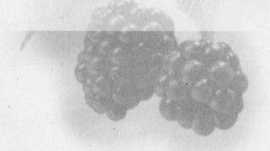

Since no man knows the future,
    who can tell him what is to come?
No man has power over the wind to contain it;
    so no one has power over the day of his death.

Ecclesiastes 8:7–8

Chapter 13

Leaving

How Parenting Teaches Us to Handle Control and Fear by Leading Us to Trust and Hope

Have you ever noticed how you read the Bible differently in your thirties and forties than you did in your teens or twenties? Some verses I wouldn't have thought twice about a couple decades ago I now find quite chilling. One such verse is Matthew 4:22. When Jesus called James and John, "immediately they left the boat *and their father* and followed him" (emphasis added). Twenty years ago, this verse didn't move me much because I thought of myself as a James or a John, setting out on an exciting adventure. I was the young son, and in that parting I saw only the upside of what lay ahead.

Now I think of myself as the father, watching my dear children depart — children for whom I have sacrificed and for whom I would gladly give all that I own. It feels *very* different to be the one left at home.

Letting go of our children can reveal the generosity of our heavenly Father's heart. In this case, God doesn't ask of us anything that he hasn't already done. When the heavenly Father sent his Son, he knew he was releasing him to a world that, for the most part, wouldn't appreciate his deity. On the contrary, they'd accuse him of joining the devil's team, and then they'd beat him and ultimately murder him. If, knowing that ahead of time, God still released his Son into the world, how can we hold back our own children? Just as God released his Son on our behalf, so sacred parenting calls us to release our children on his behalf, for the sake of his kingdom.

Though it's difficult to do — and it differs with each child — we can sanctify the pain inherent in this process as a way to more fully understand and appreciate God's great sacrifice on our behalf.

A Slow but Steady Process

Letting go of our kids makes up a valuable, though painful, part of spiritual formation. Children initiate the leaving process (for that is what it is — a process) faster than most parents like. For moms, it often starts when an infant goes from breast-feeding to bottle- or cup-feeding. Rachel Cusk admits how difficult it felt for her to watch the first time her husband offered a bottle to her daughter:

> When evening comes, I prepare the bottle. Her father is to give it to her, for we are advised that this treachery is best committed not by the traitor herself but by a hired assassin. I watch as he nudges her lips with the rubber nipple. She gnaws at it obligingly, wrinkling her nose. Presently she takes the hint of his persistence. This is not, as she had at first thought, a strange new game. She stares at the bottle, and I see the realization dawn. Her head snaps round and her eyes lock with mine. Her gaze is wondering and wounded. She sees that I am officiating over this crime. She begins to cry. I move to retract, to propitiate; my hand goes automatically to my shirt buttons. I am told to go upstairs, and I go. I sit on the bed, tearful, a pain in the pit of my stomach. Minutes later I creep back down and peer around the corner. They are sitting in a pool of lamplight. The room is warm and silent. The baby is sucking the bottle. I rush back upstairs as if I had witnessed an infidelity.[1]

I remember when Lisa breast-fed our children. People would often ask, "When do you plan to wean them?" and I would often say — half seriously — "the question isn't when we're going to wean the *baby;* the question is when we're going to wean *Lisa.*" That was particularly true with our last child.

After weaning from the breast, a child graduates to wean herself from her parents' idealistic expectations, exerting her own personality. By the time she reached seven years old, Kelsey became an enthusiastic advocate of the color purple. When asked to pick out clothes, she always picked purple. When we moved into a new house and the kids got to paint their own room, of course she chose purple. For her tenth birthday party, she decided to have a "purple party." Some of the food was purple, everyone dressed in purple, and they drank purple drinks and ate purple candy. She can't wait until she turns sixteen, because for some reason (though she has been duly informed to the contrary), she thinks she's going to get a purple Jeep for her present.

My wife doesn't subscribe to many magazines, but I do remember her reading *Victoria* early on in our marriage. I don't recall a single photograph of a little girl wearing purple clothes and living in a purple room. Kelsey has little affinity for the dresses that young girls in *Victoria* wear. She recently said to Lisa, "Will you please just have another little girl so that she can wear dresses and I can wear pants?"

Parenting is one long process of gradually releasing our grip on the reins. When our children are infants, we control virtually everything about their environment. We choose what they see, what their crib decor looks like, what they eat, what they wear, and who gets to be around them. A baby is 100 percent dependent on her parents. We have all the control, and you know what? As humans, we *like* control.

Then our kids become grade-schoolers. Suddenly they play on other coaches' teams; they spend occasional nights at other parents' houses. They go away to school and leave the house for six to eight hours at a time, choosing their own friends and eating whatever meals they can barter for with the lunches we gave them.

Then comes the sledgehammer of adolescence, removing any sentimental notion that our kids belong to anyone but God. We can't give up on our children at this time. Family should still supply the central relationships in their life, but teenagers do have their own lengthy and secretive phone conversations. They may spend weekends, and occasionally even weeks, away at camp or at youth group retreats. They start to drive cars, and even if we trust our children's ability to drive, we can't control the cars coming at them. All of a sudden, our sense of control becomes a myth.

Parents must learn the crucial spiritual lesson of caring deeply and passionately for our children, while at the same time letting them naturally grow away and be independent from us. *Our care must shift from control to influence.* Evelyn and James Whitehead put it this way:

As we [see] our children develop in unanticipated directions, we may be tempted to restrain them or to abandon them in disappointment. Restraining them, we try to force their growth according to our designs. We remind them that they are "ours." Our care insists on control, and in this we recognize that our deepest desire is more to reproduce ourselves than to serve new life on its own terms. Or we abandon them . . . , bitter that they do not appreciate "all I have done for you."

We mature, psychologically and religiously, as we acknowledge that our children . . . are not our possessions. The asceticism at the heart of parenting is to learn to continue the investment of our care but gradually to diminish our control. . . . Can we still give ourselves to the next generation . . . when we realize that they are not going to be "just like us"?[2]

We may get tested most in this area with regard to our faith. Out of a good and holy desire — our children's salvation — we Christian parents can try to control our kids' destiny with what amounts to an almost comically obvious choice. When we say to a three-year-old, "Johnny, do you want to spend all eternity in heaven with Mommy and Daddy and Grandma and Grandpa and with Jesus, surrounded by all the angels, where there is no crying or any pain at all, or do you want to spend the rest of eternity burning in hell with the devil?"

You know what? That's not a particularly difficult choice for a three-year-old. He or she isn't likely to say, "I'll get back to you on that, Dad." Of course the child is going to say, "I want to go to heaven," so we lead them in "the sinner's prayer" before they may even understand what they're committing to and what they're receiving. If we think their choice ends at that moment, we fool ourselves. When our kids enter high school and college, they won't be controlled by how *we* present the decision; they'll have their own questions and they'll seek their own answers.

At that crossroads — whether high school or college — control becomes a myth. In fact, the more we try to control, the more likely we will push our children away from us. Still, we can leave a legacy of influence. If they see an authentic example in us, they may well want what we have. If they witness a fear-driven religion based on control, they will likely run as fast and as far as they can in the other direction.

My wife and son have been training our golden retriever puppy for the past several months. Recently, while on a walk, I saw my wife do something that surprised me as much as it impressed me. We were on a trail that had one short section running next to a street. Our puppy decided to wander out toward some oncoming cars. In a panic, I rushed after Amber, which only encouraged her to go further in the wrong direction. My wife kept her head and walked away from the danger. Suddenly Amber took an abrupt turn and went after Lisa, toward the safety of the trail. In the training process, Amber learned that she should remain by Lisa's side. A well-trained dog sees its master as the most important piece of information. When Lisa turned, Amber knew she was supposed to turn; so when Lisa walked away from the danger, Amber instinctively followed.

Too many parents do what I did — we chase our kids *into* the danger. Instead, we should take our cue from Lisa by setting an example of walking away from the danger and inviting our kids to follow. Both Jesus and Paul did this, but it's much harder to do than it sounds. Think for a moment about the concern Jesus must have felt as he contemplated leaving his church in the hands of a few cowering disciples. He knew that, following his death, the disciples would gather behind locked doors, terrified and wondering what would become of them. He knew before he died that Peter, the "rock" on whom the young church would be built, would deny that he even knew Jesus — not once, but three times.

If he had been a fear-driven control freak, Jesus never would have gone to the cross; the disciples, you see, never would have been "ready enough." But Jesus let go. He trusted in the work of the Comforter, the Holy Spirit, to confirm the lessons he had taught — just as we have to trust the Holy Spirit to remind our children of the spiritual truths they have learned. Jesus returned to the Father, and though no one would claim the church is perfect, it has survived and thrived for over two millennia. Once again, we face that great irony: Although the bachelor Jesus never physically fathered another child, the process of parenting takes us to the same spiritual places that Jesus inhabited while he walked this earth.

Trusting God

The attitude of surrender develops our spiritual integrity by moving us to trust and rest in God rather than accuse God when things don't turn out quite the way we planned. One mother of a child who has Asperger Syndrome (a disorder resembling autism) found herself in a season in which she seriously questioned God's care for her son. "I went through a time where I thought God didn't love Michael," she told Cathy Carpenter, a physician. "Why would a loving God allow all this pain to happen to him? I really had a problem believing God loved Michael. That was my lack of trusting God. I felt bad for Michael that he would not have the kind of life other people have."[3]

Autistic children often have trouble reading social cues, so Michael's mom bought him a copy of *How to Win Friends and Influence People* to carry in his backpack to middle school. What most people pick up naturally — how to tell if someone is angry, what becomes offensive to others, and so forth — Michael had to learn by rote. He lacked the innate sense in social situations to know when to back off, and he couldn't pick up the signals to tell when people were reaching their breaking point.

On his very first day in middle school, with the *How to Win Friends* book in his backpack, Michael tapped an older student on the shoulder to ask him a question. It's not at all unlikely that Michael "tapped" with a bit too much vigor. Maybe he persisted for too long. When an autistic person does the tapping, any number of possibilities exist, and Michael's mom realizes that. At any rate, the tapping annoyed the older student. He told Michael to knock it off or he'd punch him.

Michael didn't process the boy's warnings. Unless people with autism have experienced that very same situation before, they're not really sure how to act; so, wanting more information, Michael tapped the older boy on the shoulder once again to ask him what he meant — and got decked.

Michael's mom realized that because of the way Michael is — the way God has allowed him to be — encountering a situation like this seemed inevitable. The older teen had never met an autistic boy, so while you might have hoped he would have responded more patiently, you can understand how, out of ignorance, he responded the way he did. But that begs the question: Why does God allow Michael to face such cruel treatment?

Interestingly, Michael doesn't seem to share his mom's questioning heart. During one summer spent with Campus Crusade for Christ, as he and other teens reached out to tourists on the Ocean City boardwalk in New Jersey, Michael called his mom and said, "Mom, it's okay if I never get married, because Jesus is my best friend, and I'll never be lonely."

Michael's mom confesses, "I always worried about Michael's relationship with God, because if he could never get close to a human, how would he understand God? When it comes to Michael's life, I tend to underestimate God. God touched him in a deep way in Ocean City that summer."

When most of us parents watch our kids leave home, we feel the normal sense of concern about how they're going to make it — but just imagine what it must be like to let loose a boy with autism! Michael's mom learned a valuable lesson: We do not parent as people who have no hope. *We have a God who watches after our children.*

Once out of college, Michael ended up in a different state. His parents worried about him being so far away from home, but they let him leave, and they placed him in God's hands. In his good providence, God led Michael to a small church that welcomed him with open arms. They sensed something "different" about him, so the pastor's wife called Michael's mom and spent an hour learning about his history and the medical diagnoses he had received. The congregation has welcomed Michael with an outpouring of generous compassion and love.

All this led Michael's mom to reconsider her earlier fears. "To me it is about being at peace with what God is doing. I thought with my limited human understanding that somehow Michael's handicap was limiting God. I thought that Michael would have trouble understanding God, like he had trouble understanding people. That was just stupid. God has again shown himself to be much bigger than my assessment of what God could do with Mike."

Maybe your child doesn't have autism. Maybe he or she has a learning disability, a moral weakness, a flawed personality, or a physical challenge. You've spent hours wondering what will happen to this child. How will he or she ever make it in the world? Please don't forget that God doesn't cast your child into the world alone. He gave your child a caring parent — you! — and he has provided a Comforter, a guide, to go with your child where you can't go. Even if your child has rejected him, God works overtime to woo him or her toward the light.

Granted, it may have seemed easier to trust God with your soul than it is to trust God with your firstborn, your second born, or your last born — but welcome to graduate school! Sacred parenting is designed to stretch your faith.

It's hard to watch our kids leave; it's hard to let go. Sometimes the leaving isn't about distance; it's about death. What will our faith have to say about that?

Surrender Within

Kevin Conlon faced perhaps the ultimate battle of surrender when his three-and-a-half-year-old son named Kevin Christopher (or K.C.) lay dying at Boston Children's Hospital. As his boy gallantly but unsuccessfully fought against the ravages of his disease, Kevin decided to compose his thoughts in the form of a letter. Here are a couple of excerpts from one of the most moving pieces I've ever read:[4]

Dear K.C.,

As I lie in bed holding you, I am so painfully aware that you will be with us for only a few minutes or hours. The hour is late, but my feelings are so strong that I leave you with your beautiful and loving mother to find a place of refuge in the hospital to compose my thoughts in this letter to you.

My heart breaks when I think of the struggles you have endured in the last eight months to get that "rock" out of your head. I would give anything to switch places with you. Nothing would make me happier.

As you close your eyes and decide when you want to go to heaven, please remember how proud I am of you. From the day you were born to today, you have brought me only joy and happiness. You have exceeded my highest expectations of what fatherhood would be like. You have not only been my son, but my dearest friend and constant companion; when I was at work or out of town, I ached to be with you.

Kevin mentions many of the fun times he and his son had together, then talks about what a wonderful brother K.C. was to his younger sibling, Cody. But now, in the midst of the sadness, listen to the amazing spirit of surrender that this father maintains in the face of watching his son die.

> Yes, K.C., I will miss you day to day, on our trips, but also on special days like Christmas. Last year you were too sick to enjoy Christmas, and for the last eight months I have dreamed of making this Christmas a special one. I can't imagine the day without you ripping open your presents or playing with Cody and your cousins.
>
> I will miss you terribly. All I have learned from you validates that my life is on the right course and that my values are in the proper place. How else could I have such a wonderful boy as you? For this I thank you.
>
> Since December of last year, your life has been dominated by the struggle to get well. You fought as if you were an army of 10,000 men. You were so brave.
>
> As you prepare to go to heaven, please know that Mommy, Cody, your grandparents, cousins, uncles, aunts, friends, and I passionately love you. We will never forget all the joy and happiness you brought us each and every day. I am the luckiest man in the world to be your father and friend. I love you madly.
>
> So, K.C., it is okay to close your eyes and rest peacefully. You do not have to fight anymore. You have won life's greatest battle: You have become a completely full and beautiful person and for this God has invited you to His house in heaven. Thanks for being my son.
>
> Love Always,
> Daddy

Faith too often gets presented in some Christian circles as the spiritual ability to "overcome" many of life's obstacles and trials through prayer — the thought being that if we have enough faith, cancer will never take the life of someone we love. But we see real faith oozing out in this letter Kevin Conlon wrote to his son. After all is said and done, *faith is not the power to get whatever we want; it is the spirit to accept whatever God gives.* Yes, Kevin prayed for K.C.'s healing, but when God chose to take K.C. home, Kevin showed that it takes even more faith to gracefully receive a "no" answer than it does a "yes."

Clearly, you've just read the words of a man of faith — and there comes a time when a parent has to prepare a child to die rather than hold out a false hope. That's *not* an anti-faith approach. It is the height of faith, the true measure of faith. Jesus prayed that the Father might remove the cup of sorrow from which he was about to drink. When the Father said, "No, you need to drink this," Jesus' faith manifested itself in his surrender: "Not my will, but yours be done" (Luke 22:42).

We have no guarantees in this fallen world. *Every day* in the United States, approximately 350 parents bury a child.[5] Such a loss will mark a parent for life. Singer Cindy Bullens admits as much when she talks about her daughter, Jessie, who died from cancer at age eleven:

> I still want to see that face. That will never go away.... Not in five years. Not in ten. Never. I can laugh today, something I couldn't do two years ago. I can have a good time today. But I always have sadness. I will live with my sadness until the day that I die and I am with Jessie again.[6]

The smallest things may trigger the pain anew and bring it roaring back to life. Seeing another child with red hair. Less laundry in the laundry basket. Passing up your child's favorite cereal box in the grocery store. Coming across one of your child's favorite programs as you channel surf. The pain is real and ongoing, and none of us can say anything to make someone "feel better." In fact, it is cruel to take away a grieving parent's pain, in that the pain may be their last remaining link to a very precious love. We can hurt with them, but we can't heal them.

I can't remove the threat of death, and as a writer I'd be dishonest to discount it. The fact is, from a Christian worldview, death is a just judgment leveled by a holy God on a sinful world. But as we'll see in just a moment, this lethal judgment and the early act of leaving can point to our greatest hope and focus our parenting like nothing else can in this earthly journey.

The Ultimate Departure

I got myself into a bit of trouble one day in York, Pennsylvania, when I told how a friend of mine spent nearly $600 at the vet's office try-ing to nurture a stray cat back to health. "My empathy for stray cats runs out at about six bucks," I confessed. "I look at it this way. A large bucket of balls on the driving range, or a stray cat; a large bucket of balls on the driving range or a stray cat — usually the large bucket of balls will win."

A veterinarian sat in the audience, as well as a number of pet lovers, and I heard from all of them! As the next session started, I dug myself an even deeper hole when I sarcastically commented that I'm actually a big fan of our kids having pets. "For instance," I said, "I'm very grateful our daughter Kelsey has a fish. I've found that fish are very valuable pets because they teach kids about death."[7]

A large number of the audience laughed heartily, but I dug the hole a little deeper with the animal lovers in the group. Yet a serious spiritual truth lies behind what I said. Death is the ultimate letting go, a journey we all must take. How will we as parents learn to let go when the letting go points to our *own* deaths? Since most of us will die before our children, most of us will face this spiritual passage first.

As I wrote this book, I watched Graham's Boy's Club basketball team win the championship for their division. During a break before the fourth quarter, Graham ran into the locker room. I followed him to give him a tip on a particular play, and the two of us spent about three or four minutes talking — about the refs, the opposing team, and what Graham and his teammates had to do to preserve their lead. That's just what Graham and I like to do — we like to talk things out.

One time, when Graham was barely more than a toddler, and I was traveling, Lisa was surprised to see Graham watching a football game. Two colleges from Florida were playing for the national championship.

Lisa has learned to tolerate my enjoyment of watching sports on television, but she rebelled at the thought that it had been passed down to my son.

"Graham, what are you doing?" she asked. We've never lived in Florida, so Lisa couldn't figure out why Graham cared about this game. Nevertheless, Graham remained persistent, so Lisa gave him twenty-five minutes to watch a bit more. When the twenty-five min-utes had elapsed, Graham started up the stairs toward bed, but he sensed Lisa's displeasure, so he paused to say, "Mom, you know why I wanted to watch that game?"

"Why?"

"I knew Dad would be watching it in his hotel room, and I figured that if we couldn't be together tonight, at least we could watch the same game at the same time, and it would be kind of like being together. And then we'll talk about it tomorrow when he calls."

That's the sort of the relationship Graham and I have: We like to talk things out. What hurts me most about the thought of death is realizing I'll want to be there to help Graham work through my death, to talk to him about it — about how he's the man now — but I won't be there. He'll have to face this one on his own. I remember Frank Schaeffer talking about the time he called his dad, Francis, shortly after he had died. Not until the fourth or fifth ring did Frank remember that his father was no longer there to answer the phone.

That kind of thought tears me up. It causes me more grief than I can imagine to think that when Graham faces the loss of his father, I won't be there to talk it out with him. When my daughters realize their father isn't there for them anymore, when they lose that sense of history — that "relational life net" — I won't be able to hold them should they cry. I won't be able to leave little notes of encouragement around their rooms. I won't be able to pray with them or build them up. Who will do all that when I'm gone?

Yet faith reminds me that, even as a parent, I'm not the center of the universe for my children. It doesn't mean I'm not an important or influential presence, but it does mean I'm not the ultimate presence. In his fine book *The Barnabas Way,* my friend and editor John Sloan writes about losing his father when he was just eight years old. He admits initially, "I felt the world slip out of its course. I thought there would never be another hour of happiness in my life." But God took over: "At that moment a series of men began to appear, one after the other, who by simply being there for me kept putting the hope in my heart that God was still alive."[8]

It may indeed cause me pain to think about leaving my children, but the same providence of God that would allow me to face an early death would also give Allison, Graham, and Kelsey the grace to work through that death. Even an early departure needn't be colored by fear; on the contrary, it should be painted with hope, confidence, and faith in God.

In fact, this very real concern can motivate us to accomplish the most important task of any parent: working for the salvation of our children. In a talk, C.J. Mahaney describes why he seeks to find new ways to discuss the gospel with his son. After he confesses to his listeners that he doesn't know how many years he has to live, he says this:

> I pray I'm able to be there for my son as he grows older; I pray I'm able to be there for my son when and if he marries. I pray I will able to be a grandpa to his children. But as I think about the future, I have no guarantee I will live through *this* day. Even in the best-case scenario, my days are numbered. So I work back from my death and ask, "What is the purpose of my life?" The purpose of my life is to prepare [my son] for his death; and not just his death, but for the judgment he will encounter upon death.... The most important task is to prepare my son for that day when he stands alone before God and answers to God.[9]

Knowing that the time to leave will come — perhaps even sooner rather than later — can keep us focused as parents on what really matters. On that final day, I won't care much about Graham's golf handicap. I won't be thinking about the Boy's Club championship basketball game. I won't feel impressed that his room was always clean, or that he looked adults in the eyes as he greeted them and shook their hands. All that will be fine enough, but of much greater importance to me, of ultimate importance to me, is that he will hear his God say to him, "Well done, my good and faithful servant; enter into your rest!"

So I want to baptize every day with this one aim: doing what I can to ensure that my children embrace the gospel. I want them to know the God who will welcome them into eternity. I have only so much time to impress on my children the urgency of this task, but at the very least, the reality of death serves as a great reminder of this responsibility.

In my first book, *Seeking the Face of God*, I wrote an entire chapter that explored how the great Christian classics considered it a spiritual duty to always keep the thought of death in the forefront of the mind. They believed this to be an essential discipline to maintain the proper attitude toward growth in holiness and mission, and to preserve an eternal mind-set. One of those writers — John of the Cross — lived in a room covered with crosses and pictures of skulls. He didn't want to forget his mortality, so occasionally he'd even eat out of a bowl fashioned from a human skull.

I can't imagine doing that, but as a father I don't have to keep skulls around to remind me of death. Having children and facing the fears of loving someone so much serves that purpose quite well. Raising children surely serves as a masterful school of spiritual formation. The journey is wonderful and it's exhausting, yet fulfilling from start to finish. Although none of us know who will first leave this earth and enter eternity, we can rest assured that God will indeed finish the work he has started, shaping the souls of those he loves so dearly.

Sacred Presents

Erin Bescheinen was three years old when doctors diagnosed her mom (Marsha) with breast cancer. The second time Marsha received the diagnosis, Erin was thirteen and more aware of events. This case involved a new tumor on the other side of Marsha's body. Because of the first scare, doctors caught it early and treated it with radiation instead of chemotherapy.

The third and final time the cancer appeared, Erin was sixteen. Marsha developed a form of lung cancer that not infrequently plagues breast cancer survivors. Within four prolific months, the cancer spread through her lungs and esophagus until it eventually attacked the covering of her brain.

Somehow, at the very onset of the third diagnosis, Erin's mom seemed to know that this time she would "strike out." She *knew* something was different about this cancer. And she knew she wouldn't survive.

Marsha decided to go out in style. She put away all the common glasses and silverware and brought out the china and crystal.

"It was pretty cool," Erin remembers, "getting to eat cheerios out of a china bowl and drinking orange juice out of crystal glasses."

Determined to give her family a smooth transition, Marsha started making plans as soon as she knew she wasn't going to make it. She wrote her own obituary and planned her memorial service. She went through the house and wrote various names on certain possessions to eliminate bickering about who got what after her death.

"I want this to go to Erin [or Kellie or Scott], and this is why . . ."

Erin particularly treasures the "why" side of these requests, as it infused seemingly common items with real sentiment.

Erin grew up in Grand Junction, Colorado, which had a public school system she remembers as "terrible." Erin struggled with her grades, and when her mom and dad scheduled a meeting with the principal and teachers, Marsha actually got rebuked: "Look, Mrs. Thomas," she was told, "Erin isn't on drugs, and she's not pregnant, so what are you so worried about?"

That's all Marsha needed to hear. "Erin won't be returning," she said, and promptly enrolled Erin in a private boarding school, which explains why Erin was away from home when Marsha received her third diagnosis of cancer. Erin's parents waited until she got home from school before they told her the cancer had returned.

That summer, two of Marsha's children got married. She felt particularly sad when the doctors told her she wasn't well enough to attend her son's wedding. She'd have to fly to get there, and the doctors told her there was no way she would endure the commercial flight.

The rest of the family flew out to celebrate, minus Marsha and Erin's dad, Lew. Imagine the kids' joy when they got a call informing them that Lew and Erin's grandfather had decided to charter a private jet. Marsha was a determined woman. Doctors or no, she would show up at her son's wedding!

On the way back from the wedding, Erin's parents dropped her off at school, but Erin felt reluctant to stay there. Her mom had grown so sick she felt afraid to leave her, but she knew that's what she had to do.

Two weeks into the school year, Erin called home and burst into tears when her father answered the phone.

"I *need* to come home this weekend," she cried.

Erin's practical dad knew that Erin had tickets to fly home in two weeks. "You've got to be kidding me," he said. "Erin, you're going to be fine." But Erin wasn't fine. She was shaking, bawling, hyperventilating, practically screaming, *"I just want to come home this weekend!"*

"Erin, I know it's hard for you to be away, but school is where you need to be."

Erin felt so angry she hung up on him, then called her sister: "Kellie, I want to go home; will you please call Pop and tell him I need to come home?"

Kellie took the same approach Erin's dad had taken: "Erin, what's the matter with you? You're coming home in a couple weeks!"

So Erin hung up on *her* and called home once again. This time her dad agreed to put Marsha on the phone. In a weak, tired voice, Marsha said, "Yeah, I'd love for you to come home."

That's all Erin's dad needed to hear. "I'll call the airport," he said. "Your ticket will be waiting for you at the counter."

Erin packed her bags, took a cab to the airport, flew home, and spent the entire weekend by her mom's side. By this point, Marsha's cancer had spread through her esophagus, causing severe coughing attacks. These attacks scared Erin more than anything else, because Marsha sometimes sounded as though she'd never come out of them.

On Sunday, just a few hours before Erin's scheduled departure, her mom had the worst coughing attack ever. The two were alone in the house.

"It was the scariest moment of my life," Erin remembers. "I thought she was going to die."

Marsha finally came out of it, took some sips of water, and Erin's dad came home twenty minutes later to a defiant daughter who told him, "I'm not leaving."

"Erin, you can't do this. It's your senior year; you're applying for colleges," he said. "You *have* to go back to school."

"No way. I'm not going back."

Erin's dad started to protest once again, but all arguments ceased when Marsha grabbed her husband's and her daughter's hands and said, "I don't want Erin to go."

Marsha died the next morning.

Erin still tears up when she thinks about it. "She knew, and God knew — and somehow God got through to me that I just had to be there."

Though she did get to see two of her children get married the summer before she died, Marsha knew she would miss a number of major life events and milestones in her children's lives. That's what hurt the most — wanting to be a part of those pivotal moments that many of us take for granted. Facing this sad reality head-on, Marsha got very creative before she died. Unknown to her children, she wrapped several presents and left them in the family safe, where she knew her husband would find them after her death.

Which is why, on her eighteenth birthday, Erin's eyes teared up when she recognized the familiar handwriting on a beautifully wrapped box:

To Erin, on her 18th birthday

Erin couldn't believe it. The last thing she expected on that day was a present from her mother, but she eagerly opened the box and discovered her mom's wedding ring. Marsha had taken out the center diamond (which she set in a ring for Erin's dad), and replaced it with an amethyst. Erin felt so touched that her mom had found a way to stay involved in this special day. Even though she was no longer physically present, spiritually she remained a major force in her daughter's life.

Several years later, Erin graduated from college. The night before commencement exercises, her dad held out another box containing that same familiar writing. This present held Marsha's watch.

"That gift was powerful," Erin says, "because there were some things I always wondered where they went; things that were 'trademark Mom,' things I remember seeing her wear every day. Mom was the queen of accessorizing, so I always wondered what happened to some of that stuff. This watch was a gift she had gotten on her fifth wedding anniversary. It's a Rolex, and it's really neat to see that on my wrist now. It's a reminder of my mom that I carry with me every day."

Several more years passed, until Erin finally met the man of her dreams. They dated and then got engaged. As she planned her wedding, Erin missed Marsha more than ever. A young woman just wants her mother to be with her when she's planning a wedding; she's not supposed to have to do everything on her own. Erin admits she felt a little sorry for herself, but even more, she just really missed not having her mom there for such an important day.

While Erin was getting ready in the bride's dressing room, talking to her bridesmaids, her father knocked on the door. Erin had asked her dad to come in to put on her garter. When her dad walked in the room, however, he wasn't carrying a mere garter; he had another of those classic boxes.

Erin recognized it right away as another present from her mom. She gently took the present from her father's hands, and there, once again, was that familiar scrawl, this time saying:

To Erin, on her wedding day

Erin opened up the package and gasped at the sight of the diamond earrings that sparkled back at her. When she put them on, it was as though her mom was giving her a warm embrace or taking Erin's head in her soft hands. Erin wore those earrings as she walked down the aisle, and though her mind overflowed with thoughts of her future and the man who waited for her in front of the church, she also remembered the woman who gave her life.

In spite of the odds, Marsha had found a way to attend Erin's wedding.

Erin doesn't know if any more gifts wait for her; her dad won't say, although he did mention, as he handed over the wedding gift, that "this is one of the last gifts." Erin doesn't know if it means one of the last gifts for everyone — which means no more for her — or one of the last gifts for her.

"More than anything, I just praise God for preparing her," Erin told me. "There's no way my mom could have pulled off what she did without the Lord. I believe there was a lot of guidance there.

"All the gifts are neat rememberings," Erin went on, "but I praise God for her and the woman that she is."

As a writer, I catch Erin in a grammatical error and inform her that she used the word "is" instead of "was" when referring to her mom.

"I definitely still feel some guidance from her," Erin admits. "I often think of her — what would my mom do, what would my mom say, what would make my mom proud? I don't think of her still being here, but I do kind of feel like she's looking over me."

As Erin has gotten older — a relative phrase since, as I write this, she is still in her twenties — her mom's friends and relatives frequently rave over the way Erin resembles Marsha. "They say, 'Wow,' because we look alike, but it's more than that. They say it's our mutual tone of voice, our love for the Lord, our mannerisms. God has brought me full circle. My mom is definitely a part of who I am today; without question, she has helped shape me into the person I've become."

Erin's story tells us that we never really leave our children; we just say good-bye for a time. Though we must physically part their company, we remain, in a very real sense, a part of them. Sometimes it may be gifts; other times it may be memories. At the very least, it's our genes and DNA.

We have no guarantees. We may die, our children may die, or our kids may simply rebel and avoid us. We have no control — but we can have profound influence. But even that doesn't mean half as much as having a God in whom we can trust, a God who points us to a place — and who offers an invitation to that place — where leaving will be no more.

This is truly the heart of sacred parenting: learning to rest, trust, and have faith in God as we usher our children to a final refuge.

This puppy pack of boys would derail my career but link me inexorably to my soul and to the Almighty and to the present and to the forever. ... These wriggly children captured me in the fleeting moment that is now, and ultimately drew me toward the peace I had always tried desperately to reach.

Iris Krasnow

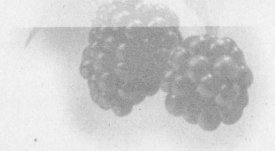

Receive Your Reward

When Lisa was a young first-time mother, I wrote a short story to inspire her. I called it "White Spots" and couldn't find a single magazine willing to publish it. But I still think the message is important — which may be why it didn't work as a story.

The "White Spots" referred to the physical evidence of Lisa's nursing, which had a way of marking most of her shirts and requiring frequent loads of laundry. Our first child spit up quite a bit; if Lisa had changed her blouse every time she got a spot on it, she would have run out of clean shirts within six hours. Over time, Lisa became frustrated and embarrassed about always wearing semi-stained clothes.

Lisa, like most young mothers, had some difficulty adjusting to this change in her lifestyle. Just a few years before, she had been in what our culture would call her "prime," looking her best, working out at the gym, doing whatever she wanted to do on a Friday and Saturday night, and having lots of fun. Now she was married, a mother, staying home with a child, trying to get her own body back into shape, covered in her own milk and the baby's spit-up, and unable to do anything without first getting a baby-sitter.

In the story, the young mother feels great surprise to discover that her act of welcoming this child into the world is the very act so highly regarded by Jesus at the judgment:

For I was hungry and you gave me something to eat, I was
thirsty and you gave me something to drink, I was a stranger
and you invited me in, I needed clothes and you clothed me,
I was sick and you looked after me.

Matthew 25:35–36

Who gets hungrier than a newly awakened baby, eagerly searching out her mother's breasts? Who is more naked than a recently
born child? Who is more a stranger than an infant who comes into
this world knowing no one? Who gets sick more often than a little
one, who seems inclined toward ear infections, diaper rash, and
colic?

When a mother welcomes a child into the world, feeding her and
giving her drink and clothing her and holding her when she gets sick
(and, at least with the first child, boiling the pacifier when it drops to
the floor, and rushing her to the emergency room when her temperature reaches 99.5), she is doing exactly what Jesus tells us will be
most rewarded in heaven.

"But how can caring for your own child result in a heavenly
reward?" some might ask. "Surely Jesus didn't mean *that*, did he?"

People who ask such a question don't understand that the children we raise, ultimately speaking, are not ours. God creates each
child, and he has such a deep, passionate love for every boy and girl
that he never misses a single event in their life: "I tell you the truth,
whatever you did for one of the least of these brothers of mine, you
did for me" (Matthew 25:40).

Understanding God's joy in his own creation is one of the more
profound spiritual experiences we will ever know. I took my son and
his best buddy to California for his twelfth birthday to spend three
days at various theme parks. Because of some frequent-flier tickets
and a couple of free nights in a hotel, the trip wouldn't be horren-
dously costly, but it would still cost enough to make me think twice
about it. One day as I contemplated it, I got the distinct sense of
God's pleasure over what my son and his friend would soon experience. The boy who would travel with us harbors dreams of becoming a pilot, but he had never flown on a large commercial airliner,
and it was as though God were imparting his own joy to me in antic-
ipation of what this boy and my son were about to experience. God
himself delighted in our trip.

It was a strange and quizzical sensation, and it certainly affected the way I look at children, particularly with regard to how God remains so passionately concerned about them. Any time we can bring them joy, we bring a smile to God's face. And any time we violate their innocence, we earn a fierce enemy: "If anyone causes one of these little ones who believe in me to sin, it would be better for him to have a large millstone hung around his neck and to be drowned in the depths of the sea" (Matthew 18:6).

Mothers and fathers, when you give your tiny infant a bath, you are washing God's baby. Pause a moment in your busy day and look up to heaven. When you minister to that youngster, can you imagine God smiling down at you? When you fix that hungry six-year-old a peanut butter sandwich, you are feeding one of God's children. Listen carefully — you may hear God laughing in pleasure. When you hug an adolescent whom others have teased mercilessly at school, you are comforting God's teenager. Are those God's tears dampening your shoulder?

In the process of caring and loving, you bring God great pleasure. At that very moment you become his provision, his comfort, his passion. Learn to swim in that joy, and you will never look at parenting the same way again.

You could have rejected this child. You could have spurned the demands on your time, your resources, and your emotional well-being. But instead you accepted this child, through great pain you gave birth to this child, and with even greater pain you make daily sacrifices to love this child. Your heavenly Father doesn't miss a second of this sacrifice. He sees it all. He cries with you and he laughs with you and he takes great joy in the good work you are doing.

When I see children in public now, I try to tune in to God's passion for them. Sometimes I'll say a prayer for them. If I sit by them in a plane, I'll talk to them and try to take some of the burden off their parents, since I know traveling with children isn't easy. On one flight into Seattle, I sat by a delightful family with a very sociable little girl and her amazingly well-behaved eighteen-month-old brother. Near the end of the flight, the two kids were climbing all over me because I was sitting by the window and we were passing Mount Rainier. They naturally wanted to see the mountain. Once the plane landed, the little girl looked up at me and said, "I sure hope we meet again sometime."

"I do, too," I replied, realizing that God wouldn't spare any expense to protect, love, nurture, and bring this child to him — and in that sense, I loved her very much.

Whether we are parents or not, we have incredible opportunities to participate in this passion that God has for children. I'm sure God is present in the sanctuary of a church, because Jesus says that wherever two or more come together in his name, he is there (see Matthew 18:20). But if we *really* want to live in the presence of God, we may want to hang out at the playground, Sunday school rooms, and nursery.

There is no way God is missing what is going on there.

A Sacred Call

Over a decade ago, I commuted to work on the highways outside of Washington, D.C. I had to leave the house by 5:30 a.m. at the latest. If I left at 5:45, it took an extra thirty minutes to get to the office; if I didn't leave until 6:00 a.m., I might not get to work before lunch.

One morning I paused for a few extra moments before I left for the day. Usually I rushed out the door, but this day I had a feeling that something miraculous was taking place.

I went back upstairs and checked in the kids' rooms; two of them had left their beds. I returned to the master bedroom and saw Lisa fast asleep, her arm around little Kelsey, whose tiny nostrils (she was just a baby back then) gently flared with every breath. Three-year-old Graham had wedged himself in by the foot of the bed, making the three of them look like pieces of a jigsaw puzzle. They were sleeping peacefully, contentedly. Allison, knocked out to the world, lay tangled up in her bedsheets and blankets, as is her custom.

There is a certain holiness in the quiet hours of the morning, when a simple house — even a town house or an apartment — becomes a sanctuary, a cathedral. The silence brings to my mind God's peace and presence. While laughter may roar throughout the day — and, not infrequently, tears — nothing speaks so loudly to me as the quiet of the early morning.

Finally I stepped outside into the dark, unusually satisfied. My soul felt completely full. Feminists may fault me for this, but there aren't many better feelings for a man than going to work while your family contentedly sleeps. Something tells you that this is the way it's supposed to be. My father did it, my grandfather did it, and his grandfather did it, too.

Physically I sat in a small Honda Civic as I drove toward Route 66, but spiritually I sat in a lap — God's lap — enjoying the peaceful sensation that the Lord provided me. The sun had yet to peek above the horizon, but driving through the darkness, I realized I had caught an illuminating glimpse of what sacred parenting was all about. I felt eager to meet whatever challenges lay ahead of me in this wonderfully amazing journey.

The challenges haven't stopped; the learning continues. But one thing I know: Being a parent is a sacred calling.

Notes

Chapter 1: Papa God

1. Though it's interesting to note that in this same verse Paul continues, "In regard to evil be infants, but in your thinking be adults."
2. Rachel Cusk, *A Life's Work: On Becoming a Mother* (New York: Picador, 2002), 8.
3. Cited in Rick Reilly, *Who's Your Caddy?: Looping for the Great, the Near Great and Reprobates of Golf* (New York: Doubleday, 2003), 59.

Chapter 2: The Hardest Hurt of All

1. David McCullough, *John Adams* (New York: Simon and Schuster, 2001), 226.
2. Rick Reilly, "The Weak Shall Inherit the Gym," *Sports Illustrated* (14 May 2001), 96.
3. Cited in Marilee Jones, "Parents get too aggressive on admissions," *USA Today* (6 January 2003), D1.
4. Jim Schmotzer, personal communication.
5. David Brooks, "The Organization Kid," *Atlantic Monthly* (April 2001), 43.
6. Brooks, "The Organization Kid," 44.
7. Brooks, "The Organization Kid," 54.
8. You can order this tape (and many others) online by logging on to www.sovereigngraceministries.org.
9. Gary Thomas, *Sacred Marriage* (Grand Rapids: Zondervan, 2000), 237.

10. Yes, I realize the actual quote is "My God, my God, why have you forsaken me?" (Matthew 27:46), but I've taken what I believe to be legitimate license here to make the point. Whatever title Jesus chose, the words "why have you forsaken me?" are what really hurt.

11. Cited in Rabbi Nancy Fuchs-Kreimer, *Parenting as a Spiritual Journey: Deepening Ordinary and Extraordinary Events into Sacred Occasions* (Woodstock, Vt.: Jewish Lights, 1998), 162–63.

Chapter 3: The Gold behind the Guilt

1. See Rabbi Nancy Fuchs-Kreimer, *Parenting as a Spiritual Journey: Deepening Ordinary and Extraordinary Events into Sacred Occasions* (Woodstock, Vt.: Jewish Lights, 1998), 115.

2. Lisa Belkin, *Life's Work: Confessions of an Unbalanced Mom* (New York: Simon and Schuster, 2002), 119.

3. Belkin, *Life's Work*, 120.

4. Cited in Merrell Noden, "Marty Liquori, Dream Miler," *Sports Illustrated* (5 June 2000), 18.

5. I was privileged to read an early draft of Carolyn's book *Feminine Appeal: Seven Virtues of a Godly Wife and Mother* (Wheaton, Ill.: Crossway, 2003), in which she makes this observation.

6. For this story, I'm indebted to Dr. Robert Stone, who used it in a sermon delivered to the members and guests at Hillcrest Chapel in Bellingham, Washington, on October 13, 2002.

Chapter 4: Seizing Heaven

1. Cited in Dennis Rainey, *Ministering to Twenty-First Century Families* (Nashville: Word, 2001), 216.

2. Frank Buchman, *The Revolutionary Path* (London: Grosvenor, 1975), 2–3, emphasis added.

3. Buchman, *The Revolutionary Path*, 5.

4. Gordon Smith, *On the Way: A Guide to Christian Spirituality* (Colorado Springs: NavPress, 2001), 72.

5. Cited in Peter Howard, *Frank Buchman's Secret* (London: William Heinemann, 1961), 13.

Chapter 5: Joy!

1. Cited in Rick Reilly, "The Gold Standard," *Sports Illustrated* (4 March 2002), 88.

2. Account taken from Reilly, "The Gold Standard," 88.

3. Carol Lynn Pearson, *On the Seesaw: The Ups and Downs of a Single-Parent Family* (New York: Random House, 1988), 4–5.

4. Cited in Elton Trueblood, *The Humor of Christ* (New York: Harper and Row, 1964), 22.

5. Barna Research Group, "Surprisingly Few Adults Outside of Christianity Have Positive Views of Christians"; view at Barna Research Online (www.barna.org/cgi-bin/PagePressRelease.asp?PressRelease ID=127&Reference=F).

6. Cited in Trueblood, *The Humor of Christ*, 23–25.

7. Cited in John and Susan Yates, *What Really Matters at Home: Eight Crucial Elements for Building Character in Your Family* (Dallas: Word, 1992), 141.

8. Trueblood, *The Humor of Christ*, 32.

9. C.J.'s tape is entitled "Gospel-Centered Parenting." Carolyn and the girls can be heard on "Mothers and Daughters." These tapes are available through www.sovereigngraceministries.org.

Chapter 6: Vicious Vulnerability

1. Cited in Albert Kim and Mark Mravic, "The Beat," *Sports Illustrated* (11 June 2001), 40.

2. Iris Krasnow, *Surrendering to Motherhood: Losing Your Mind, Finding Your Soul* (New York: Hyperion, 1997), 149.

3. Dennis Rainey, *Ministering to Twenty-First Century Families* (Nashville: Word, 2001), 223.

4. Cited in Cal Fussman, "Al Pacino — the Legend," *Esquire* (July 2002), 48.

Chapter 7: Burning Love

1. Augustine, "Enchiridion," vol. 3 of *A Select Library of the Nicene and Post-Nicene Fathers of the Christian Church*, ed. Philip Schaff (Grand Rapids: Eerdmans, 1998 reprint), 249.

2. Rachel Cusk, *A Life's Work: On Becoming a Mother* (New York: Picador, 2002), 79.

3. Cusk, *A Life's Work*, 79–80.

4. Cusk, *A Life's Work*, 80.

5. C. S. Lewis, *Reflections on the Psalms* (New York: Harcourt, Brace and World, 1958), 30.

6. Lewis, *Reflections on the Psalms*, 31–32.

7. Hans-Cristoph Hahn, "Anger," *The New International Dictionary of New Testament Theology*, vol. 1, ed. Colin Brown (Grand Rapids: Zondervan, 1975), 109.

8. See Duane Miller, *Out of the Silence: A Personal Testimony of God's Healing Power* (Nashville: Nelson, 1996).

9. Dan Allender and Tremper Longman III, *Cry of the Soul* (Colorado Springs: NavPress, 1994), 74.

10. Joy Davidman, *Smoke on the Mountain* (Philadelphia: Westminster, 1974), 67–68.

Chapter 8: The Glory behind the Grime

1. Rabbi Nancy Fuchs-Kreimer, *Parenting as a Spiritual Journey: Deepening Ordinary and Extraordinary Events into Sacred Occasions* (Woodstock, Vt.: Jewish Lights, 1998), 26.

2. Rachel Cusk, *A Life's Work: On Becoming a Mother* (New York: Picador, 2002), 69–70.

3. Cusk, *A Life's Work*, 70–71.

4. Cusk, *A Life's Work*, 138.

5. Iris Krasnow, *Surrendering to Motherhood: Losing Your Mind, Finding Your Soul* (New York: Hyperion, 1997), 74–75.

6. See Patrick Carnes, *Out of the Shadows: Understanding Sexual Addiction*, 3d ed. (Center City, Minn.: Hazelden, 2001), 87.

7. Carnes, *Out of the Shadows*, 88.

8. Krasnow, *Surrendering to Motherhood*, 86–87.

Chapter 9: Walking on the Wild Side of Parenting

1. Cited in David McCullough, *John Adams* (New York: Simon and Schuster, 2001), 548.

2. Cited in McCullough, *John Adams*, 634.

3. Cited in Elton Trueblood, *The Recovery of Family Life* (New York: Harper Brothers, 1953), 50.

4. Trueblood, *The Recovery of Family Life*, 50–51.

5. Trueblood, *The Recovery of Family Life*, 56–57.

6. One form of the story is cited in Rabbi Nancy Fuchs-Kreimer, *Parenting as a Spiritual Journey: Deepening Ordinary and Extraordinary Events into Sacred Occasions* (Woodstock, Vt.: Jewish Lights, 1998), 59.

Chapter 10: A Very Boring Chapter in the Bible (That Can Change Your Life Forever)

1. Account taken from Richard Wheeler, *Iwo* (New York: Lippincott and Crowell, 1980), 79.

2. Cited in Terrence Rafferty, "The Evil Do-Gooder," *GQ* (June 2002), 83.

3. Rabbi Nancy Fuchs-Kreimer, *Parenting as a Spiritual Journey: Deepening Ordinary and Extraordinary Events into Sacred Occasions* (Woodstock, Vt.: Jewish Lights, 1998), 10.

Chapter 11: Xerox R Us

1. George Gilder, *Men and Marriage* (Gretna, La.: Pelican, 1986), 192.
2. Gilder, *Men and Marriage*, 192–93.
3. Cited in Ivan Solotaroff, "Pride of the Confederacy," *GQ* (October 2002), 279.
4. See Patrick Carnes, *Out of the Shadows: Understanding Sexual Addiction*, 3d ed. (Center City, Minn.: Hazelden, 2001), 5.
5. Carnes, *Out of the Shadows*, xviii.
6. Carnes, *Out of the Shadows*, 5.
7. Cited in John Stott, *Guard the Gospel* (Downers Grove, Ill.: InterVarsity Press, 1973), 27.

Chapter 12: Sacrifice

1. Jeremy Schaap, "A Father's Gift," *Sports Illustrated* (7 January 2002), 28.
2. Rachel Cusk, *A Life's Work: On Becoming a Mother* (New York: Picador, 2002), 29–30.
3. Cusk, *A Life's Work*, 30.
4. Elton Trueblood, *The Recovery of Family Life* (New York: Harper Brothers, 1953), 92.
5. Cited in David McCullough, *John Adams* (New York: Simon and Schuster, 2001), 236–37.
6. Quoted in Dan Rafael, "Full Force Tyson . . . ," *USA Today* (18 October 2000), 2C.
7. See "Spending Time with Tyson," *Sports Illustrated* (20 May 2002), 38.
8. Iris Krasnow, *Surrendering to Motherhood: Losing Your Mind, Finding Your Soul* (New York: Hyperion, 1997), 166–67.
9. Trueblood, *The Recovery of Family Life*, 30.
10. Cusk, *A Life's Work*, 65.
11. Thomas Kelly, *A Testament of Devotion* (New York: Harper and Brothers, 1941; rereleased 1992 by HarperCollins), 75, emphasis added.
12. Kelly, *A Testament of Devotion*, 75.
13. Francis de Sales, *Thy Will Be Done: Letters to Persons in the World* (Manchester, N.H.: Sophia Institute Press, 1995), 60.
14. De Sales, *Thy Will Be Done*, 86–87.
15. Cusk, *A Life's Work*, 41.
16. See C. S. Lewis, *The Lion, the Witch and the Wardrobe* (New York: HarperCollins, 1994 reprint), 154–55.
17. This story is based on a column written by Rick Reilly, "'Twas the Fight before Christmas," *Sports Illustrated* (27 December 1999), 144.

Chapter 13: Leaving

1. Rachel Cusk, *A Life's Work: On Becoming a Mother* (New York: Picador, 2002), 107–8.
2. Evelyn and James Whitehead, *Marrying Well: Possibilities in Christian Marriage Today* (Garden City, N.Y.: Doubleday, 1981), 243–44.
3. Cathy Carpenter, unpublished manuscript, 74 (shared in a personal communication).
4. Cited in Bob Greene, "A Father's Farewell to His Dearest Friend," in *Chevrolet Summers, Dairy Queen Nights* (New York: Viking, 1997), 243–45.
5. Cited in Greg Barrett, "A Child's Death Leaves an Unfillable Void," *USA Today* (1 August 2001), 10D.
6. Barrett, "A Child's Death Leaves an Unfillable Void."
7. To be fair, I got this "insight" from my good friend Paul Petersen.
8. John Sloan, *The Barnabas Way* (Colorado Springs: WaterBrook, 2002), 7–8.
9. C.J. Mahaney, "Gospel Centered Parenting, part 2: The Imperative of Instruction," available on CD through Sovereign Grace Ministries at www.sovereigngraceministries.org.

Gary Thomas

Please feel free to contact Gary. Although he can't respond personally to all correspondence, he loves to receive your feedback. For information about Gary's ministry, link to his website from: www.zondervan.com/desk/profile.asp; you may write to Gary at the following address:

Gary Thomas
P.O. Box 29417
Bellingham, WA 98228-1417
email: GLT3@aol.com.

For information regarding his speaking dates or to inquire about the possibility of Gary speaking in your church or community, please call the Center for Evangelical Spirituality at 360-676-7773, or email Laura@garythomas.com.

The Center for Evangelical Spirituality (CFES) is a ministry dedicated to fostering spiritual growth within the Christian community through an integrated study of Scripture, church history, and the Christian classics. We believe evangelical Christians can learn a great deal from historic Christian traditions without compromising the essential tenets of what it means to be an evangelical Christian. Accepting Scripture as our final and absolute authority, we seek to promote Christian growth and the refinement of an authentic evangelical Christian spirituality.

Sacred Pathways

Gary Thomas

Some Christians effortlessly spend hours in contemplative prayer. Just being around them makes you wish you were that way. Or maybe you find that others are far better at showing God's love in practical ways, or courageously standing up for God's kingdom. Why can't you be like them?

Maybe you weren't designed to be.

In *Sacred Pathways*, Gary Thomas strips away the frustration of a one-size-fits-all spirituality and guides you toward a path of worship that frees you to be you. If your devotional times have hit a snag, perhaps it's because you're trying to follow someone else's path. This book demolishes the barriers that keep Christians locked into rigid methods of worship and praise.

Sacred Pathways unfolds nine distinct spiritual temperaments—their traits, strengths, and pitfalls. Illustrated with examples from the Bible and from the author's life experience, each one suggests an approach to loving God, a distinctive journey of adoration. In one or more, you will see yourself and the ways you most naturally express your relationship with Jesus Christ. You'll also discover other temperaments that are not necessarily "you" but that you may wish to explore for the way they can stretch and invigorate your spiritual life.

Perhaps you are a Naturalist. Prayer and praise well up within you when you're walking a forest path or drinking in a mountain's jagged beauty. Or maybe you're an Activist. Taking a stand for God's ways is your meat and drink. Whatever temperament or blend of temperaments best describes you, rest assured it's not by accident. It's by the design of a Creator who knew what he was doing when he made you according to his own unique intentions.

If your spiritual walk is not what you'd like it to be, *Sacred Pathways* will show you the route you were made to travel, marked by growth and filled with the riches of a close walk with God.

Softcover 0-310-24284-3

Pick up your copy today at your local Christian bookstore!

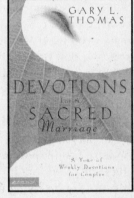

What If God Designed Marriage to Make Us Holy More Than to Make Us Happy?

Sacred Marriage

Gary Thomas

"This isn't a book that seeks to tell you how to have a happier marriage. This is a book that looks at how we can use the challenges, joys, struggles, and celebrations of marriage to draw closer to God." —Gary Thomas

Scores of books have been written that offer guidance for building the marriage of your dreams. But what if God's primary intent for your marriage isn't to make you happy . . . but holy? And what if your relationship isn't as much about you and your spouse as it is about you and God? *Sacred Marriage* invites you to view your marriage in a new and different light, as a spiritual discipline, a means whereby you can come to know God more fully and intimately.

Gary Thomas writes, "The ultimate purpose of this book is not to make you love your spouse more—though I think that will happen along the way. It's to equip you to love your God more and to help you reflect the character of his Son more precisely."

The respect you accord your partner; the forgiveness you humbly seek and graciously extend; the ecstasy, awe, and sheer fun of lovemaking; the history you and your mate build with one another—in these and other facets of your marriage, *Sacred Marriage* uncovers the mystery of God's overarching purpose. Like no other spiritual discipline, marriage reveals your deep need to draw strength and life from Jesus Christ alone; consequently, it is unsurpassed for releasing his character and vision in your life.

Sacred Marriage may alter profoundly the contours of your marriage. It will almost certainly change you. Whether it is delightful or difficult, your marriage can become a doorway to a closer walk with God and to a spiritual integrity that, like salt, seasons the world around you with the savor of Christ.

Softcover 0-310-24282-7

Pick up your copy today at your local Christian bookstore!

GRAND RAPIDS, MICHIGAN 49530 USA

WWW.ZONDERVAN.COM

Authentic Faith

Gary L. Thomas

What if life wasn't meant to be perfect but we were meant to trust the One who is?

Isn't it startling how God reveals himself most profoundly in places we least expect to encounter him? He is intent on showing himself Lord in all our circumstances—in the highs and the lows alike.

Best-selling author Gary Thomas helps us sharpen our spiritual vision and fortify our commitment by examining ten disciplines God uses to forge a fire-tested faith. A biblical view of these disciplines can safeguard us from disillusionment when—not if—difficulties surface in our lives. How we respond will determine the depth and vitality of our walk with God.

Sharing scriptural insights, the wisdom of Christians through the centuries, and cogent personal observations, Thomas explores the disciplines of:

- Selflessness
- Persecution
- Mourning
- Hope and Fear
- Waiting
- Social Mercy
- Contentment
- Suffering
- Forgiveness
- Sacrifice

As Gary Thomas reminds us, Jesus said that in this world we will have trouble. Paul exhorted believers to mourn with those who mourn. James wrote that God chooses the poor of this world to be rich in faith. Clearly, faith is about something other than a smooth ride through this fallen world. Rather, authentic faith is shaped, tempered, and purified in the flames of struggle.

Authentic Faith reveals the rich benefits that derive from embracing the harder truths of Scripture. This eye-opening look at what it means to be a true disciple of Jesus will encourage you, bolster your faith, and help you rise above shallow attachments to fix your heart on things of eternal worth.

Softcover 0-310-25419-1

Pick up your copy today at your local Christian bookstore!

We want to hear from you. Please send your comments about this
book to us in care of zreview@zondervan.com. Thank you.

GRAND RAPIDS, MICHIGAN 49530 USA

WWW.ZONDERVAN.COM